Intermediate
ART & [illegible]N

Norman Binch

Oxford University Press 1996

Oxford University Press, Walton Street, Oxford OX2 6DP

Oxford New York
Athens Auckland Bangkok Bombay
Calcutta Cape Town Dar es Salaam Delhi
Florence Hong Kong Istanbul Karachi
Kuala Lumpur Madras Madrid Melbourne
Mexico City Nairobi Paris Singapore
Taipei Tokyo Toronto

and associated companies in
Berlin Ibadan

Oxford is a trade mark of Oxford University Press

First published 1996

ISBN 0 19 832795 1

Printed in Hong Kong

Contents

[introduction]

What is a GNVQ?

(General National Vocational Qualification)

A GNVQ in Art and Design is a qualification which is intended to enable you, eventually, to become employed as a professional designer, artist, or craftsperson.

There are three levels of qualification:

1 **Foundation** – roughly equivalent to four GCSEs at Grades D – G

2 **Intermediate** – roughly equivalent to four GCSEs at Grades A*– C

3 **Advanced** – roughly equivalent to two A Levels.

GNVQ is different from GCSE and A Level because it is more concerned with the skills and knowledge that you will need in employment than with general educational aims.

Some basic differences between a GNVQ and GCSE or A level

GCSE and A Level are aimed at increasing your general knowledge and ability across a broad area of the subject. These will be helpful to you in many different situations. They might be important in your future job but they are also likely to enable you to enjoy the rich variety of things which make up the field of art, crafts, and design. For example, you might simply enjoy making things for your own personal satisfaction; you might enjoy visiting exhibitions; you might enjoy collecting art objects. General studies in art and design help you to develop your own tastes and sense of 'style' and to choose things for your own use because you like the way they are designed and made. In time you will develop an aesthetic sense of your own which can be applied to many aspects of life.

Of course, GCSE and A Level also enable you to progress into further and higher education, although you may not choose to specialise in art, craft or design. In other words, they are just like all the other subjects which you study as part of your general education. Once you have chosen a particular career direction you will have to study subjects which are related to that career.

The Intermediate Art and Design GNVQ is also a general qualification, but it is general *within* the field of art, craft, and design. The course you will follow should cover a very broad range of study and you are unlikely to specialise in one particular area until you have made up your mind what you want to do, either in employment or in higher education. (In the same way, a GNVQ in Business Studies would not be designed to enable you to become an accountant or a business manager but would aim to prepare you for making a choice of such specialisation.) GNVQ is designed to give you a sound general foundation in all aspects of art, craft, and design and to experience a wide enough range of specialisms to enable you to make a choice of a particular area for further study or employment.

As you progress from Level 2, the Intermediate qualification, to Level 3, Advanced, you will probably begin to concentrate more on one particular specialism which you would like to study further – for a Degree or Higher National vocational qualification. The

GNVQ in art and design is therefore one of the ways through which you can gain access to higher education. There are other ways, for example, studying for GCSE and A Level then enrolling on a pre-degree Foundation course before applying for a place on a Degree course. The main difference between these two routes is that in the GNVQ courses your studies will be focused on art, craft, and design throughout, whilst in the other, only the Foundation course will be specialised.

Many students choose to do both a GNVQ course and GCSE or A Level in art and design. This increases the range of qualifications they obtain. This is sometimes an advantage when applying for grants and for a place on a degree course.

For further advice and information on careers in art, craft, and design, you can consult the book produced by the National Society for Education in Art and Design:

A Guide to Courses and Careers in Art, Craft, and Design. Charlton A. 5th Edition Revised 1993. Available from the NSEAD, The Gatehouse, Corsham Court, Corsham, Wiltshire SN13 0BZ. Price at time of writing £12.15 inc. P. P.

EMPLOYMENT IN ART, CRAFT, AND DESIGN

▲ Albert Irvin working in his studio

▲ Lawson Oyekan

▲ Frances Soubeyran

▲ Julian Gregory

The range of possible employment in art, craft, and design is considerable. Most of you will know about the more highly-publicised careers – graphic design, fashion, and fine art – but there are many other occupations which are less well-known. For example, look at the table opposite which shows you an extensive list of occupations in the crafts.

SECTOR	SUB-SECTOR
Glass	Furnace work
	Glass engraving
	Glass painting
	Heat forming
	Stained glass
Graphic Crafts	Bookbinding
	Calligraphy
	Decorative crafts
	Illustration
	Lettering
	Letterpress
	Paper making
	Paper shaping
	Printmaking
Iron and Stone	Stone and monumental masonry
	Stone carving and sculpture
	Wrought iron
	Blacksmithing
Jewellery and Allied Crafts	Enamelling
	Fine metalwork
	Jewellery
Leather	General leatherwork
	Hornworking
	Saddlery
Pottery and Ceramics	Ceramic sculpture
	Ceramics
	China painting
	Pottery

SECTOR	SUB-SECTOR
Rural Crafts	Dry stone walling
	Thatching
	Wheelwrighting
	Woodcrafts
Textiles	Embroidery
	Fashion
	Knitting – hand and machine
	Lace making
	Patchwork and quilting
	Soft furnishing and upholstery
	Spinning, weaving and dyeing
	Surface pattern
Toys and Instruments	Automata
	Dolls
	Gunmaking
	Horology
	Models and replicas
	Musical instruments
	Toys, toy settings, games and puzzles
Wood	Basketry, cane seating and rush work
	Furniture and upholstery
	Picture framing
	Wood specialities
	Woodcarving
	Woodturning
	Woodworking

Table extracted from the Occupational and Functional Mapping Report of the Crafts Occupational Standards Board, January 1994. Reproduced by kind permission of the COSB.

NVQs (National Vocational Qualifications)

The table on the previous page raises an important issue about qualifications which are specifically vocational. They are concerned with the work that people actually do, and can be gained whilst at work as well as through a course of study in a college or a training centre. These are known as NVQs. They are not yet fully developed to cover the full range of art, craft, and design occupations. For example, there are no NVQs in the crafts yet but there are in design. **The main difference between a GNVQ in art and design and a NVQ is that one is general and the other is specialised and mainly about skills, or competences.**

As you embark on your career you will be able to plan the way in which you can gain additional qualifications while you are at work. These qualifications can be obtained by accumulating the required number of units over whatever period of time suits you. It may be possible in the next few years to begin to accumulate NVQ units alongside GNVQs.

Accreditation of Prior Learning

One final thought in this section – although you may embark on a course of study in art, craft, and design, the term 'general' means that you can change courses if you wish, and some of the studies you have completed will be taken into account when you enrol on a new course. Similarly, if you enrol on an art and design course after some time in employment, or on another course of study, that experience can be credited to you. This is known as Accreditation of Prior Learning (APL).

THE STRUCTURE OF THE ART AND DESIGN GNVQ

If you look closely at the list of things that artists, craftspeople and designers have to be able to do in Chapter 3, and compare them with the **Performance criteria** on the next page, you will see that the GNVQ is constructed to cover all of these skills. These skills are included in more detail in what are known as **Competences** within each **Unit** of the GNVQ.

The qualifications are made up of Units which you must complete in order to gain an award.

Intermediate GNVQ has 9 units: 4 mandatory, 2 optional, and 3 core skills. (**Advanced GNVQ** has 15 units: 8 mandatory, 4 optional, and 3 core skills.)

Mandatory Units mean you **must** study the 4 units.

Optional Units mean you have a **choice** of doing 2 units from the range offered.

The Core Skills are mandatory and you **must** complete them successfully in order to gain an award.

Additional Units are designed to allow you to develop further, probably more specialised, skills in chosen aspects of art, craft, and design, and again you will have a **choice** of units.

The Awarding Bodies

The qualification you will obtain will be awarded by one of three Awarding Bodies:

BTEC (Business and Technology Education Council)

City and Guilds (The City and Guilds of London Institute)

RSA (The Royal Society of Arts)

The GNVQ structure and Mandatory Units are the same for each Awarding Body, but the Optional and Additional Units are different. You can see all of the Unit specifications in the booklets provided by each of the Awarding Bodies.

Your school or college will choose the Awarding Body.

The Intermediate GNVQ

Mandatory Units – 4

Unit 1 *2D visual language*

1.1 Explore 2D visual language

1.2 Use 2D media, technology, processes, and techniques

Unit 2 *3D visual language*

2.1 Explore 3D visual language

2.2 Use 3D materials, technology, processes, and techniques

Unit 3 *Exploring others' art, craft, and design work*

3.1 Explore historical and contemporary contextual references

3.2 Investigate professional practice

Unit 4 *Applying the creative process*

4.1 Clarify the brief and carry out research

4.2 Originate and develop ideas

4.3 Produce final work

4.4 Evaluate and present work

Optional Units – 2

(from the choices provided by the awarding body)

Unit 5*

Unit 6*

Unit 7*

Unit 8*

**The unit specifications will be different for each awarding body. The booklet produced by your awarding body will tell you what they are.*

Core Skills Units – 3

Communication

2.1 Take part in discussions

2.2 Produce written material

2.3 Use images

2.4 Read and respond to written materials

Application of Number

2.1 Collect and record data

2.2 Tackle problems

2.3 Interpret and present data

Information technology

2.1 Prepare information

2.2 Process information

2.3 Present information

2.4 Evaluate the use of information technology

It may help you to understand the structure a little better if you study the chart below. It shows how each Unit is constructed.

Unit The Unit has a title which indicates what it is about, and it consists normally of two or three elements. For example, the title for Unit 2 is *3D visual language* and it has two Elements – *2.1 Explore 3D formal elements*, and *2.2 Use 3D materials, technology, processes, and techniques.*

Elements Each Element has a short description of what it is about then a more detailed breakdown of what it consists of. An Element consists of the following:

Performance criteria	These are lists of the things you have to be able to do to successfully complete the Element.
Range	This is a list of the areas of skills, knowledge and understanding which you must cover in each Element. The words printed in bold type in the Performance Criteria are headings used in the Range.
Evidence	These tell you what evidence you must provide in order to show that you have successfully completed the Element.

The following example from Unit 2, *3D visual language*, will give you some idea how the Unit Specifications are normally presented. You may find the language difficult at first but it is important that you learn to understand it, because you will be the one mainly responsible for checking that all of the components have been properly completed. Your college or school will probably provide you with a checklist based on the Unit Specification but it is better for you if you have read and understood it yourself.

Example:

Unit 2 3D visual language

Element 2.1 *Explore 3D visual language*
Element 2.2 *Use 3D materials, technology, processes, and techniques*

Each of the Unit Specifications will be dealt with in some depth in the following Chapters and this example is simply to help you to understand the structure.

The Unit has two Elements. The first number – 2 in 2.1 and 2.2 – means that each of the Elements belongs to Unit 2. Elements for Unit 3 would be numbered 3.1, 3.2 and so on.

It may be helpful to work through one of the Elements and to explain what the terms mean.

Unit 2, Element 2.2 *Work with 3D materials, technology, processes, and techniques*

Performance criteria

This term means the list of things you have to be able to do in order to be assessed for an award.

1 develop skills in the use of 3D materials, technology, processes, and techniques

This means:

- that you have to show that you can manipulate chosen materials properly e.g. that you can model clay, shape or carve resistant materials, and join materials together in constructing things.
- that you have developed appropriate techniques, including the use of hand tools, for controlling, shaping and joining materials.
- that you understand and can use the processes involved in creating objects from three-dimensional materials, e.g. the sequence involved in throwing a pot on a wheel or in making a coil pot.
- that you can use properly the equipment or machinery involved e.g. using an electrically-operated potter's wheel or a kick wheel to make a pot.
- that you have developed skills to a level where you can produce work of the quality required for Intermediate Art and Design GNVQ.

2 explore working characteristics, potential, and limitations of materials

This means:

- that you have understood what it is possible to do with the materials you have chosen: what their potential and limitations are. For example, clay can be pressed, squeezed and rolled into different shapes but if you try to stretch it, it will pull apart – you can also model with clay by adding pieces and taking pieces away to create a particular form.

The characteristics of clay are:
- that when it is moist it is 'plastic' and easy to shape by most means but not stretching
- that it then dries and becomes very brittle and fragile – it can also be destroyed by water since it is in an impermanent state
- that it can be fired (heated to a high temperature) to change its chemistry and make it permanent
- that it can be decorated by impressing the surface when moist, adding clay patterns, putting slip on to the surface and by glazing it after it has been fired once.

3 select and use 3D materials, technology, processes, and techniques creatively to meet specified intentions

This means:
- that you have been able to select appropriate materials, techniques and technology most suited to what you wanted to make (your intentions).

4 follow the 3D health and safety procedures associated with studio and workshop practice

This is a very important part of your education and training and is concerned with using materials, tools and equipment safely. You have to show you were aware of the possible dangers and that you were able to avoid them by observing correct safety procedures. It is also useful to know something about your legal obligations and about the relevant legislation.

Hazards may include possible danger to other people in the way that you work and whether or not the thing you have made might be dangerous – for example, by using the wrong kind of paint on a child's toy you might cause poisoning; or something which uses electricity has to conform to legal safety standards.

5 discuss and review the effectiveness of own use of 3D materials, technology, processes and techniques

This means:
- that you are able to discuss the skills, materials and technologies which you used in making things
- that you are able to review or look back over what you have done and make some judgements about how well you did it or how you could have done it better.

Range

3D materials: card, clay, metal, plastics, textiles, wood

• This is the list of materials which you are expected to have used in covering this Element. Whatever is included in the list *must* be explored in some way, although you wouldn't be expected to have experienced using them all to the same extent. For example, your centre's facilities for dealing with metal may be limited and you probably wouldn't be able to do any welding or other hot metal treatments. On the other hand, there may be very good facilities for textiles and you could use many different textiles materials.

Technology, processes and techniques:

• These are the means by which you cut, form and join 3D materials.

• **Technology** will involve some kind of machinery or special equipment.

• **Processes** means how you make something over a period of time. For example, the process of making something in metal may involve you in cutting shapes out of a sheet of metal, bending or beating them, joining them by soldering or braising, and finally polishing the finished object.

• **Techniques** are similar to processes but usually mean particular ways of working. For example, cutting techniques could involve you in using different saws, knives, or hot wire to cut polystyrene.

Specified intentions:

• These are simply to do with the reasons for making something. For example, you may be making something for a client or customer, in which case the intentions would be to do with what your client wanted, how you planned to do it, and what you expected the outcome to be. Or, you may be making something only for yourself, in which case your intentions would be personal – to do with your tastes and ideas.

Health and safety procedures:

• These are very important and they are covered by law. You have to be aware of possible dangers to others (known as hazards) and to yourself, and you have a shared responsibility to ensure that nothing you do creates unacceptable risks. There will be strict regulations covering some activities and general codes of conduct for others. Your tutors will make sure that you are aware of the procedures but, mostly, safe working practices involve common sense, sensible behaviour, and being careful.

Evidence indicators

These are the kinds of work that you have to show in your portfolio or in other coursework. You have to provide **evidence of study** in the form of notes and records as well as showing the required range of art, craft and design work. In this Element, you have to provide evidence of two complex activities, including examples from the process of making something as well as the finished work. The evidence must be from at least two of the contexts of art, craft and design.

The Evidence indicators will be the basis of your Unit assessment and may be checked by someone from outside your centre, known as an **External Verifier**.

It is important to recognise that in all of the Units you will not only have to do the required practical work but you must also be able to undertake some investigation and explain what you have been doing. In each Unit this means there will be written work as well as discussion about your work. (This will be assessed under the core skill Communication.)

Final Assessment

When you are finally assessed at the end of your course you may be interviewed by an External Verifier. He/she will be employed by the awarding body you have worked under. They will check to see that you have achieved the required standards. They are known as **Verifiers** because their main job is to verify, or confirm, the assessments made internally by yourself and your tutor.

THE STRUCTURE OF A GNVQ COURSE

Although the GNVQ Unit Specifications are presented as separate components, most courses don't actually teach them separately. The most usual methods are to devise assignments, projects or specific tasks for you to do which combine a number of the Units. You could be engaged in work which relates to almost all of the Units or it may involve only a few.

For example, an assignment which requires you to undertake the whole process of designing and making a product would probably involve all of the four Mandatory Units; but one which was aimed mainly at developing your drawing ability might only involve Units 1 and 3. The assignments are designed so that by the end of the course you will have done all of the required Units. This means your tutors have to construct them in such a way that all of the Units are covered and that you have to check that you have actually done them. You must keep all the evidence needed to show that this has been the case.

To design assignments to cover the required Units in sufficient depth is very complicated and difficult. For you, it may at first seem to be incomprehensible. However, as your course progresses, you will get used to the system of checking or 'referencing' the work you have done against the Unit Specifications. So, don't be put off by the apparent complexity – it really does become understandable as the course progresses.

Let's take Unit 2, Element 2.2 again (*Work with 3D materials, technology, processes, and techniques*) as an example. You will soon get used to checking that you have done what is required:

- referring to the list of Performance Criteria
- the Range statement will help you to see if the breadth of the work which you have done covers all of the things in this list.
- your portfolio can then be arranged so that the Evidence for each Element is properly identified and labelled.

WAYS OF APPROACHING YOUR STUDIES

When you begin your course you will be introduced to a range of different methods of working, different materials and techniques and given a broad foundation in the kinds of work you will be doing in more depth later on.

A very important feature of a GNVQ course is that you will be expected to assume a lot of responsibility for the planning and direction of your own work. This is important because it prepares you for being a professional artist, designer or craftsperson but it is also the aspect of your work which will enable you to gain a higher grade of pass.

Pass, Merit, and Distinction Grades

If you can only complete your set assignments with the help of your tutor you will probably obtain a **Pass** grade.

If you can work independently and show that you can carry out successfully an assignment on your own, then you could get a **Merit** or a **Distinction**. (An assignment is a particular task or design problem which your tutor will have given you to do within a specified time.) You will, therefore, need to develop your own methods of approaching the tasks you are given which demonstrate clearly that you can work independently.

There are many ways of approaching an assignment and the one you choose will probably depend on what you are expected to do. For example, an assignment in the early stages of your course might be mainly concerned with helping you to develop the skills of investigation and research and you may not be expected to produce a finished product. In this case, the emphasis will be on finding out where you can get information, learning to select from what you have found, analysing and interpreting the information, and recording it in ways which enable you to make full use of it in developing your ideas.

Later in the course, an assignment is likely to include the full range of skills required to complete the whole process of creating something.

In this case you may be involved in most of the following:

• **planning** the direction of your work

• **generating ideas** from any appropriate source

• **researching and investigating** sources of information which you may need, including the work of other artists, craftspeople, and designers, and some aspects of the contexts in which similar work occurs – in different times, places, and cultures, for example

• **recording** the results of your investigations

• **researching** the market to see what other products already exist and what you might do which is different or better

• **exploring and experimenting** with different materials, tools and techniques to discover which are the most suitable for your purposes

• **learning any new practical skills** which you need in order to do the work

• **making final decisions** on the product you want to make and taking it to a proper degree of finish – this will involve you in a complex process in which you will constantly have to make judgements about the work in hand and make any modifications to your ideas and techniques which will enable you to complete it successfully

• **evaluating** the final outcome – this again will mean making judgements about how well you have succeeded and being critical of your own work

[By this stage you should have an idea of the quality of work expected of you. Your tutor will set general standards but you should be prepared to develop your own personal ones.]

• **recording, documenting, and presenting** your work

Of course, you will also have to use the **core skills** whenever they are appropriate to the assignment. You may need to do calculations, use the computer to analyse, store, and extract information or develop your design, write about your work, correspond with clients, and record research findings.

'Action' words

The words in bold type are important for you to understand because they tell you the kinds of activity you are expected to undertake.

Planning

This will involve you in thinking about how you will go about your work. For example, you might prepare diagrams, charts and lists of materials or things to do, and you will have to consider how long each stage of the process is likely to take (managing your time). You will need to decide what sources of information you have to find and the people you may need to consult, e.g. professional designers and experts on things you don't know much about. You will need to plan for using any particular tools, equipment and techniques which you may need, and you will have to think about how you will record and present your work.

Generating ideas

This is one of the most important parts of any creative process – you will have to find ways of stimulating ideas. They come from all kinds of sources, sometimes they simply come when you're least expecting them – from your sub-conscious mind – and at other times they only come from a long process of looking at things and from your investigations. They can be generated by looking at other similar kinds of work, through your feelings about something, and, most importantly, from your imagination. Of course, they very often come from talking to other people – 'brain-storming' is often useful.

One of the main reasons for keeping sketchbooks and notebooks is that they can be used for jotting down ideas when they occur to you. Some writers keep a notebook by their bedside so that if they wake up in the night with an idea in mind they can note it – otherwise it will probably be forgotten.

In art, craft, and design, ideas are most often generated in visual form – in drawings, sketches, models, and photographs. The sources for such studies can be found everywhere – found objects, natural forms, and made objects, for instance, but one of the most important sources is other art, craft, and design work. Visiting galleries, museums and exhibitions should be something you do as often as you can and, if possible, you should visit artists, craftspeople, and designers in their studios.

When you make such visits you should get into the habit of making notes and studies in your sketchbooks and carrying a camera to record things you have seen. A camera can prove to be one of the most useful pieces of equipment you can buy.

Finally, you must develop the habit of looking carefully at things which interest you. Learning to look is one of the most important skills you can acquire if you want to become a professional artist, craftsperson, or designer. The act of drawing something carefully actually forces you to concentrate on its visual appearance and to spend time on it. Many things nowadays only require us to look briefly to get the message (think of advertising on TV) but it's only when you spend time in looking that you begin to really understand what you are seeing.

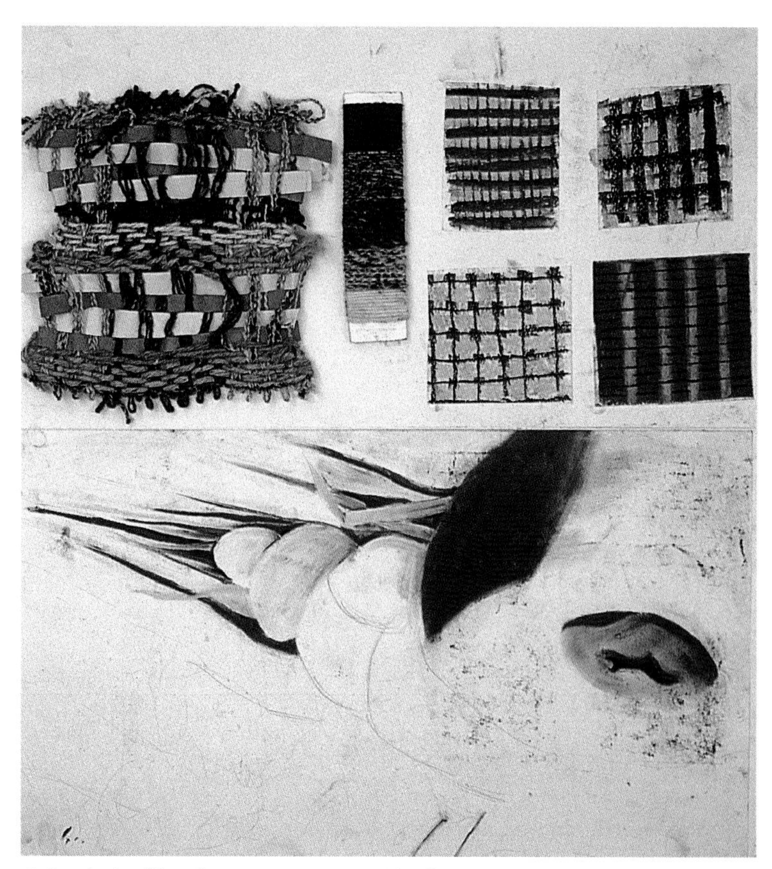

▲ **Developing ideas for woven patterns starting from an analytical drawing**

Researching

This is often confused with investigating but it is a different process. Research involves finding, selecting, storing, recording, and interpreting information. You might need statistical information on a possible market for a product. For example, the kind of people who might buy it, how many there might be, where they are most likely to be located, how much they might be prepared to spend and so on.

You may need information about a range of products which could compete with your own, in which case you will need to research the field to find out what there is, who makes and sells it, how much it costs, what patents exist on its design, and how many are sold each year. Or, you may need to research the history of a range of products so that you understand how they have been developed. Such research will involve you in using computers and is one of the main areas within the core skill of Information Technology (IT).

▼ **Examples of research notes**

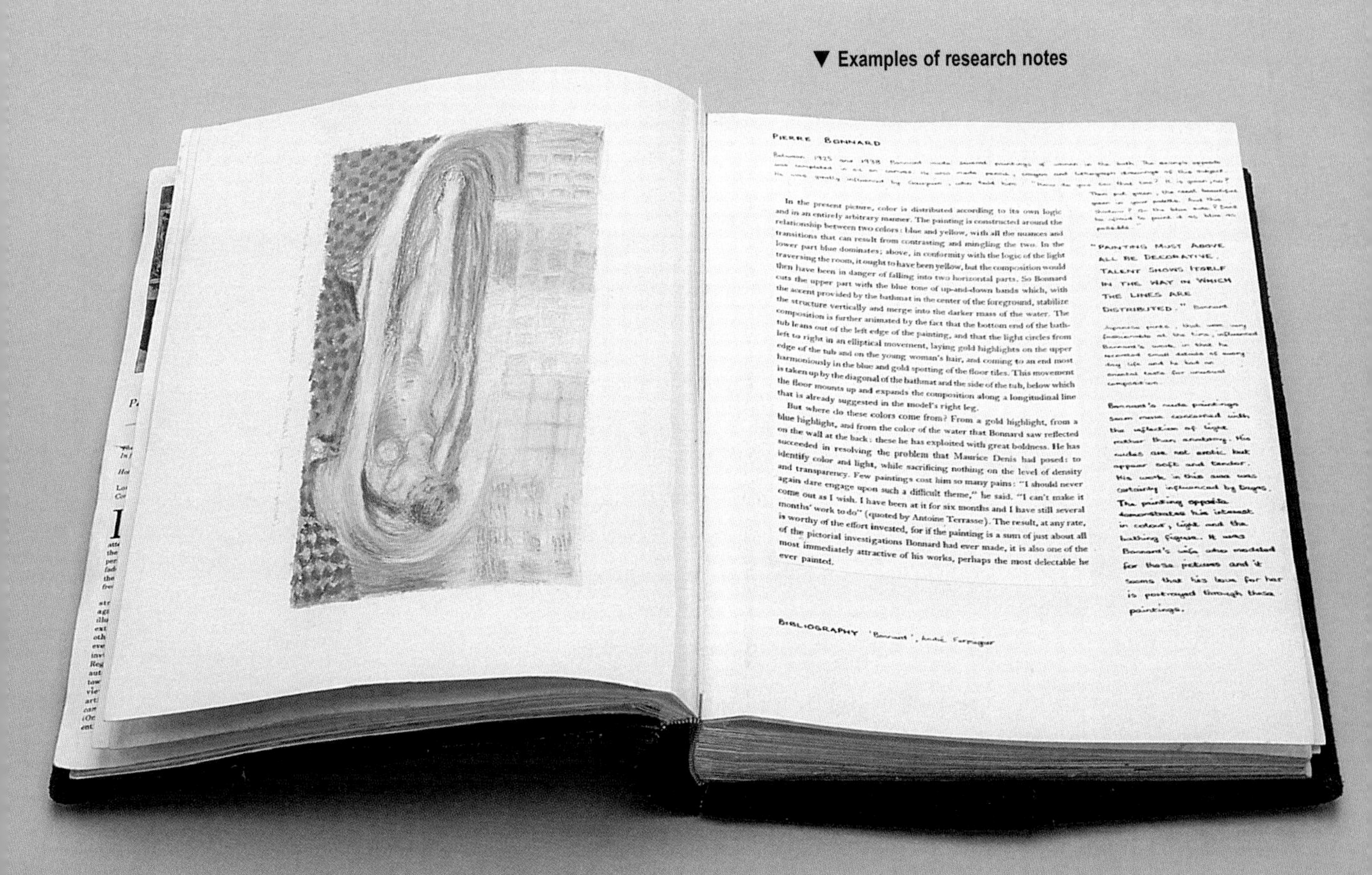

PIERRE BONNARD

In the present picture, color is distributed according to its own logic and in an entirely arbitrary manner. The painting is constructed around the relationship between two colors: blue and yellow, with all the nuances and transitions that can result from contrasting and mingling the two. In the lower part blue dominates; above, in conformity with the logic of the light traversing the room, it ought to have been yellow, but the composition would then have been in danger of falling into two horizontal parts. So Bonnard cuts the upper part with the blue tone of up-and-down bands which, with the accent provided by the bathmat in the center of the foreground, stabilize the structure vertically and merge into the darker mass of the water. The composition is further animated by the fact that the bottom end of the bath-tub leans out of the left edge of the painting, and that the light circles from left to right in an elliptical movement, laying gold highlights on the upper edge of the tub and on the young woman's hair, and coming to an end most harmoniously in the blue and gold spotting of the floor tiles. This movement is taken up by the diagonal of the bathmat and the side of the tub, below which the floor mounts up and expands the composition along a longitudinal line that is already suggested in the model's right leg.

But where do these colors come from? From a gold highlight, from a blue highlight, and from the color of the water that Bonnard saw reflected on the wall at the back: these he has exploited with great boldness. He has succeeded in resolving the problem that Maurice Denis had posed: to identify color and light, while sacrificing nothing on the level of density and transparency. Few paintings cost him so many pains: "I should never again dare engage upon such a difficult theme," he said. "I can't make it come out as I wish. I have been at it for six months and I have still several months' work to do" (quoted by Antoine Terrasse). The result, at any rate, is worthy of the effort invested, for if the painting is a sum of just about all of the pictorial investigations Bonnard had ever made, it is also one of the most immediately attractive of his works, perhaps the most delectable he ever painted.

"PAINTING MUST ABOVE ALL BE DECORATIVE. TALENT SHOWS ITSELF IN THE WAY IN WHICH THE LINES ARE DISTRIBUTED."

BIBLIOGRAPHY

Investigating

This is similar to research in that its main purpose is to find out things that you need to know, but in art and design it is mainly done visually. You will probably draw, model and take photographs to obtain visual information – how an object was constructed, how something grew, what its structure or colour range is, what its surface is like and so on.

▲ **Examples of investigative drawings and an original photograph – Advanced level student**

For example, if you were doing a project involving a study of trees you might make lots of drawings and take photographs of different aspects of trees, building up a range of visual references. By doing this you not only have a useful record of your investigations, but you will also be able to draw some trees from memory and from the knowledge of trees which you have absorbed. Some people describe this as building up a 'visual vocabulary' which is retained in your memory in much the same way that you remember words.

Of course, at the same time as you develop your skills of observation you will also develop your drawing skills. You will discover how to represent something you are observing carefully, and what are the most suitable materials and techniques.

Recording and documenting

This is something you do when you are researching, investigating and thinking about any ideas you may have. In its simplest form it is just about making a visual record of what you are looking at, an objective drawing or a photograph for instance. Again, you will probably use drawing, painting, modelling, and photography but sometimes you have to record things which are not possible to do in this way. You will then have to use other methods, such as making notes, tape recording, video recording or a combination of the whole range. You will also record images from memory, imagination and from things you experience, in which case the visual records will not be objective drawings in the sense described above.

Remember that the Evidence indicators tell you what kinds of records and art, craft or design work you need to provide for assessment. You will get used to checking or 'referencing' your work against the Evidence indicators, Performance criteria, and Range.

▶ Recording figures in action from short poses – Intermediate level student

Exploring and Experimenting

These terms are easy to understand since they mean just what they say. Remember that in the Unit Specification you are often expected to show that you have done sufficient exploration and experimentation. It is important for you to feel free to choose what you do and how you do it, because many new and unexpected ideas can emerge from truly creative and open-minded experimentation. You need to develop some methods which suit your own personality. Some people will be much happier working methodically, while others will rely on their imaginative responses. However, you must do a reasonably substantial range of work in order to demonstrate your ability to work thoroughly and persistently until you have enough work from which to make proper choices for the final piece.

► **Recorded evidence of the progression of an idea and its development**

Learning new skills

Mostly, you will be taught the skills you need for particular assignments and for developing your general capabilities, but you should always look for new things to learn and show that you are keen to learn them. An example might be that you want to duplicate an image a number of times in order to try out different patterns and colour combinations. There are many ways in which this can be done, some of which you may have been taught. However, you realise that the most efficient way might be to use a drawing programme on a computer. If you haven't been taught the necessary skills to do that, you might need to set about learning them.

You should try to increase the range of skills you have at every opportunity.

Making Decisions

Again this sounds fairly obvious, but the range of decisions you will have to make and justify is considerable. If you think about the activities already described, all of them involve you in making some decisions. Most obvious are the decisions you make when you choose what to make, investigate or research, but there are others which are important to the process of creating something which you may not be aware of. Every time you make a mark on a piece of paper or an impression in a piece of clay it changes the appearance and you are immediately faced with a decision on what to do next. You are not necessarily aware of this process taking place; you make the decisions intuitively. But you are making decisions and you will often be asked to say why you did something at a particular time and won't really know why. In evaluating your own work, one of the important things to do is to reflect on what you have done and try to become aware of the reasons for the decisions you made, some apparently without much thought.

Other decisions will require you to be logical and to think a problem through. Often this process will be accompanied by drawings and notes which will provide important evidence for your assessment. You must learn to keep all such evidence in your portfolio or files.

Evaluating

This has already been mentioned in the last activity and it is a very important part of your course of study. You are expected to be able to consider the work you have just completed, or partially completed, and make reasoned judgements about it. This means you will have to be able to say how successful you think the project has been and what you could have done to improve it if you weren't very successful. You will learn to use the right kind of language and become involved with unfamiliar terms. For example, if you are asked to say how good something you've made looks you will probably have to talk about things like colour, shape, line, surface texture, balance, and composition. These are known as the 'formal elements' of art – they are used to describe the 'form' as opposed to the 'content' of a piece of art or craftwork.

You may also be required to make written evaluations and this is another example of where you will be using the core skill of Communication.

It is very important for you to try to evaluate the *quality* of your work.

Presenting

This is another very important part of your course – you have to be able to show your work to the best advantage. There are different kinds of presentations – you might simply arrange your work in an attractively organised portfolio for presentation to a client (or an assessor), or you might need to arrange a substantial exhibition which involves you in mounting your work and creating an imaginative display.

There are particular skills associated with presentation and you must ensure that you learn them thoroughly as the course progresses.

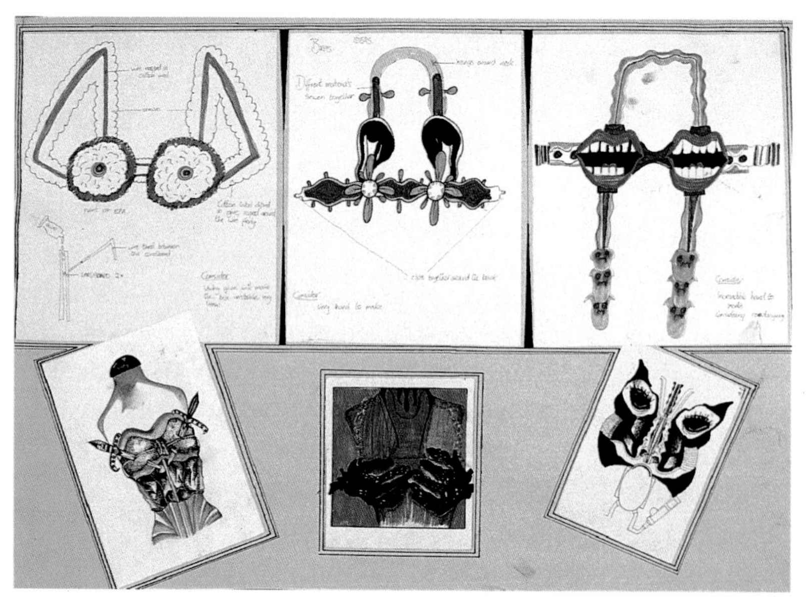

◀ **An example of a mounted sheet of work for portfolio or display – Intermediate level student**

Core skills

You might be tempted to think that artists, craftspeople, and designers don't really need to be able to write particularly well or be able to add up and measure things. Some of you may even have chosen to do art and design because it doesn't involve much English and Mathematics. In some forms of art and craft this may be so, but like all occupations, you will need to be reasonably literate and numerate. Certainly, there are few design occupations where you wouldn't need such skills. If you already have GCSEs in English, Maths, and Computing you should have no difficulty in coping with the Core skills' requirement, but if you haven't, you must be prepared to work at it so that you develop the necessary abilities. You must recognise that, apart from being a requirement of the GNVQ, competence in each of the Core skills is a necessity in most professional occupations.

You will become familiar with the Core skills as your course progresses. They are:

- **Application of Number**
- **Communication**
- **Information Technology**

They are called Core skills because they apply to all GNVQ courses. They are the same for Art and Design as for Business Studies. The idea is that we all need such Core skills in whatever job we do and for general needs in our personal lives, so the intention is to **integrate** them into each area of study rather than teach them as separate subjects. For example, the Mathematics you do won't be simulated, it will be applied to real situations where you can see and understand its purposes.

This means that the Core skills are taught and learnt in the **context** of the different specialist studies of Art and Design, Business Studies, Health and Social Care, Leisure and Tourism and so on. At school you would have been taught Maths, English and probably Computer Studies separately in specially timetabled periods. In the GNVQ they are incorporated into your programme of study and relate to the specialist work you are doing.

The Core skill, *Application of Number*, is concerned with processing numerical information. This could involve you in calculating quantities of materials for a construction project, taking measurements for a cutting list, or making measured drawings. It can also involve data collection, calculations on the data, and drawing statistical conclusions. Of course, these number skills are also transferable – what you learn in one context can be used in others.

Communication covers the skills of writing, discussing, explaining, reading, listening to others and understanding what they are saying, adding descriptive text to illustrations and drawings, and so on.

Information Technology includes a range of skills in the use of computers, particularly the processing and presentation of information. An example would be processing data and presenting it in the form of pie charts and bar charts. This will involve you in developing the ability to use a variety of software programmes to sort, store, retrieve and present information.

In art, craft, and design, computer-assisted design (CAD) is commonplace, as we will discuss later. This involves specialised skills which may not be applicable to other contexts and they are not, therefore, strictly Core skills. However, since CAD often involves processing images and text you might be using the Core skill *Communication*.

The structure of the Core skills Units is the same as in the Art and Design Units. Each *Unit* contains a number of *Elements* which are broken down into *Performance criteria, Range statements* and *Evidence indicators*. These specify what you must do, but again they do not constitute a Syllabus, you do them in appropriate situations along with the other work you are doing. An important thing to remember is that you are mainly responsible for the referencing of the Core skills within your work. You have to get used to identifying and noting when you are using a particular Core skill and ensuring that it is noted and assessed. This will be a familiar part of all of the work you do and your tutors will explain how to cover the requirements. You will also, of course, be given instruction and help with developing Core skills, sometimes in the form of specialist sessions where a particular skill will be taught.

Some of you may have difficulty with parts of the Core skills requirement. For example, if you are dyslexic you are likely to experience some difficulties with *Communication*. If you have any form of disability you can get help. For example, difficulties with writing can be overcome by finding other means of recording and expressing things, such as using tape recorders and videos. Sometimes you may require specialist help and you must make sure that your tutor understands your needs. Don't try to solve all of your problems by yourself – nobody will want you to fail your course because of a disability.

Those of you whose first language is not English may find the requirements to write, discuss, explain, and evaluate things that you do particularly demanding. Don't be put off – if you persevere you will find that it becomes easier to do this kind of work, and people will be very helpful if they know that you are experiencing problems.

This book does not attempt to deal with Optional and Additional Units since they vary according to which Awarding Body offers them. Therefore, the four main Chapters which follow deal with the Mandatory Units only. However, much of this material will also be relevant to Optional and Additional Units since they are designed to provide for more specialised study in aspects of art, craft, and design covered by the Mandatory Units.

1

unit 1

2D visual language

ELEMENT 1.1

EXPLORE 2D VISUAL LANGUAGE

ELEMENT 1.2

USE 2D MATERIALS, TECHNOLOGY, PROCESSES, AND TECHNIQUES

2D visual language is the title of the first of the four Mandatory Units and, as you can see, there are two Elements. In this chapter, each of the Elements will be explained in some detail with examples of the kinds of work which you should do.

2D visual language is concerned with work which is done mainly on flat, or two-dimensional, surfaces (it has length and breadth but not depth), such as drawing, painting, printmaking, photography, film, and video. 3D visual language (Unit 2) is used in relation to work which is three-dimensional, or 'in the round', such as modelling, carving, and construction.

The term **visual language** can be difficult for you to understand. It is a term used to describe all of the different means through which you can communicate with others, work out your own ideas, and express your personal feelings and intuitions **visually**. The difference between this and spoken or written language is simply that the means you use are visual – you 'talk' to other people and 'read' through pictures, signs, and symbols. There are certain ways of doing this which are commonly used and, therefore, have 'rules' in the same way that a written language has rules – such as those relating to grammar. In art, craft, and design, however, these rules are not absolute. There will be occasions when you will want to use your own variations, but if you use language, signs, and symbols which other people can't understand then, obviously, you won't communicate very well.

Symbols are things which, by general agreement, represent or stand for something else. For example, the *cross* is commonly accepted as the symbol for Christianity, the colour *white* is a symbol for purity, the *dragon* symbolises evil or paganism, and the *lion* symbolises courage. **Signs** are similar, in that they too stand for something else by general agreement and, although their definition is quite complicated, it may be useful for you to think of them as they commonly appear, in the form of road signs, livery, heraldic emblems, logos, direction signs and so on. As you study for Unit 3, *Exploring others' art, craft and design work,* you will learn more about some of the ways in which signs and symbols have been used at different times in history, how they are used in different cultures, and how they are used by contemporary practitioners. If you don't understand the meaning of such signs and symbols it will be difficult for you to know what the art and design work is about, i.e. what the content is.

▲ An aircraft tail fin emblem

▲ *Paolo Uccello (c.1397-1475), 'St. George and the Dragon'.* The myth of St George and the Dragon in Medieval and Renaissance times symbolised the triumph of Christianity over Paganism. The dragon was a symbol for evil. In Chinese mythology the dragon is a symbol for good rather than evil.

You will learn to 'read' paintings and works of art, craft, and design similarly to the way in which you learnt to read books, and it will be helpful to think of art, craft, and design as a language.

It is important that you begin to understand the relationship between **Content** and **Form**. As we have said, content is the work's subject matter – what it is about and what it means – whereas form is what it looks like and how it is composed or constructed – its appearance. Most of the work you will be expected to do in this Unit is to do with form, but you will nevertheless become increasingly involved in content as part of visual language as you progress through the course.

▲ ***Ben Nicholson, 'Painting', 1937.*** **This painting by Ben Nicholson is essentially about form rather than content.**

The main basis for this visual language is a set of terms – sometimes referred to as a **vocabulary** – which are used in art, craft, and design. They are concerned with the **appearance** of 'art objects' and they are therefore about **formal** considerations. They are known as the **formal elements**. The use of the word element indicates that they are single categories which can be isolated from each other because they have different characteristics, but they are mostly combined with each other to create many different effects. Chemical elements are thought of in a similar way and are also combined with each other to create different composites. It is the extent of the possible range of combinations which creates the enormous diversity in the appearance of art, craft, and design objects. For the purpose of this chapter we shall mainly consider a range of basic elements separately, but with appropriate references to their most common combinations.

ELEMENT 1.1

EXPLORE 2D VISUAL LANGUAGE

Performance criteria

1. *explore and practise **mark-making techniques***
2. *explore **2D formal elements** and explain the elements used*
3. *use 2D visual language to communicate **information***
4. *use 2D visual language to express **ideas and feelings***
5. *show awareness of the potential of 2D visual language in work produced*
6. *discuss own and others' use of 2D visual language*

Range

Mark-making techniques: collage, computer-aided, drawing, lens-based, painting, print-making

2D formal elements: line, light, colour, tone, contrast, shape, scale, proportion, perspective, texture, pattern, design, composition

Information: representation of space and form, images, objects, people

Ideas and feelings: personal responses, moods (given, self-identified)

Evidence indicators

Studies showing the use of 2D visual language, covering the range for mark-making techniques and 2D formal elements. The studies should be supported by records to show that the student has:

- explained the formal elements used.
- discussed the use of visual language in their own and others' work

Evidence of two complex activities, including developmental and final work. These activities should be set in at least two of the following contexts:

- art
- craft
- design.

This is the standard form of presentation which you will recognise in all of the Units. It simply tells you what you must have done in order to complete the Unit. **An important thing for you to understand is that this specification is not a syllabus. It is a check-list for assessment of the work you have done**. If it were a syllabus you would have to follow it exactly and study 2D visual language as a Unit on its own. In your course you are unlikely to do this, since you will normally work in many different ways and cover parts, or the whole, of several Units in one project. When you come to assess your work, you will refer to the specification and, with your tutor, make judgements about your work's quality and whether or not you have done all that you were expected to do. This process is commonly known as **referencing**.

The main requirements are for you to **explore** the formal elements, mainly through practical work and experimentation. Later, at Advanced level, the emphasis will be on the **use** of formal elements for specific reasons. By that stage, you will be expected to explain and justify their use as well as to demonstrate that you understand how they work in relation to the formal qualities of art, craft, and design objects.

You now need to learn what the terms used in the Performance criteria and Range statements actually mean.

We shall consider the terms and suggest what work you should do and how you might go about it.

Performance criteria and Range statements

The most important thing for you to realise is that the Performance criteria and the Range statements are closely related. For example, the second of the list of Performance criteria **'explore 2D formal elements and explain the elements used'** is described in more detail in the second sentence in the Range statement – it provides a list of the formal elements you will be expected to explore.

The list of words included in the Range statement on **formal elements** may seem to be pretty daunting. It is an extensive list and each term used has its own complex set of theories attached to it. However, at your stage of development, it will be better to simplify the list and to begin to understand some of the very basic uses of the formal elements in art and design.

Perhaps the simplest list might be:

- Line
- Tone
- Shape/Form
- Colour
- Pattern
- Texture

Line

Line, as used in drawing, is a **convention** (a practice based on general consent) which artists use to create the illusion of three-dimensional form on a two-dimensional surface. A line is basically one-dimensional having only length, but you can have fun arguing about how true this is. It can be said that lines, as we use them in art, don't exist in nature. For example, a drawn outline of a figure consists of line which represents the point at which we can no longer see its surface – the sides and the back of the figure are out of sight. A line drawing of a leaf is a representation of its shape, but if we add lines to show the veins and the stem we begin to describe its form and structure. We can go further by using lines to create the illusion of light and shade, thereby suggesting its volume. If you think about how to represent a cylinder using only line you will find that you will probably want to use lines to indicate its sides then create the illusion of three-dimensions by drawing the ellipses at the top and bottom of the cylinder.

▲ Line is used by itself to create the illusion of a cylindrical form

Line can be very 'expressive'. We have already mentioned the way in which drawings can indicate mood and you can experiment with a wide variety of materials and methods to explore the expressive properties of line. You can try drawing sensuous or sinuous lines, lines which suggest speed or violent movement, lines which are 'still', peaceful, in repose and so on.

◄ *R A Bertelli, 'Head of Mussolini', 1933 (48.75 cm high).* The object is cylindrical, made on a potter's wheel, but the outline produces the profile of Mussolini.

The materials and methods you use have a direct effect upon the 'quality' of line and you should try to make your exploration of a particular medium as extensive as possible. For example, try drawing rapidly with a soft pencil until it has been used up, then try as many different variations in the strength of line which you can make with pencils of different grades. These are very basic ways in which you can get to know your materials but it is surprising how many people simply accept what media and materials seem to be able to do and don't explore their full potential.

▲ **An experiment to try out the potential of pencils as a medium**

▲ ***Roy Lichtenstein, 'Whaam!', 1963 (17.27 x 40.64 m – measure this out on a wall to see how big this painting is).*** **In this painting the linear element is dominant and suggests extreme reactions.**

Line is, of course, mainly used in combination with other formal elements, such as tone and colour, but it can be confusing to think about the complexity of such combinations. What you will learn to do is to recognise how line has been used in different contexts and how to apply such uses in your own work. This is one of the reasons why Unit 3, *Exploring others' art, craft, and design work*, is so important to your studies. As you begin to see how other artists and designers have used the formal elements, you will begin to be able to use your developing knowledge of a visual language to 'read' works of art.

▲ *Shuncho, 'A promenade through rice fields', 1796 (Japanese woodcut)*

◀ *John Sell Cotman, 'Norwich Market Place', 1806 (pencil and wash)*

Two illustrations showing line combined with different elements. Cotman's drawing is in pencil with a tonal wash added, and the Japanese image is a colour print from a wood block.

Line is often used in relation to other formal elements. The following examples will give you some idea of its different uses.

Perspective

In Western European art, the drawing system known as perspective drawing is highly developed. It stems from a desire to represent things as we see them from a particular viewpoint. You will be familiar with the example of the railway tracks appearing to converge as they recede and of street scenes where the houses appear to diminish in size. These examples generally use only a single viewpoint but you can use as many as you need. For example, if a road winds away into the distance and goes up and down hill you would need many points to create this illusion. Similarly, if you want to suggest a cube (e.g. looking at the near corner of a house) you would need at

▲ **This photograph is an example of single point perspective**

least two points. You might like to consider how unnatural this kind of representation actually is – we hardly ever see anything in this way, frozen permanently in time, we see things as we move and they move and the knowledge which comes from such seeing enables us to encapsulate them in a single representative image.

The full theory of perspective drawing is complex and very sophisticated but, initially, you will mainly need to understand those parts which you need in order to be able to work reasonably well. The main thing is to **LOOK** very carefully at the objects you are trying to draw and to find appropriate ways of representing them.

▼ **This is an example of two-point perspective**

◀ ***John Sell Cotman, 'Mousehold Heath, Norwich', 1810.*** **This shows the use of multi-point perspective.**

Many other cultures do not use perspective drawing and represent things in different ways. For example, some represent things as they **know** them rather than as they see them. In Western European twentieth-century art, similar ways of representing things have been developed. The Cubists tried to represent things in this way so that their knowledge of an object, which came from seeing and experiencing it throughout a period of time, was reflected in the multi-faceted nature of their paintings.

▲ ***Georges Braque, 'Still life with violin and glass'.*** **A 'Cubist' painting which is an example of the attempt to 'represent' things as we naturally see them in time and space from many different viewpoints.**

◀ ***Shivago on horseback, central India.*** **Perspective is not used in this painting.**

It is worth remembering at this stage that art mainly consists of illusion. It is very much concerned with the different ways in which we see or perceive the world and represent or express those perceptions. We all see things differently to some extent, even when we are looking at the same thing. Look at paintings of the same object by several artists and you will see just how different their perceptions and interpretations seem to be. Try it with your friends and compare the results.

When we try to understand how our eyes and brain work in enabling us to see things, we encounter all kinds of problems and enter the world of psychology and neuro-physiology. Scientists are constantly trying to understand the workings of the brain and as they find out more, so the theories change and so do the conventions we use in art. How we see colour is one field in which there is considerable interest and research, for example.

However, for the purpose of this book it will suffice to alert you to some of the perceptual problems that psychologists have investigated and then you can do more reading on the subject if you are interested.

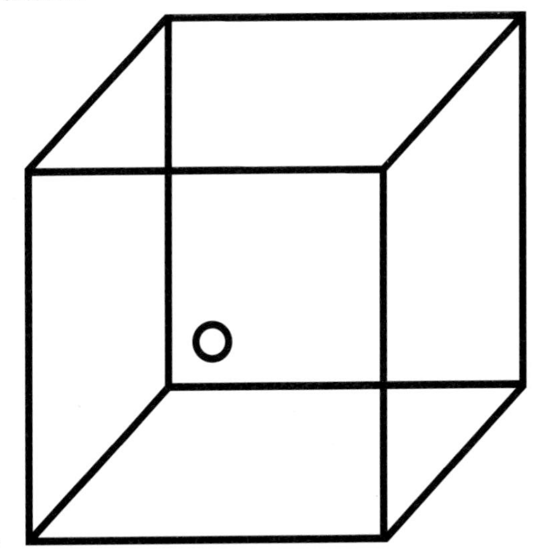

Look at these **ambiguous** images: in the first, you oscillate between seeing a vase and two faces nose to nose. You have no control over when the image changes. This is concerned with the relationship between object and ground (see also the series of paintings by Piet Mondrian on page 52). In the second, another ambiguous image oscillates between being a cube seen from above and from below. Again you have no control over when the image changes – your brain registers the two alternative viewpoints but never makes up its mind which is correct!

▲ *MC Escher, 'Belvedere', 1958.* How does the ladder fit into the structure?

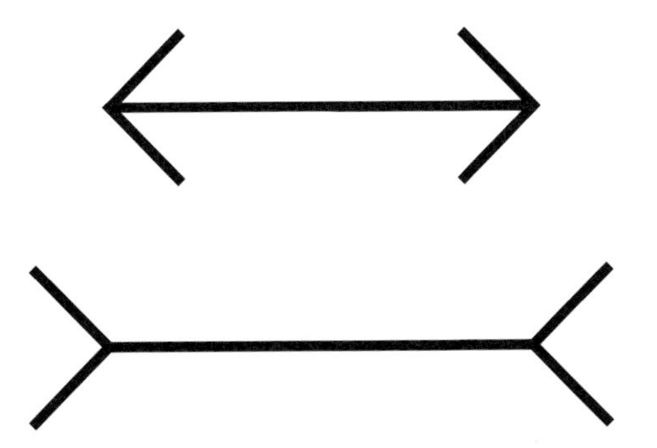

► **A Pair of Muller-Lyer 'Arrow' Illusion Figures**

Another famous example is of two lines of the same length placed side by side. One has an arrow shape extending from the ends of the line, the other has an inverted arrow at the same position. The one with the inverted arrow looks shorter than the one with the extended arrow and you believe this, even though you know that the two lines are identical in length.

Then there are paradoxical figures – 'impossible images' – which at first glance look fairly normal then we realise that they are impossible in real life. The most famous illustrations in this field are by M C Escher, a Dutch artist. In the engraving of 'an impossible house' (opposite) you can see how the columns supporting the arches rest on a base at opposite sides of the building – an impossible construction. You can have fun inventing similar images of your own and learn a lot about illusion and perspective at the same time.

Movement and direction

This follows on from the last reference to the Cubists, since another pre-occupation of some twentieth-century artists has been to try to create the illusion of movement. What they were attempting to do was to incorporate into their work the fourth dimension – **time** – and this is very difficult to do when the materials you use remain permanently still. You have to find ways of creating the illusion of movement or direction in a motionless form, unless you are using media such as film or video.

◄ ***Marcel Duchamp, 'Nude descending a staircase, No. 2', 1912, oil on canvass (145 x 87.5 cm)***

Shape and the illusion of form

Line is often used to describe shape, usually a thing's outline or total configuration. Form is different and usually includes an indication of a thing's structure – e.g. the shape of an umbrella can be drawn without including any of the things which contribute to its form, such as the internal structure of the rib supports.

▲ *Patrick Heron, 'January 1973: 14', 1973.* **Flat shapes and colour are used to create this abstract painting.**

◄ **Glueing sunshades in Thailand. The form of the sunshades can be understood by comparing the finished umbrella with the bamboo structure of the unfinished ones.**

Structure

This usually refers to the way something was made or built, or in nature, the way something has grown. For example, the structure of a tree would refer to the relationship between the roots, trunk, branches, twigs and leaves.

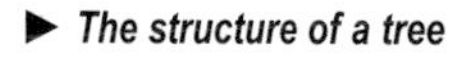

► ***The structure of a tree***

Pattern

Pattern can be created by repeating lines or shapes constructed through the use of lines. Line is also important in relation to the 'structure' of a pattern or the 'grid' on which it is based; and in patterns produced by means of line, such as in weaving.

▲ Design for wallpaper from 'Documents Decoratifs', 1902, Plate 29

► African textiles: cotton cloth woven on a man's narrow loom, Ewe, Ghana

Tone

Line can be used to create tonal variations by techniques such as cross-hatching or closely drawn lines to suggest the effect of light on an object.

◀ ***Rembrandt van Rijn, 'The Drunken Lot', 1633 (Black crayon)***

Texture

Similarly, texture can be created or suggested by using a finer, less regular pattern of linear marks.

Tone

Tone is monochromatic, i.e. shades of one colour or a mixture of black and white; and colours have 'tonal' values in that they vary between light and dark.

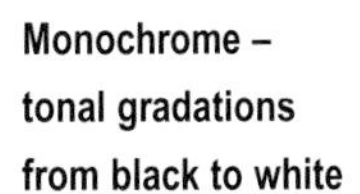

Monochrome – tonal gradations from black to white

Monochrome – one colour mixed with black or white

One dark and one lighter colour mixed to create tonal as well as colour variations

Polychrome – examples of colours which have different tonal values

▲ Examples of tonal variations in black and white, one colour, and mixed colours

Volume and solidity

Tone, in two-dimensional work, can be used to create the illusion of volume and solidity by suggesting the source of **light** falling on an object through the use of light and dark areas of shading. It is often used in conjunction with line. For example, the drawing of a cylinder discussed in the last section, can be enhanced by the use of tone to make it appear more three-dimensional.

A major part of your drawing studies should be to develop your skills in using tone effectively.

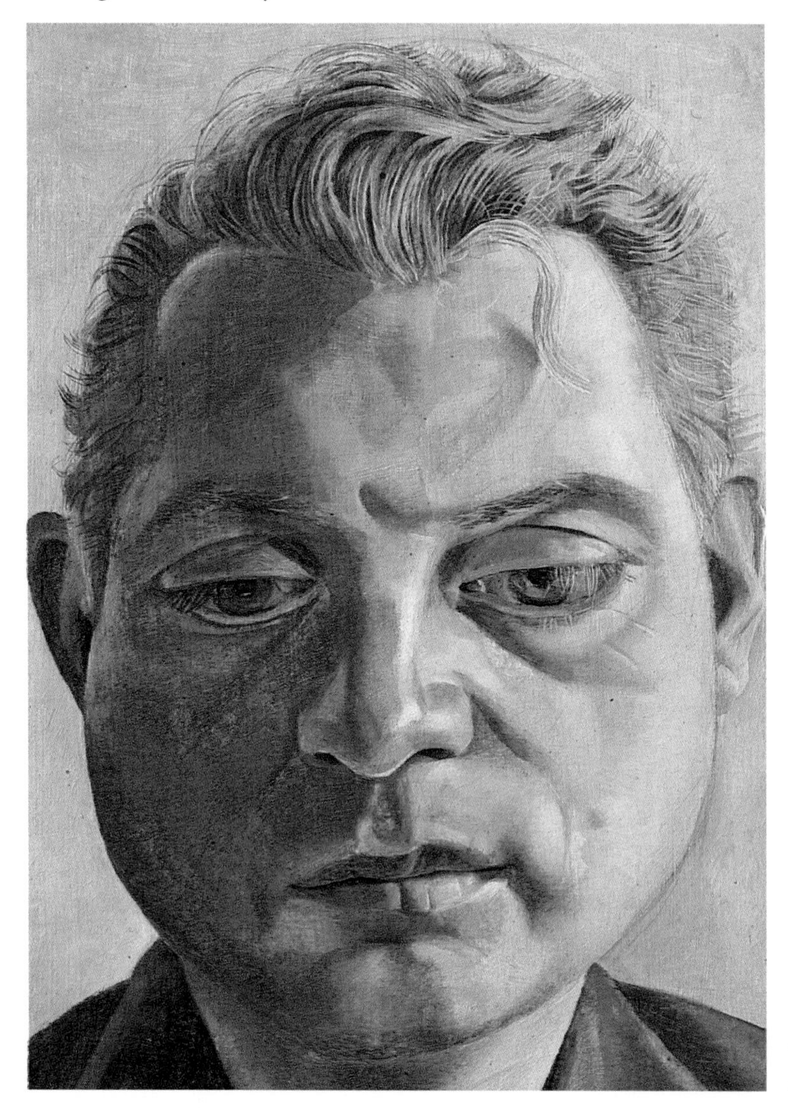

◀ *Lucian Freud, 'Portrait of Francis Bacon', 1952*

The illusion of depth and distance

Tone can also be used to create the illusion of depth in two-dimensional work. One important area is known as **aerial perspective**. You might be familiar with landscapes on misty days when receding hills are seen mainly as simple silhouettes. As well as the shapes diminishing in size, which is suggested by linear perspective, the tonal values become lighter as each successive shape recedes into the distance. This is the simplest example of aerial

▲ **Aerial perspective – distance is indicated by receding tones**

perspective and there are other important means of creating the illusion of depth. For example, the contrast between light and dark tones on the nearest objects are greater than those on objects in the distance. Sometimes, the tonal balance is reversed and the darker tones are in the background with strongly lit shapes in the foreground.

▲ ***David Cox, 'Landscape with sunset', c.1835 (63.75 x 94.75 cm).*** **Depth is suggested by the tone of the distant hills**

► ***Paul Nash, 'Winter Sea', 1925-37 (1.02 x 1.52 m).*** **Depth is suggested by lines of perspective and strong contrasts between light and dark in the foreground with weaker ones in the distance.**

The relationship between ground (background) and object (foreground) is important in understanding the relationship between the formal elements, since all of the area of a two-dimensional piece of work is equally important to your composition. When working with tone and colour in particular you should remember that the spaces in between can be as important as the object itself.

◀ ***Piet Mondrian, 'Red tree', 1908 (67.5 x 100 cm)***

◀ ***Piet Mondrian, 'Tree II', 1911 (55 x 75 cm)***

◀ ***Piet Mondrian, 'The gray tree', 1912 (75 x 105 cm)***

This series of paintings, which are progressing towards an abstract image, shows the importance of the relationship between ground and object in paintings

Shape and form

These two terms can be confusing but, as we have said in the section on Line, a simple way of distinguishing between them is to think of shape mainly in relation to outline and form relating to the whole structure of an object.

Single shapes and forms

A useful way to begin to understand the relationship between shape and form is to study single shapes initially. A shape or form can often be analysed or simplified in order to understand its basic structure – squares, circles, cubes, cylinders and so on. It is often very useful when working with natural forms to try to do this since once you understand the basic structure of an object it is usually easier to draw or paint.

Simplifying a head and shoulders portrait by reducing it to the basic shapes of a cube, cylinder and triangle

'Families' of shapes

There are often useful similarities in natural and made forms which enable you to group them into categories, especially when considering their basic shapes. **Compositions** consisting of multiple shapes and forms can be complex and the really important part of a study of the formal elements lies in the infinite range of possibilities in using them in combination.

◀ *David Inshaw, 'The Badminton Game', 1972-73.* Simplified natural forms relate to each other and the cube of the hedge relates to the house.

▲ *Georges Braque, 'Chateau de la Roche Guyon', 1909 (77.5 x 57.5 cm).* Simplified forms of buildings in this early Cubist painting.

▼ *Georgia O'Keeffe, 'Radiator Building – Night, New York', 1927*

It is easier to begin making compositions, or to analyse the appearance of an apparently complex scene, by trying to see the range of components in their simplified or basic form. By using or looking for shapes which are similar, you can begin to understand the relationship between them more easily. Many modern or contemporary buildings are actually constructed from 'units' and it is easier to understand their structure if you understand the form of each unit and how they are combined.

◀ ***David Nash, 'Crack and Warp Column', 1985.***
An example of wood 'units' cut from planks and used to create a column reflecting the form of the original tree.

In nature and in made forms, **rhythm** and **pattern** are features which we are attracted to. Perhaps this is because as human beings we need to establish a sense of order in what we see, experience and make. Seeing things in groups or categories and recognising patterns and rhythms is an important part of the process of satisfying this need.

◀ *Vincent van Gogh, 'The Starry Night', 1889*

▼ *Utagawa Hiroshige, 'Bizen Ukazan', from the series 'Mountain and Sea compared like Wrestlers', mid nineteenth century (wood block colour print)*

Examples of rhythm and pattern in two very different styles of painting

Structure

Another important part of the process of understanding things is to analyse their structure. For example, to understand the form of a tree it is necessary to work out how it has grown in order to support its mass and withstand different weather conditions. To understand the human figure, you need to know about its skeleton and how the muscles relate to it. Understanding its structure is enormously helpful when you come to making a representation of a form.

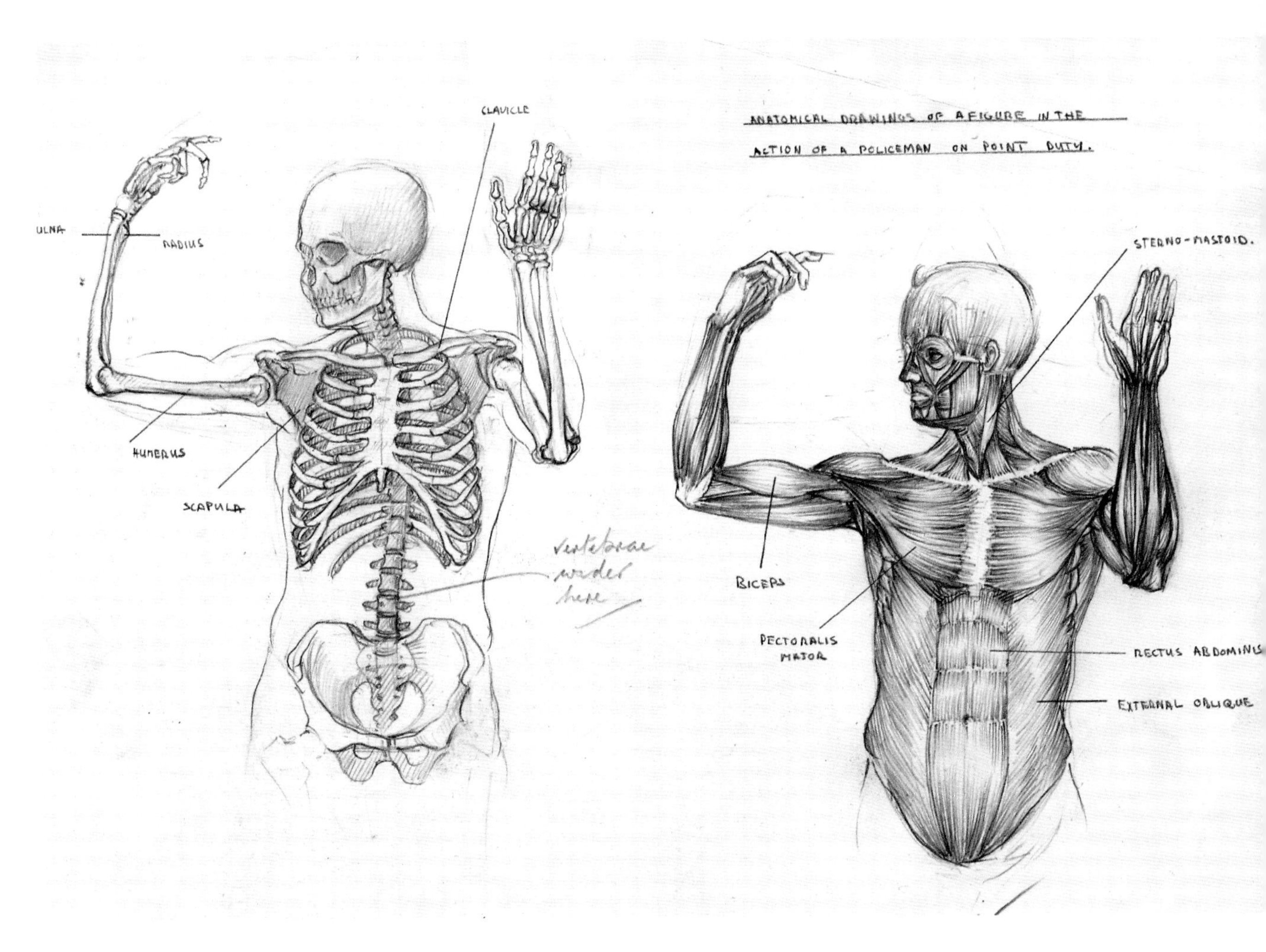

Colour

This is a very big topic and you'll never stop learning about it. There are theories which can be helpful in understanding colour, but they are constantly being revised in the light of increasing scientific knowledge of the way in which we see things – how our eyes and brain work. Basic colour theory can be understood by studying and experimenting with the **colour wheel**. You will have to understand this basic theory in order to do some of the Unit tests, but it is as important to learn about colour through continuous exploration and experiment.

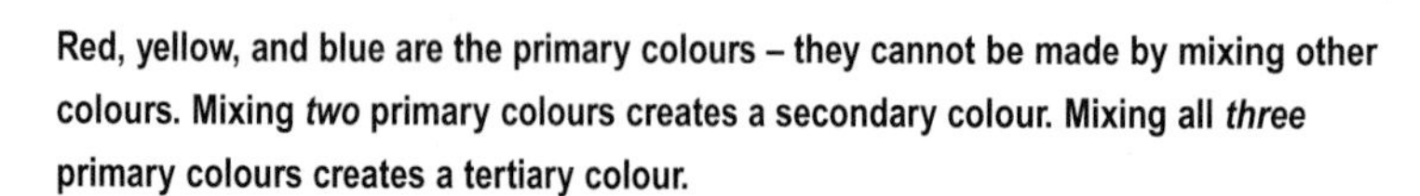

Red, yellow, and blue are the primary colours – they cannot be made by mixing other colours. Mixing *two* primary colours creates a secondary colour. Mixing all *three* primary colours creates a tertiary colour.

Complementary colours – those which are opposites on the colour wheel – provide the maximum colour contrast available to you. They can be used to create 'greys' or 'browns' called tertiary colours.

We all have different tastes and like some colours more than others and this is the basis for developing our own individual colour sense. As artists, craftspeople, and designers, a distinctly individual style in the use of colour can be a great advantage.

Colour is used for many different purposes, for example:

Colour to evoke mood or express emotion

Colour affects the way that we feel and we can express emotions through different combinations of colours. For example, cool colours such as blues and greens can suggest calmness and repose, whilst warm or hot colours can express anger, fear, and other powerful emotions. Interior designers use colours to create particular environmental conditions.

► *Howard Hodgkin, 'Rain', 1984-9 (16.38 x 17.9 m).* **Note the use of blue/orange complementary colours in this expressive, abstract painting.**

Colour for differentiation and identification

Colour is used to differentiate between components of things such as charts, graphs, signs, information displays etc.

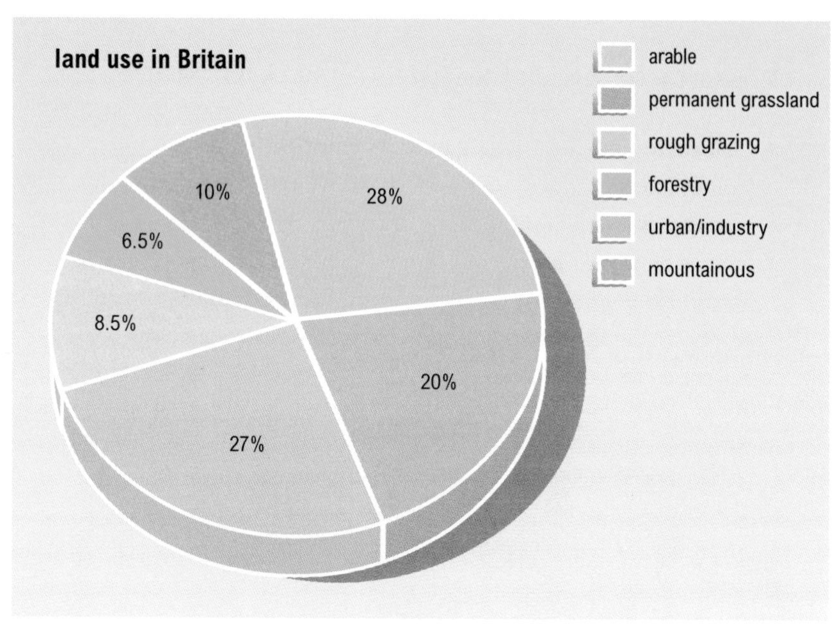

▲ An example of a computer-generated pie-chart

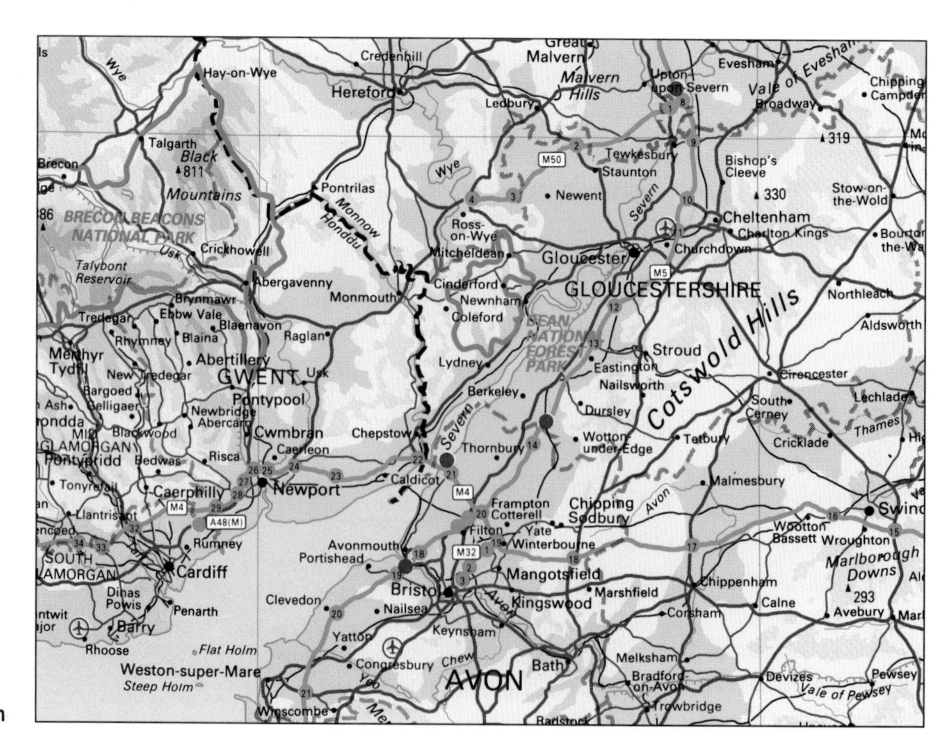

► A map showing colour differentiation

Colour is used for identification – heraldic costume, signs and emblems, military identification, flags, uniforms etc.

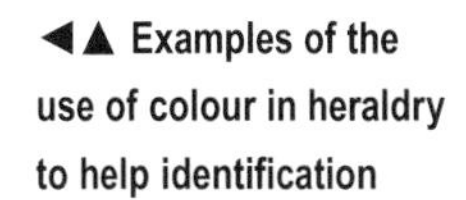

◀▲ Examples of the use of colour in heraldry to help identification

▶ Modern military emblems help to identify troops – and camouflage helps to hide them

Colour as camouflage – animals, birds, fish, insects, military equipment etc.

◀ *Henri Rousseau, 'Tropical Storm with a Tiger (Surprise)', 1891*

Colour is used to attract – in nature, advertising, display, and presentation.

◀ **A child's cassette player**

Colour in fashion – costume, body adornment, accessories etc.

► **The use of colour by fashion designer Sonia Rykiel**

Colour as symbol. The Virgin Mary in Renaissance paintings was represented wearing a blue cloak since blue was the colour symbolic of Heaven. Blue was also a very expensive colour to make which added to its significance in paintings.

► ***Piero della Francesca, active 1439 died 1492, 'The Nativity'***

Pattern

We all have a natural tendency to want to regulate our world, and one of the most powerful stabilising factors is pattern. It is predominant in nature, and most of the things we make include some aspects of pattern. Its main characteristics are **repetition** and **rhythm.**

Structures of pattern repeats

An important basic consideration is the way in which patterns are constructed. They normally consist of units repeated in different ways.

For example: Simple repeat, half-drop, O-gee, linear, counterpoint, tessellation, revolution etc.

◀ **Examples of repeat structures for patterns**

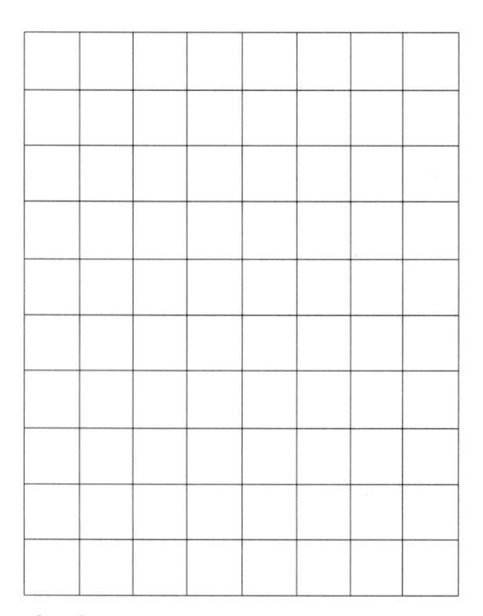

simple square repeat

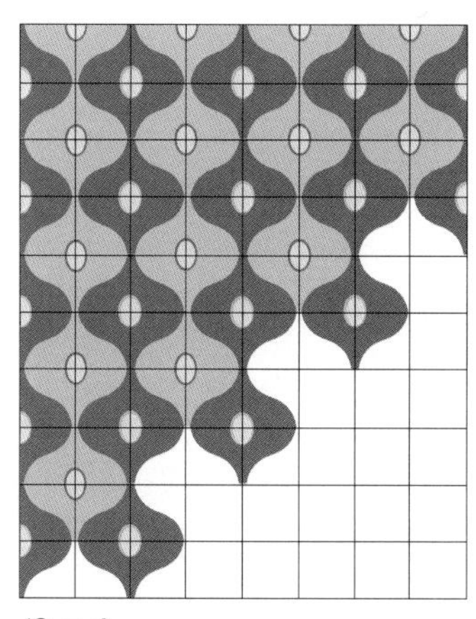

'O-gee'

'Half-drop'

'Counterpoint'

► ***'Omar' design, by C. Townsend, 1898.*** **Analysis of this pattern design shows the use of a mirror image within a basic O-gee grid structure.**

Computer-assisted design programmes will include a wide variety of different pattern variations. All are based on mathematical 'grids' and it can be a valuable exercise to try to analyse the grid structure of existing patterns to understand how the pattern was formed.

Texture

Texture usually applies to the surface qualities of an object and it can be both visual and tactile – e.g. it looks and feels rough or smooth.

It is similar to pattern in that it is normally produced by some kind of repetitive marks but usually less regular and more refined than in the deliberate form of pattern-making described above.

Pattern and texture have many common characteristics and it might be possible to agree that there are three basic kinds:

- that which is integral to the process of making – e.g. the marks left by fingers in the making of ceramic objects, marks left by the tools which shaped an object.

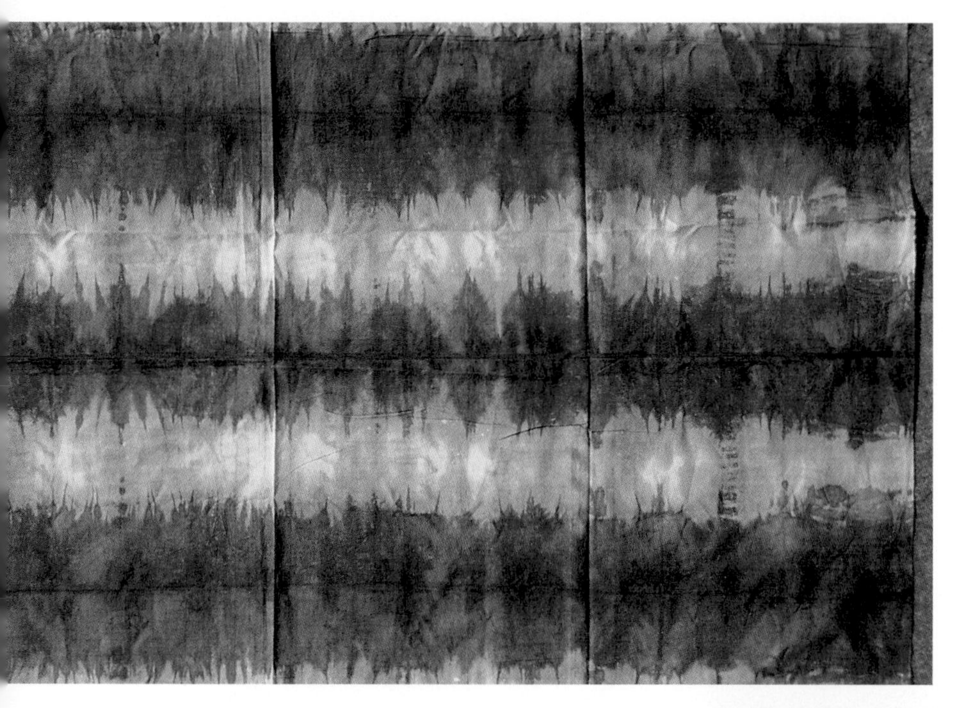

▲ Pattern and texture created by tying cloth with string

► Surface pattern made by fingers

- that which is deliberately applied to a surface – e.g. 'combed' effects, polish and applied patination, etched and sand-blasted surfaces, glazes etc.

▶ **Surface texture applied to porcelain**

▼ **Salt-glazed effect on an old chimney pot**

- that which is integral to the material – e.g. the grain of wood, the smoothness of glass, the roughness of sandstone, heavily-grogged clay, and painted surfaces.

◀ **Glazed surface of old stoneware vessels**

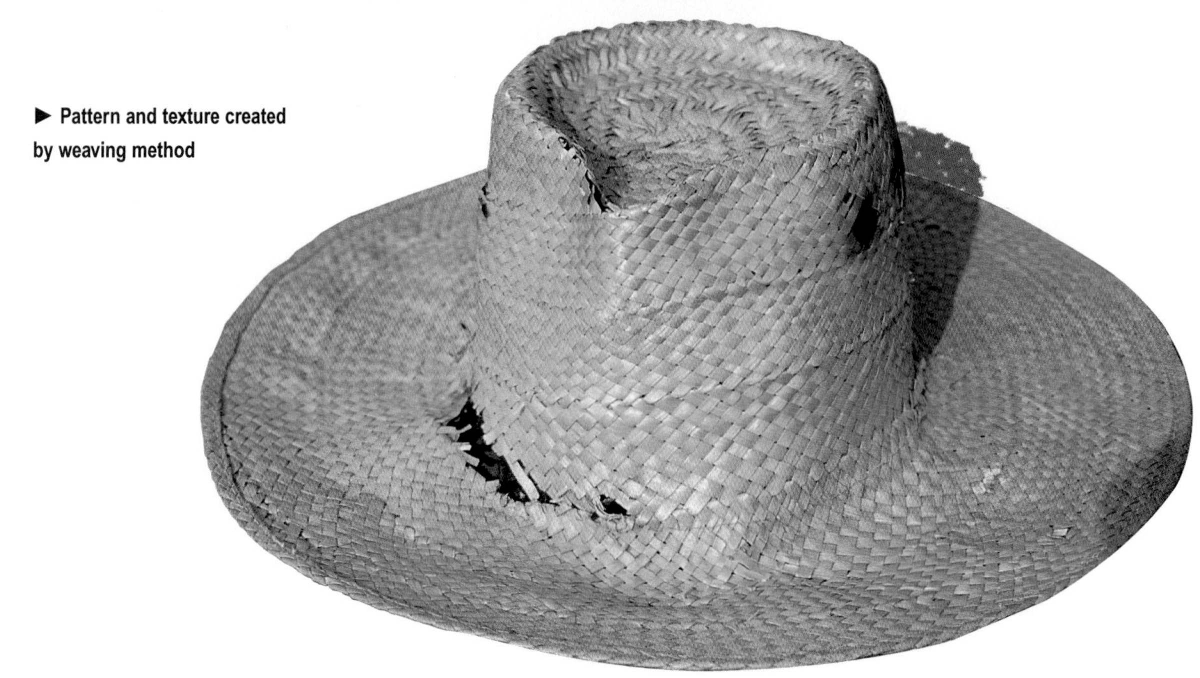

▶ **Pattern and texture created by weaving method**

ELEMENT 1.2

USE 2D MEDIA, TECHNOLOGY, PROCESSES, AND TECHNIQUES

Performance criteria

1. *develop skills in the use of* ***2D media, technology, processes and techniques***
2. *explore working characteristics, potential and limitations of media*
3. *select and use* ***2D media, technology, processes and techniques,*** *creatively to meet* ***specified intentions***
4. *follow the 2D* ***health and safety procedures*** *associated with studio and workshop practice*
5. *discuss and review the effectiveness of own use of media, technology, processes and techniques*

Range

2D Media:

- Dry – chalks, charcoal, crayons, pastel, pencil
- Wet – adhesives, dyes, inks, markers, paints
- Computer-aided applications – for drawing, graphics, paint
- Lens-based – photography, copying

Technology, processes, and techniques associated with:

- drawing, painting, collage, print-making, photography, copying, computer-based mark-making, surface treatment

Specified intentions: to communicate information, to express ideas and feelings; specified by tutor or self-identified

Health and safety procedures:
correct use of media, technology, processes and techniques; elimination of risk to self and others (burns, cutting edges, chemicals, electric shock, fumes, lifting, sharp instruments, sharp tools)

Evidence indicators

Studies covering the 2D media, technology, processes, and techniques ranged. Studies should be supported by records to show that the student has:

- followed the 2D health and safety procedures required in studio and workshop practice
- discussed and reviewed the effectiveness of own use of media, technology, processes, and techniques.

Two complex activities, including developmental and final work. These activities should be set in at least two of the following contexts:

- art
- craft
- design.

Drawing

In this unit you are mainly concerned with learning to explore and use visual language for your own purposes in making art, craft, and design. One of the most important aspects of visual language is **drawing.**

Any mark you make on a sheet of paper will begin to suggest some meaning. If you continue making marks and develop them into a drawing or an image which is a representation of something, other people are likely to recognise it too and you are beginning to communicate with them. The more highly developed and complex your drawing becomes, the more information is communicated.

▲ **The development of a drawing from the simplest marks to a more complex image**

The way that you make these marks is also important in expressing things such as **mood** or **emotion**. For example, if you make an image by means of violent strokes of a brush or vigorous, heavy black lines, you may be expressing feelings of anger or frustration. If, on the other hand, you make a careful, very fine drawing you will probably be recording what you are seeing and you will be in an objective rather than an emotional mood. Sometimes your work will be descriptive, when you will be trying to show whoever sees your work all of the things that you have observed.

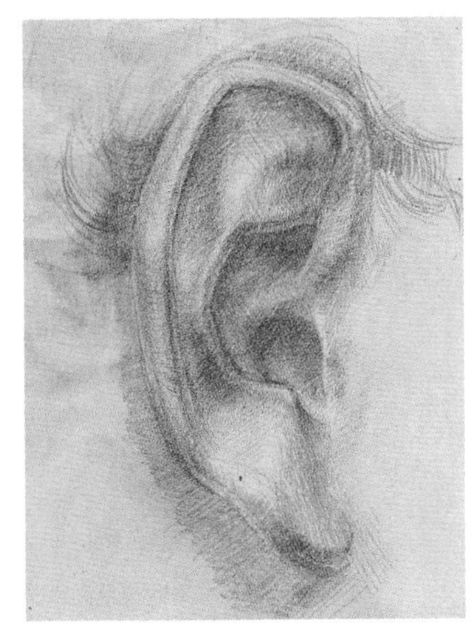

▲ Expressive drawing

◀ Fine detailed drawing

► An 'objective' drawing – a straightforward *record* of something seen

Then there are the kinds of drawings and sketches which you might do in order to develop your ideas. These are normally done only for yourself and the process involves you in thinking, making intuitive responses, experimenting with different possibilities and, perhaps, gradually coming to a conclusion about what kind of finished work you intend to attempt. This is a very important part of your course since your ability to develop ideas and to show how they were developed is given a high priority. You should make a habit of working in this way so that you really do develop the necessary skills by yourself and show that you can work **independently**. When you reach the stage of assessing this Unit, independent work of this kind can mean the difference between gaining an ordinary pass, a merit award or a distinction.

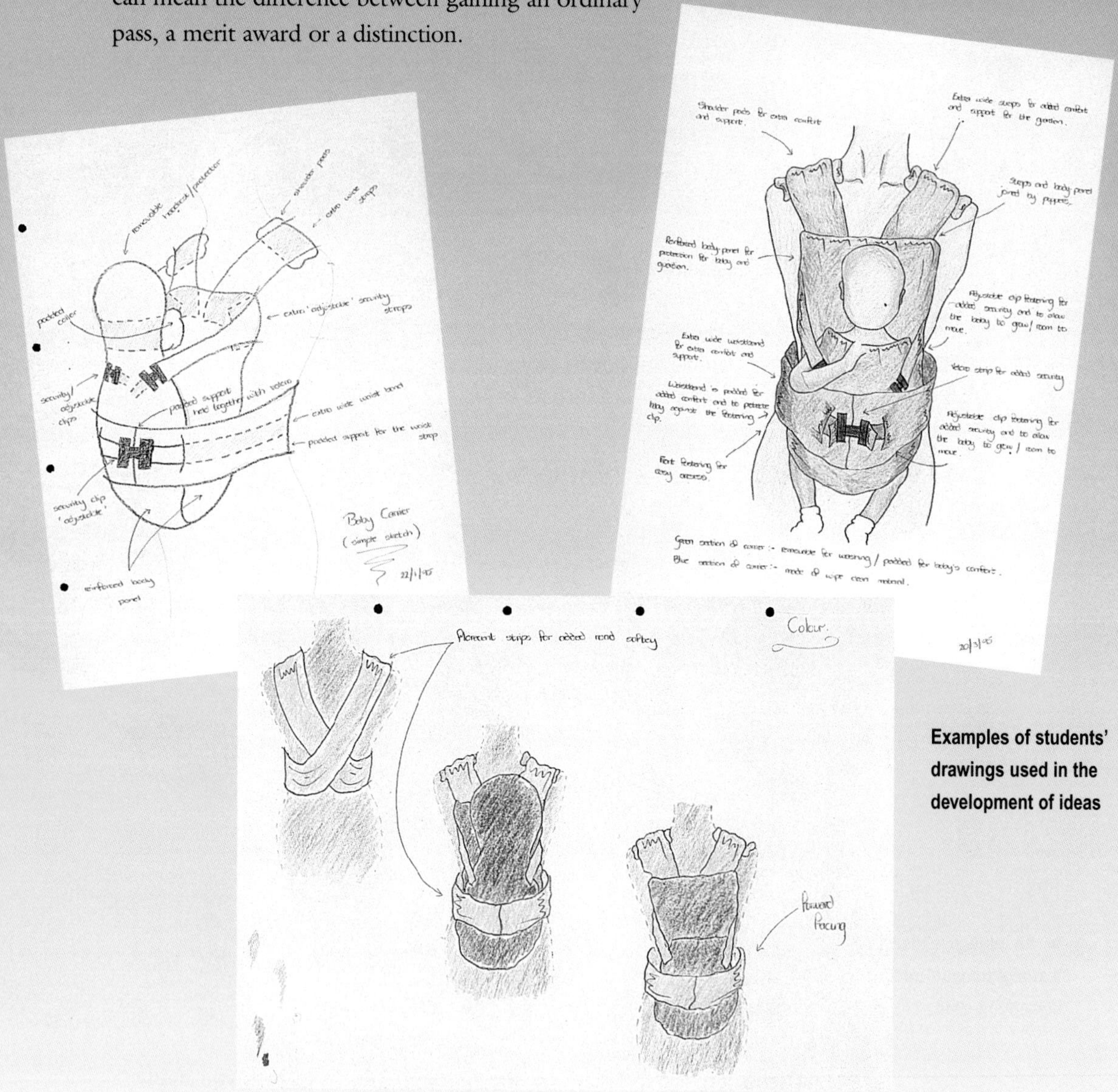

Examples of students' drawings used in the development of ideas

In design work there are particular ways of drawing which enable you to communicate things such as how an object should be made or constructed. This kind of drawing is known as **technical drawing** in that it requires you to use a common system of drawing which was designed to communicate precise information. Its main purpose is to communicate spatial information. Since many different people might use your drawings in the process of making the same object it wouldn't make sense to use a system which everyone involved didn't fully understand.

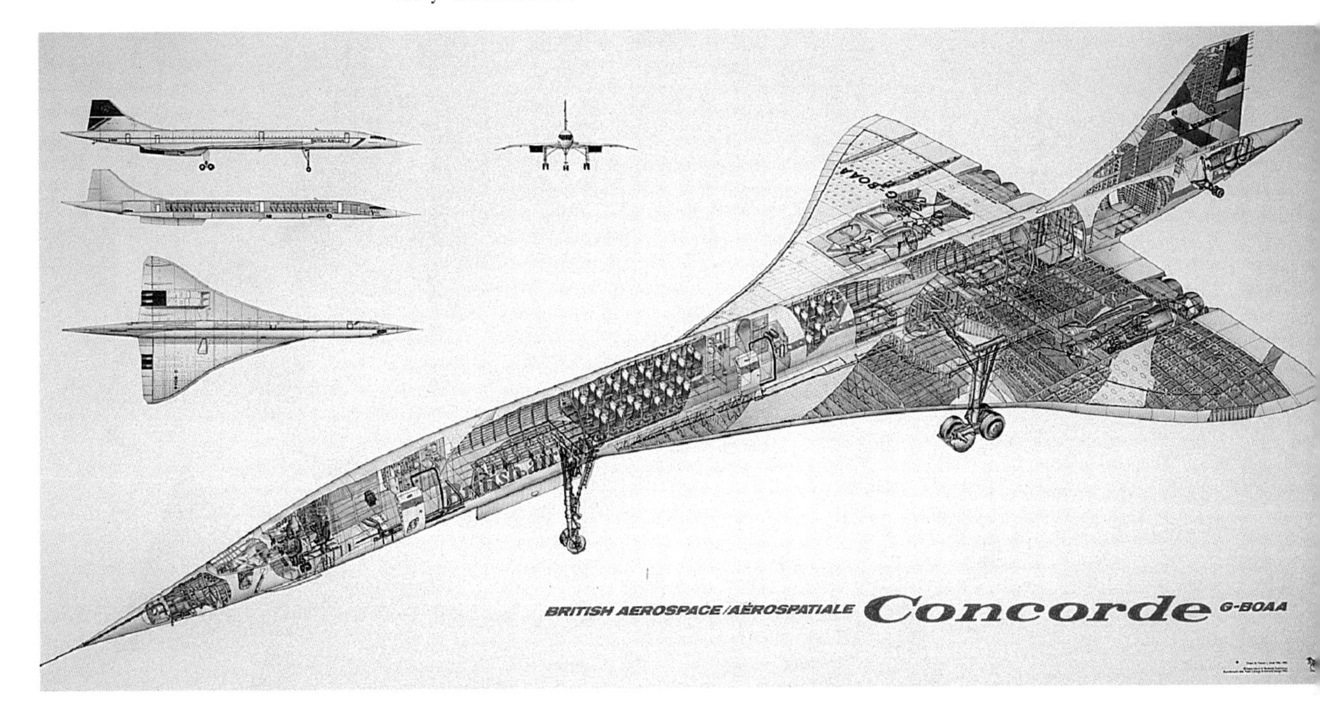

▲ **Technical drawings of Concorde**

There are many other kinds of drawing in design work which require you to be precise. For example:

- particular kinds of illustrations, such as those used to explain how to assemble something you have bought
- illustrations in books which provide important information in support of the text, for example, medical drawings
- illustrations which provide a detailed, accurate record of things in the text (books on plants, animals and birds).
- other kinds of illustration, such as those used in children's story books and comics – these allow you much more freedom to be original and creative. Sometimes you might only be illustrating parts of a story and you will have to follow the text quite closely but you can still use your own style and ideas. At other times your drawings

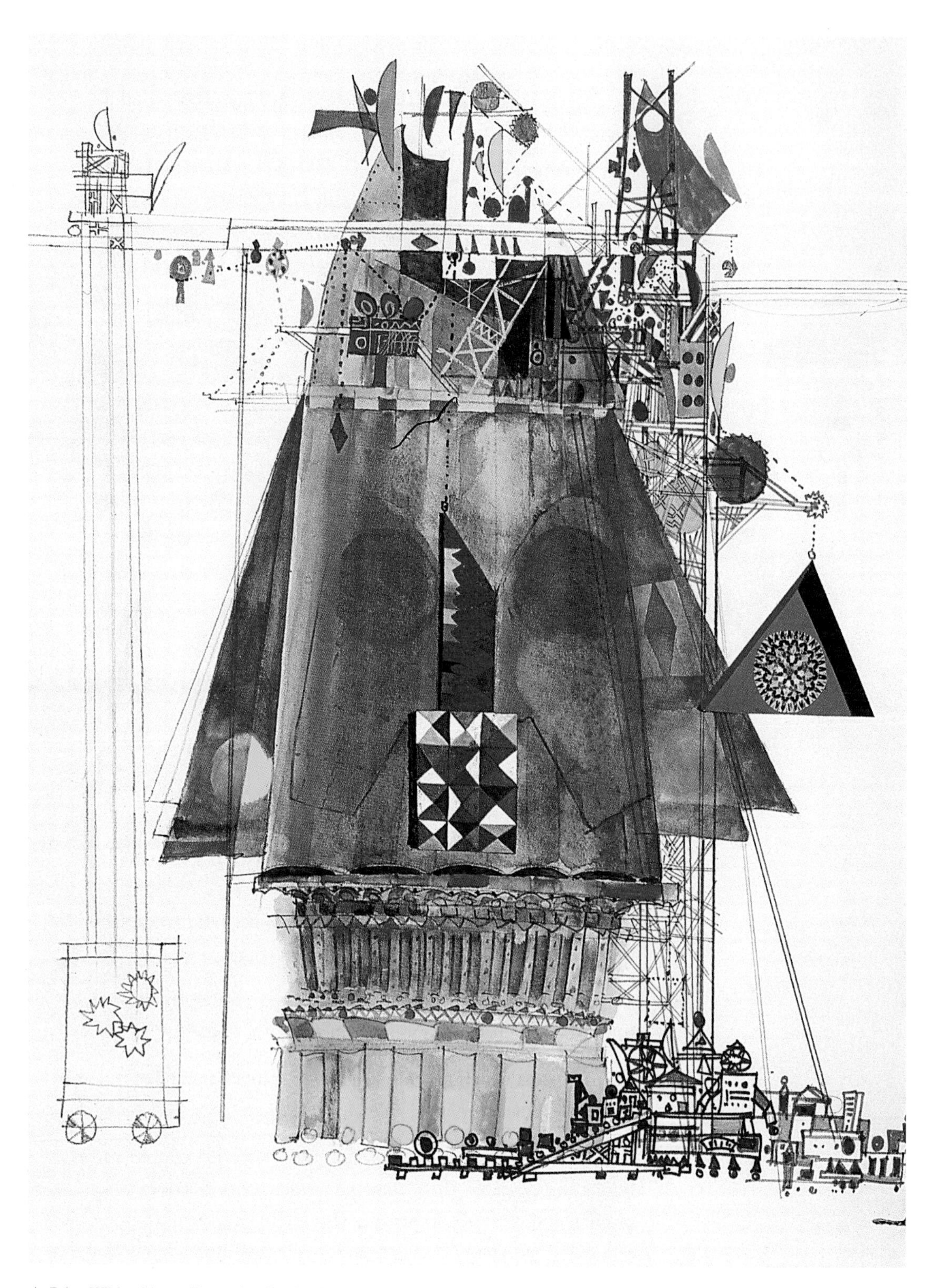

▲ Brian Wildsmith, an illustration for 'Professor Noah's Spaceship', Oxford University Press, 1980

might be the main means of telling the story and the success of the narrative will depend on how imaginative and inventive they are.

- drawings for developing ideas and a 'structure' for applied surface decoration such as in fabric printing

- drawings for the layout and design of printed text and illustrations in publications like books, or for posters, packaging, and advertising

- drawings for the design and development of products, such as domestic equipment, cars, and most manufactured objects

- drawings in support of crafts work – ideas for ceramics, jewellery, textiles etc.

The important thing to recognise is that the way you use drawing in these different contexts will vary. Often you will begin work on a project by drawing first, at other times drawing will be useful as a means of sorting out your ideas and finding solutions to problems after you have used other methods. For example, craftspeople often work directly in their chosen medium in order to develop ideas, then they may use drawing to develop them at a later stage.

These many different ways of communicating are part of a complex structure of visual language which you will come to understand, largely through practical work. You have to practice skills such as drawing constantly in order to develop and maintain them which is one of the reasons for keeping sketchbooks. Drawings in sketchbooks are also very important to those who will be assessing your work since they will tell them a lot about the way you think, develop ideas and record information for later use (independent work). It should not be assumed that a sketchbook is just for drawings – any kind of 'record' of things seen, experienced and imagined is suitable. For example, sticking found objects into your sketchbook is a good way of recording, then later that object will jog your memory and you'll be able to recall what you were doing at the time you found it and why you selected it.

Sketchbooks are very personal things and it is sometimes inhibiting to think that someone else is going to examine them. However, you should try to overcome your inhibitions and make them as interesting, lively and informative as possible.

▲ **Examples of sketchbook studies – figures by the lake**

This book cannot teach you how to draw. It can only describe different ways of drawing, the different purposes they serve and show you some of the ways in which other people use drawing. There is a common tendency to think that drawing only involves media such as pencil, pen and ink, and materials like charcoal, but in fact you can 'draw' with almost anything. You can certainly draw with paint and brushes but even when you are using materials such as clay for modelling you are still likely to be 'drawing'. You can, for example, draw with wire to create a three-dimensional representation of an object.

► An example of a three-dimensional 'drawing', using split cane

Summary of the Functions of Drawing

Drawing mostly involves you in the following:

- **Recording** what you see, remember or imagine. In this process you are simply trying to put down as much accurate information as possible so that if you need to use the drawing for reference in future work it provides a reliable and detailed record.

- **Analysing** the appearance of something, the way it has been constructed or has grown, and its formal qualities.

- **As a means of personal expression**. A way of telling other people what you think, believe, feel, imagine and see.

- **As a means of providing additional information** related to writing – as in book illustrations.

- **As a means of processing visual or spatial information** – as in working drawings, plans, and instructional diagrams.

- **As a means of developing your ideas** – as in the drawings you might do when tackling an assignment or in your sketchbooks.

It will be very helpful to you if you really learn to distinguish between these different functions of drawing. You should always try to know why you are using particular drawing methods or systems and what purposes they serve. Remember that you will be required to explain and to justify what you have done and why you have done it.

Working with 2D media, technology, processes, and techniques

In studying this Unit you will learn how to use a wide range of materials in order to communicate information, develop your ideas and design solutions, and to express your personal feelings and opinions.

This includes:

- The ability to handle many different kinds of paint, such as water colours, gouache, oil paint, and acrylics.

- To be able to reproduce images in a range of different ways, such as in printmaking and by using reprographic equipment.

- To be able to design and apply pattern and surface decoration to a range of materials, such as textiles, ceramics, paper, wood, plastics etc.

- To use photography for recording information, objects and events and for the wider range of creative uses of photography and, perhaps, to use other lens-media, such as video and film.

- To use computers to assist your design work, collate and retrieve data and for other appropriate purposes.

At the Intermediate stage, the emphasis is on exploring and experimenting in order to find out for yourself what can be done with different media, materials, and techniques. You will, of course, be taught to use them by your tutors but they can only start you off and provide guidance during the course. It's up to you to develop your skills and knowledge fully. By experimenting in an organised way you will begin to identify those areas where you need more expert guidance and your tutor will be able to help you more easily if he or she can see how you have arrived at a problem. You should, therefore, keep all of the results of your experiments so that you and your tutor can see the way that you've worked. This is also important evidence when it comes to assessment.

Dry media and materials

As a general principle you should be prepared to try out anything which will make a mark. For example, you can experiment by drawing with your fingers or a stick dipped into graphite or charcoal dust. These kinds of experiments can broaden your repertoire of drawing skills and can enable you to produce work which is distinctive to you.

Normally, however, you do need to experience the more traditional methods of working and to learn about the working characteristics of the materials used.

Charcoal is a medium suitable for broad, often large, drawings. Since it is black you will mainly be working with tone as the formal element and it is a very good medium for exploring tonal values and effects. For additional research you can find out how charcoal is produced.

▲ **Using charcoal to explore lighting effects**

▲ Pastel on grey ground

▲ Pencil – line drawing

▲ Pencil – tonal study

Pastel has similar characteristics to charcoal but colour is available and you need particularly to experiment with different ways of colour mixing. This is usually done on the working surface, unlike paints which are normally mixed before application. You need to try working from light to dark and vice versa; try the effects of cross-hatching or rhythmic strokes to create a textured mix of colour; try merging colours by rubbing them into each other; and try optical mixing where the colours remain separate but blend into each other when you look at them. (You will learn more about optical colour mixing if you study the Impressionists and Pointillists in Unit 3.)

You should also try working on different coloured paper for both charcoal and pastel. Both can be used to good effect in combination with a ground colour or toned paper. For example, you can use charcoal on grey paper for the dark and medium tonal areas of a composition then use chalk or white pastel for the light areas and highlights. Again, you should try to relate your own work to that of other artists, either contemporary practitioners or those from the past.

Pencil drawing has already been referred to earlier in the chapter. It is one of the most commonly used media in art and design, and pencils have been developed as tools to suit particular purposes. The normal

▲ Pen and ink

▲ Pencil and wash

▲ Water-colour

range of hardness or softness of pencils is from 6H (very hard, fine line) to 6B (very soft, broad, black line). You need to explore the different grades of pencil and identify those which are suitable for specific purposes or those which suit your personal style of drawing.

For example, fine drawing as a basis for further work in design or painting is generally better done using a hard grade of pencil (but don't press too hard or colour will settle into the indentations caused by the pencil), whereas dramatic lighting on an object can be better represented through the use of a 4B or even 6B.

Try to select the pencils which best produce the qualities you want to achieve and ask yourself if the pencil you are using is appropriate.

Wet media and materials

Sometimes you will be totally free to try out materials in your own way whilst at other times you will have to work within set constraints. For example, you might want to explore the medium of watercolour and you start by experimenting with a few colours, concentrating on the different qualities you can achieve by increasing the amount of water added to the paint – the more water you add the lighter the colour. You may then try superimposing layers of colour to see what

▲ Examples of exploration of a medium – watercolour

effects you can create. Then you try to work out a system for using lighter and darker colours. Unlike oil colour, you will find that you can't apply light colours over dark ones – the paint is translucent and the darker colour underneath remains dominant. This means that, generally, you start by using lighter colours and paint darker ones over them when they're dry. You need to try out different kinds of brushes – very large ones (mops) are for painting large, wet areas and producing washes. Smaller brushes can be used for different kinds of detail, for drawing and for texture. Dry-brush or drag effects can be achieved by reducing the amount of paint on the brush – and so on. The paper you use is also very important and you will need to try out different kinds. Paper which is specially made for watercolour painting is normally heavier than ordinary cartridge paper and usually has a rough surface. On heavy watercolour paper the paint will often granulate, i.e it will separate a little and settle into the indentations on the surface, whilst on smoother paper this doesn't happen. This paper normally has to be stretched by sticking down the edges of a thoroughly wet piece of paper to the drawing board with gumstrip. This is typical of the kind of techniques that you will need some help with since too many failed experiments can be expensive. This is an example of exploring the **working characteristics** of materials.

▲ A study for a cover for the book 'Operation Thistledown'

You might then be required by your tutor to prepare some illustrations for a children's story book using watercolour. In this case, you aren't totally free to experiment, you have to find ways of using the medium to meet the requirements of the brief. For example, perhaps the story is about mysterious happenings and your illustrations have to create an air of mystery. You would then have to find out what properties of watercolour enable you to achieve these effects.

The next stage might be to try out the effects of combining watercolour with other materials. 'Pen and wash' is a traditional medium in which you can either draw first in pen and ink then add watercolour washes, or use the watercolour first and draw over, or into, it with pen and ink.

▲ *Giovanni Tiepolo (1692-1769), 'Houses and Campanile' (pen and wash drawing)*

Similar effects can be created using pencil and wash or charcoal and watercolour – combining wet and dry materials.

You will then begin to understand that any combination of materials is worth exploring. Sometimes you will only create a mess and you may become disheartened and frustrated, but it is important to remember that all truly creative work involves taking risks. If you don't try something you will never know if it might have worked, and we all learn as much by our mistakes as we do through sticking to known methods.

▲ *John Piper (1903-92), 'St. Mary Port, Bristol' (mixed media)*

The range of wet media available to you is extensive, far greater than the examples given in the Range statement, and you should try to experience as many as possible. Generally there are those which are translucent, like watercolour, and those which are opaque like oil paint and gouache. The characteristics of opaque colours are quite different from those of translucent ones. If you try out the experiments suggested with watercolour then try something similar with gouache you will quickly note the difference. You should then make a record of your observations to meet the requirement to investigate the working characteristics of media and materials.

Gouache is also a water-based medium but its characteristic opaqueness allows you to use it in a similar way to other opaque media such as oil paint. In experimenting with gouache, you should be able to paint very clean, flat areas of colour which might be needed in design work, as well as to build up layers of paint to create many different textural, tonal and colour effects that you might need in a painting. You will find that you can superimpose light colours over dark ones as well as use them like watercolour (light to dark translucent layers) and this gives you a wide range of options when you use them.

▲ **The darkest tones are roughed in**

► **Half-tones and colour are added**

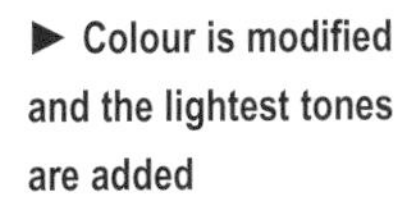

► **Colour is modified and the lightest tones are added**

Working from dark to light with opaque colours

Oil paint is a versatile medium which can also be used in many different ways, from semi-translucent layers to heavy, opaque 'impasto' effects. It is oil-based, of course, and this means that you have to use liquid vehicles such as turpentine and oil to thin out the paint. The pigment (colour) is carried by a vehicle (linseed oil in this case) and when it dries it is waterproof and permanent, whereas watercolours and gouache can be wiped out with water. You will find that oil paint can be worked for some time while it is still wet but watercolour and gouache cannot. Acrylics have similar characteristics to oil paints but their base is a plastic polymer. They are initially soluble in water but once they have dried they become permanent and are resistant to water. They can also be worked when wet but dry more quickly than oil paint. You should also try using these different paints on a range of different surfaces and do some research into traditional methods and materials. For example, find out what 'gesso' and 'tempera' mean.

▲ ***Claude Monet, 'The Thames below Westminster', 1871*** **(above – detail)**

Adhesives will be used for many different purposes and you need to understand their different properties. One of the most common uses of adhesives in two-dimensional work is in **collage**. The process simply involves you in creating images by sticking pieces of material such as paper, fabric, and card onto a surface. There is an infinite variety of suitable, cheap material available for collage and it can often be substituted for the more expensive alternatives of paint.

You may be asked to 'draw' with collage. For example, you might be asked to do a portrait using only black and white torn paper or one using an appropriate range of colour selected from printed fabric material. Using such methods forces you to 'match' the colours or tones that you observe with ones selected from the scrap material before applying them to the surface.

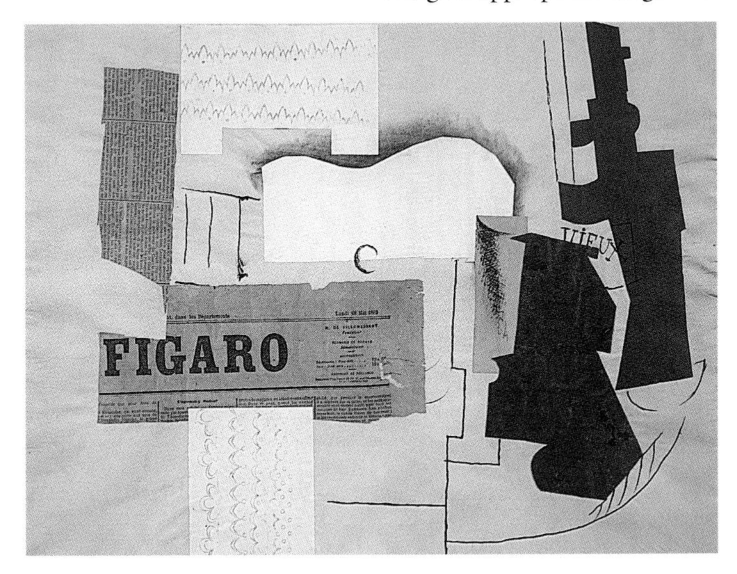

Collage can be very effective when combined with other materials. For example you could begin to work in torn paper then add paint, ink drawing and textural material to complete the image. Look for works in collage by artists such as Picasso, Braque and Schwitters.

▲ *Picasso, 'Guitar, newspaper, glass and bottle', 1913*

► **A student's study of apples using a torn newspaper collage**

Printmaking and reprographics

The range of possible work covered by the terms printmaking and reprographics is enormous and, within the constraints of the course you are studying, you will only be able to experience a relatively small amount. However, it will be important for you to understand the basic concepts and methods which characterise them. In printmaking there are basically three distinctive categories, each using different techniques and processes.

- **Intaglio:** This is a term used to describe a method of printmaking which depends upon ink being 'sucked out' of grooves in the surface of a printing plate through pressure. Etching and engraving are two examples of intaglio printing. In etching the surface of the printing plate is etched by acid, ink is then rubbed into the resulting grooves and the plate is passed through a roller press under great pressure to draw the ink from the grooves and produce a printed image. In engraving, the printing process is the same but the grooves in the printing plate are made by cutting into the surface. Etching is a potentially dangerous activity and there are important health and safety requirements which you must observe. You must not experiment with etching without proper supervision.

◀ **Rembrandt van Rijn, 'The Flight into Egypt', 1654 (etching)**

- **Relief:** Relief printing is, as the term implies, a process by which images are printed from a raised surface, rather than as in etching, from the grooves in the plate. The most common method of preparing a plate for printing is to cut away those areas of the surface that you don't want to print from and the raised areas left become the printing surface. Lino-prints or potato prints are examples of relief printing which you may have done at school. Relief printing is also extensively used in applying decoration to fabric surfaces. This is known as block-printing since the pattern is derived from repeated printing of the same block on one piece of material. You can also build up a printing surface rather than cutting away the ground and you can print from flattened found objects. Relief printing can be cheap to do and, as you can see, offers unlimited creative possibilities.

▶ **Utagawa Hiroshige, 'Marshy island off the mouth of the River Sumida, with Edo and Mount Fuji in the distance', c. 1857 (woodblock print)**

• **Screen printing:** In screen printing the image is produced by forcing ink or dye through a stencil supported by a fine, tightly-stretched mesh screen. Stencils can be made by cutting or by using screen-masking material which, when exposed to light, dissolves leaving unmasked areas through which the ink can be forced. Very detailed and accurate prints can be produced by using this method in conjunction with photographic images projected onto the sensitized masking material.

◀ *Andy Warhol, 'Marilyn Diptych', 1965 (detail)*

The term copying in the Range statement includes a huge range of methods of reproducing images through the use of appropriate technology. These range from basic letterpress printing, through lithography to sophisticated photocopying and laser printing. You will be able to use some of these processes on your course, depending on the range of equipment available.

Photography, film and video

Photography is one of the most useful mediums you can use on your course. It can serve a wide range of purposes. For example:

- **Photography as a means of recording information, objects and events.**

Photography will be very useful during research and investigation at various stages of a project and you should develop the habit of keeping a camera handy to record things which you could not note in other ways. A camera is also useful for recording something you have been drawing for future reference.

▼ ***Henri Cartier-Bresson, 'Seville', 1933.*** **Recording the effects of the Spanish Civil War.**

• Photography as a means of adding information to other work.

Photographs can be used in conjunction with text and other information, including drawings, to add to the information presented.

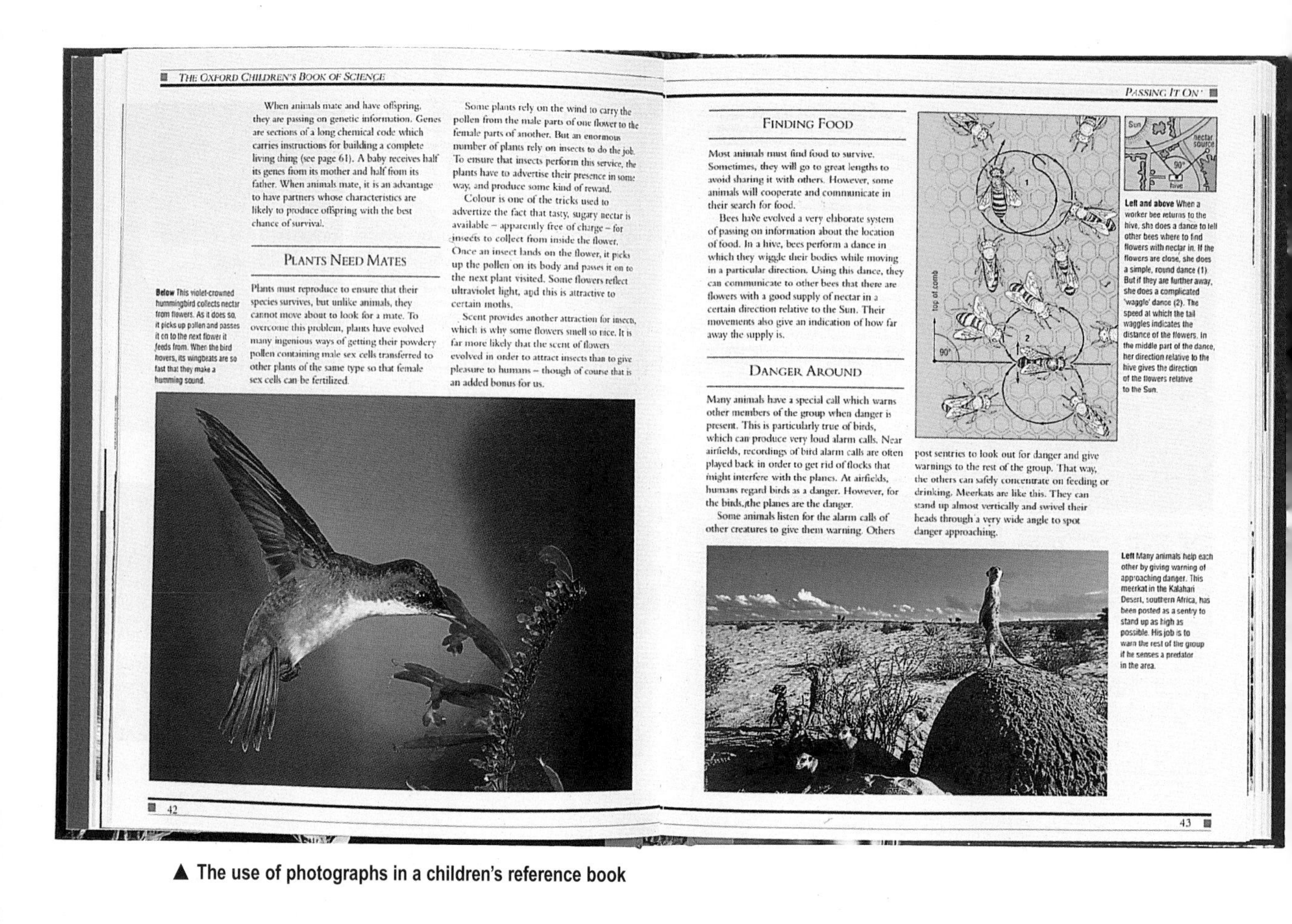

THE OXFORD CHILDREN'S BOOK OF SCIENCE

When animals mate and have offspring, they are passing on genetic information. Genes are sections of a long chemical code which carries instructions for building a complete living thing (see page 61). A baby receives half its genes from its mother and half from its father. When animals mate, it is an advantage to have partners whose characteristics are likely to produce offspring with the best chance of survival.

PLANTS NEED MATES

Plants must reproduce to ensure that their species survives, but unlike animals, they cannot move about to look for a mate. To overcome this problem, plants have evolved many ingenious ways of getting their powdery pollen containing male sex cells transferred to other plants of the same type so that female sex cells can be fertilized.

Some plants rely on the wind to carry the pollen from the male parts of one flower to the female parts of another. But an enormous number of plants rely on insects to do the job. To ensure that insects perform this service, the plants have to advertise their presence in some way, and produce some kind of reward.

Colour is one of the tricks used to advertize the fact that tasty, sugary nectar is available – apparently free of charge – for insects to collect from inside the flower. Once an insect lands on the flower, it picks up the pollen on its body and passes it on to the next plant visited. Some flowers reflect ultraviolet light, and this is attractive to certain moths.

Scent provides another attraction for insects, which is why some flowers smell so nice. It is far more likely that the scent of flowers evolved in order to attract insects than to give pleasure to humans – though of course that is an added bonus for us.

Below This violet-crowned hummingbird collects nectar from flowers. As it does so, it picks up pollen and passes it on to the next flower it feeds from. When the bird hovers, its wingbeats are so fast that they make a humming sound.

42

PASSING IT ON

FINDING FOOD

Most animals must find food to survive. Sometimes, they will go to great lengths to avoid sharing it with others. However, some animals will cooperate and communicate in their search for food.

Bees have evolved a very elaborate system of passing on information about the location of food. In a hive, bees perform a dance in which they wiggle their bodies while moving in a particular direction. Using this dance, they can communicate to other bees that there are flowers with a good supply of nectar in a certain direction relative to the Sun. Their movements also give an indication of how far away the supply is.

DANGER AROUND

Many animals have a special call which warns other members of the group when danger is present. This is particularly true of birds, which can produce very loud alarm calls. Near airfields, recordings of bird alarm calls are often played back in order to get rid of flocks that might interfere with the planes. At airfields, humans regard birds as a danger. However, for the birds, the planes are the danger.

Some animals listen for the alarm calls of other creatures to give them warning. Others post sentries to look out for danger and give warnings to the rest of the group. That way, the others can safely concentrate on feeding or drinking. Meerkats are like this. They can stand up almost vertically and swivel their heads through a very wide angle to spot danger approaching.

Left and above When a worker bee returns to the hive, she does a dance to tell other bees where to find flowers with nectar in. If the flowers are close, she does a simple, round dance (1). But if they are further away, she does a complicated 'waggle' dance (2). The speed at which the tail waggles indicates the distance of the flowers. In the middle part of the dance, her direction relative to the hive gives the direction of the flowers relative to the Sun.

Left Many animals help each other by giving warning of approaching danger. This meerkat in the Kalahari Desert, southern Africa, has been posted as a sentry to stand up as high as possible. His job is to warn the rest of the group if he senses a predator in the area.

43

▲ **The use of photographs in a children's reference book**

• Photography as narrative.

Photographs can be used to tell a complete story on their own, without the use of supporting text or other material (see opposite).

▲ A photo story from a magazine

- **Photography as an art form in its own right.**

Photographs can also be works of art, i.e. they serve the same purposes as paintings, sculpture and other art objects.

▲ *Author, 'Lock gates'*

◀ *Angus McBean, 'Portrait of Vivien Leigh'*

Film and video serve a similar wide range of functions and, depending on what facilities are available, you should try to develop some understanding of their creative possibilities.

Computer-based mark-making in art, craft, and design is commonly known as

Computer-aided design (CAD)

You should have sufficient access to computers to experience some of the increasing range of programmes which you can use in art and design. Many are specially designed to perform functions which are exclusive to art and design but there are many others which are more generally available, such as desk-top publishing programmes. The most useful from your point of view will be paint programmes which allow you to draw on screen and to use an extensive range of different colour combinations. From your initial experiments, getting used to the programme and the machine, you will begin to select programmes for specific purposes. For example, if you are working on

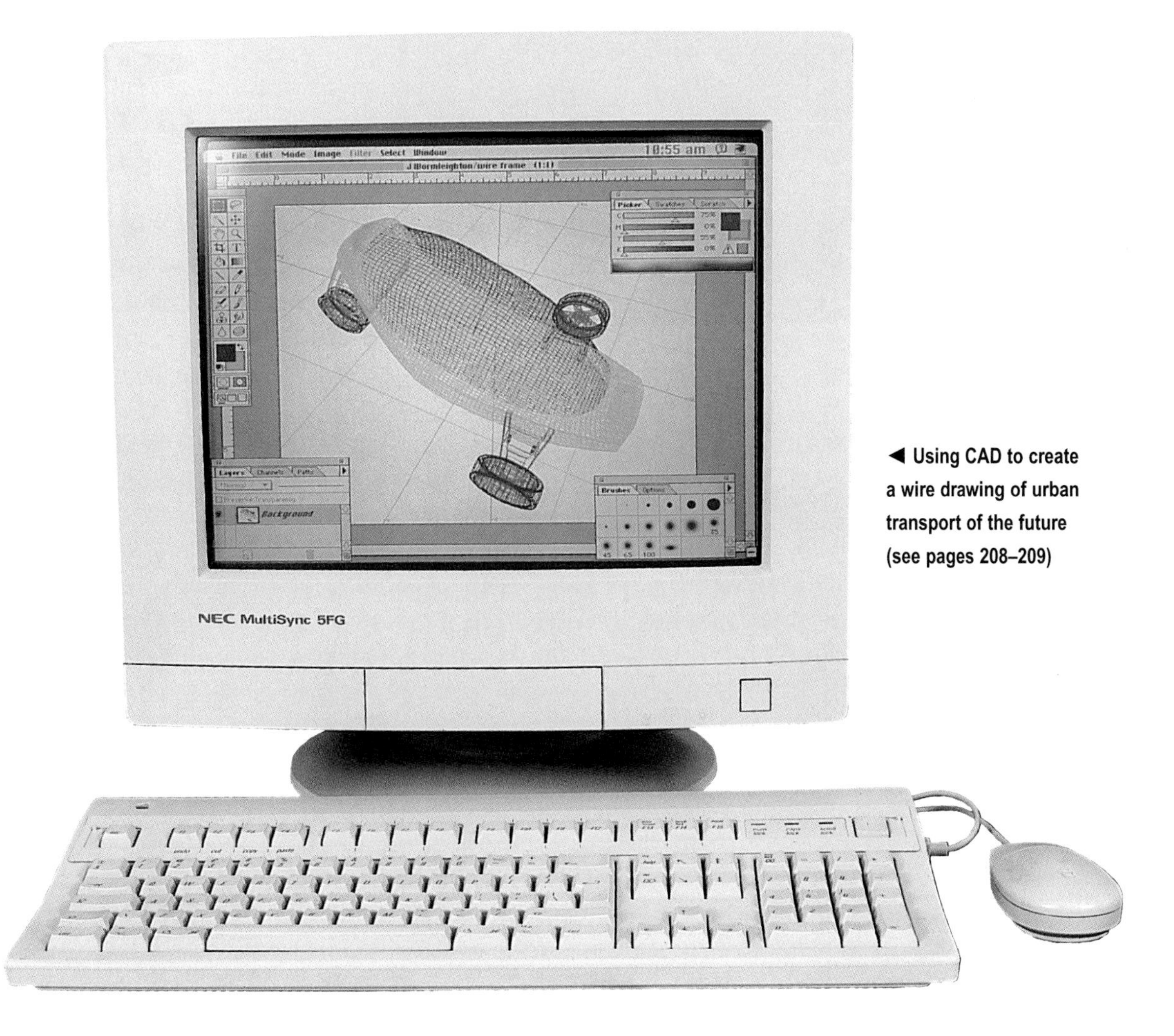

◀ **Using CAD to create a wire drawing of urban transport of the future** **(see pages 208–209)**

a design for a printed surface, there are programmes which allow you to change scale, pattern structure and colour, and to edit the work as you progress. There are other programmes which enable you to design and print your own letter fonts and to work on the complete layout and design of pages in books or other documents. Most of these allow you to import images from reference banks, or to process your own images and incorporate them into the layout.

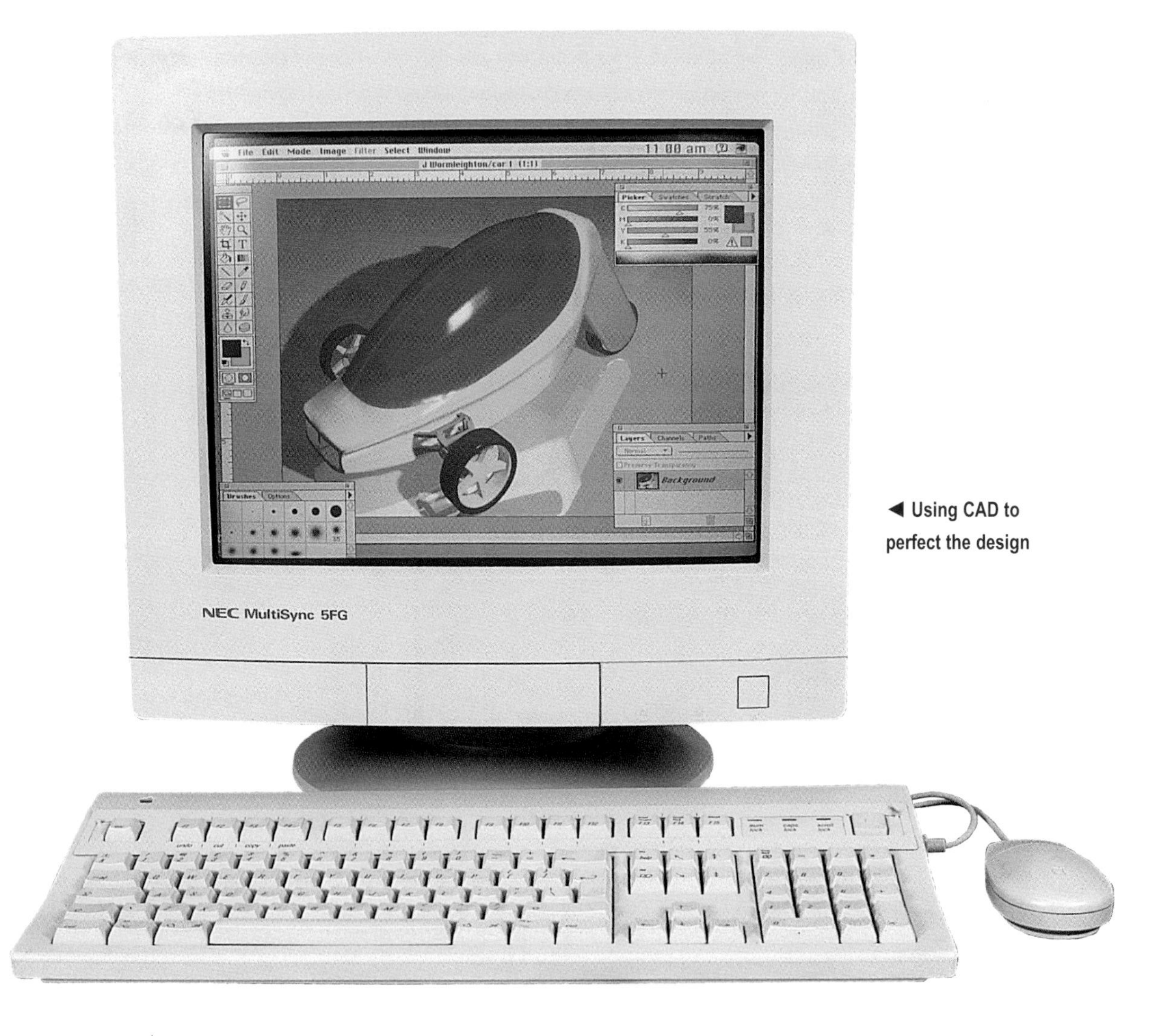

◀ Using CAD to perfect the design

Recently, multi-media facilities have become available and you can work with text, still images, video, and sound at the same time.

Remember that some of your work with computors can be assessed under the core skill of Information Technology.

Health and safety considerations associated with studio practice

There is substantial legislation covering the health and safety of people at work. The most important is the *Health and Safety at Work Act, 1974*. The legislation is mainly intended to protect employees from potential hazards and, as a student you are not technically an employee. However, the normal interpretation is that you are entitled to receive the same degree of protection as employees when you are working in your Centre. You are also expected to conform to the regulations and to observe normal safety procedures in studio practice. Safety is a shared responsibility and you have a duty to others as well as yourself.

You should make sure that you are aware of the safety procedures which apply to your working conditions and, in general, use your common sense to avoid creating hazardous situations.

2

[*unit 2*]

3D visual language

ELEMENT 2.1

EXPLORE 3D VISUAL LANGUAGE

ELEMENT 2.2

USE 3D MATERIALS, TECHNOLOGY, PROCESSES, AND TECHNIQUES

3D visual language is the title of the second of the four Mandatory Units and, as in the first Unit, there are two Elements. This Unit is similar to Unit 1 but it is concerned with work in three-dimensions, that is work which is 'in the round', such as modelling, carving, and construction.

ELEMENT 2.1

EXPLORE 3D VISUAL LANGUAGE

Performance criteria

1 explore and practise **making techniques**
2 explore **3D formal elements** and explain the elements used
3 use 3D visual language to communicate **information**
4 use 3D visual language to express **ideas and feelings**
5 show awareness of the potential of 3D visual language in the work produced
6 discuss own and others' use of 3D visual language

Range

Making techniques: cutting, forming, joining

3D formal elements: shape, structure, scale, proportion, balance, composition, colour, texture

Information: representation of space and form (of images, of objects, of people)

Ideas and feelings: personal responses, moods (given, self-identified)

Evidence indicators

Studies showing the use of 3D visual language, covering the range for making techniques and 3D formal elements. Studies should be supported by records to show the student has:

- explained the 3D formal elements used
- discussed the use of visual language in their own and others' work

Evidence of two complex activities including developmental and final work. These activities should be set in at least two of the following contexts:

- art
- craft
- design.

As we have said in Chapter 1, this is the standard form of presentation which you will recognise in all of the Units. It simply tells you what you must have done in order to complete the Unit. **An important thing for you to understand is that this specification is not a syllabus. It is a check list for assessment of the work you have done.** If it were a syllabus you would have to follow it exactly and study 3D visual language as a Unit on its own. In your course you are unlikely to do this, since you will normally work in many different ways and cover parts, or the whole, of several Units in one project. When you come to assess your work, you will refer to the specification and, with your tutor, make judgements about your work's quality and whether or not you have done all that you were expected to do. This process is commonly known as **referencing**.

Exploring and recording

The first two Performance criteria are concerned with **exploring** making techniques and 3D formal elements. This means that you should be prepared to experiment with different ways of handling materials, explore their potential and characteristics, and think about how you might use the formal elements in different ways to achieve the results you want. The Evidence indicators tell you that you should **record** your experiments and exploration in suitable ways and it is important to make a habit of keeping such records.

Making techniques

Let's now look at how you might explore making techniques. In the Range statement there is a simple list: cutting, forming, and joining. These are basic general terms to describe ways of shaping materials, but they usually become more complex when applied to a particular material.

Cutting techniques. The way that you cut materials will depend on their characteristics. For example, wood has different characteristics from metal and you would have to use different tools and techniques to perform similar operations. You might cut metal with a hacksaw, or even use an oxy-acetylene cutter. Neither of these would be suitable for wood, so you would have to use tools that were appropriate, such as a tenon saw, a chisel, or a mechanical saw (a bandsaw or jigsaw).

Forming techniques also have to suit the material. For example, forming clay might involve you in throwing, coiling, slab building, slip casting, and modelling; textiles work might involve weaving, steaming, and plaiting; and for plastics you may bend and mould them.

Joining techniques will also be different for each material. Different kinds of stitching are used to join textiles, and joining metals could involve welding, forging, braising, soldering, and riveting. Clay can be joined by simply squeezing pieces together or you might need to use slip (liquid clay) to join pieces of a slab pot.

Health and Safety

You can see how complex the exploration of making techniques can be. It can also be dangerous. As in Unit 2, there are legal requirements in terms of Health and Safety which you must observe. Mostly, they apply to your teachers, but you have an important shared responsibility to ensure that you don't endanger yourself or others. There will be rules about normal studio practice which you have to follow but you also need to learn about the risks associated with different materials and techniques for handling them.

Planning

In the early stages of a course you are likely to be given set tasks and selected materials to use by your tutor. You will also gain experience through specific 'workshops' which will be designed to give you a sound basic knowledge of the techniques and processes suitable for selected materials. However, as the course progresses, you will have more freedom to work on your own ideas and to explore materials and techniques independently. At this stage, you should begin your exploration by carefully planning what materials you intend to use, what tools and equipment will be required, and what kind of working space might be necessary. You also need to think about what technical help you might need, who can provide it, and if you want to share the exploration with other people.

It is often a good idea to work with other students to generate ideas and share possible areas of interest to begin with. You can then select aspects of the shared exploration to pursue on your own.

Modelling, carving, and constructing

It may be helpful to think about the handling and manipulation of three-dimensional materials using three broad categories since each involves a different **concept**.

Modelling

The concept of modelling consists of **adding** successive pieces of material, such as clay, until the final form is created. There are many materials which are suitable for modelling but the most commonly used are probably clay and wax. They are both used for figurative sculptural work and involve few tools. Spatulas and other simple hand-held tools are normally used to assist the sculptor in creating the final form and there are techniques for using them which you should explore. For example, spatulas are commonly used to add small pieces of clay to the surface, creating textural effects as the form is built up.

◀ *Dame Elizabeth Frink (1930-93), 'Two Heads'.* **You can see the marks made by modelling the clay before these heads were cast in bronze.**

Firing clay models

In their 'raw' state, neither clay nor wax are permanent and if the work is to be kept, it needs to undergo another process. Clay can be 'fired' in a kiln to change it to a permanent state of ceramic or pot, but it isn't usually done with solid modelling. The problem is that air can be trapped in a solid clay model and when it is fired, the air expands whilst the clay contracts, causing the model to explode. Small models can usually be fired in a solid state provided that they are thoroughly dry – any moisture left in the model will cause similar problems to those created by trapped air. Larger models should be hollow – that is they should be modelled (or hollowed out) so that there is sufficient space inside to allow for expansion. There is a name given to hollow, modelled objects of this kind – Terracotta – and there are many examples in museums and galleries which you can study.

▲ **Three terracotta figures of actors performing a mime, 1st Century AD**

Armatures and supports for clay models

Large clay models usually require supports, known as armatures, to prevent them collapsing as the form is built up. They can be in any suitable material, normally metal, which is strong and can be bent and joined to form a supporting structure for the clay. Rolled paper is often used to support terracotta pieces, which remains inside the model and is burnt out during the firing. This produces unpleasant fumes and kilns used for such firings should be well ventilated.

Casting clay and wax models or 'patterns'

Another way to make the model permanent is to make a mould from it and cast it in a material such as plaster or ciment fondue. This can be done using either a waste mould in which the mould is cut away from the cast after it has hardened, or a piece mould which can be taken apart to release the cast and used again for repeated casting.

Batch productions of pottery or ceramic figures are made in a similar way using plaster piece moulds filled with clay slip. The slip dries from the outside and when the required thickness has been reached the rest of the slip is poured out leaving the cast to dry and shrink away from the mould.

Wax objects can also be cast, and usually produce greater detail in the casting than clay models. When a mould is made from a wax object the wax can be melted out of the mould and then replaced by the casting medium. For example, gold and silver jewellery and fine metalwork are often made by this method. The wax model (called a pattern) is surrounded by a special mixture of heat-resistant liquid plaster. When it is set, it is heated to melt out the wax leaving an empty space of exactly the same form as the wax model. This is the mould from which a cast of the model can be taken in molten gold or silver.

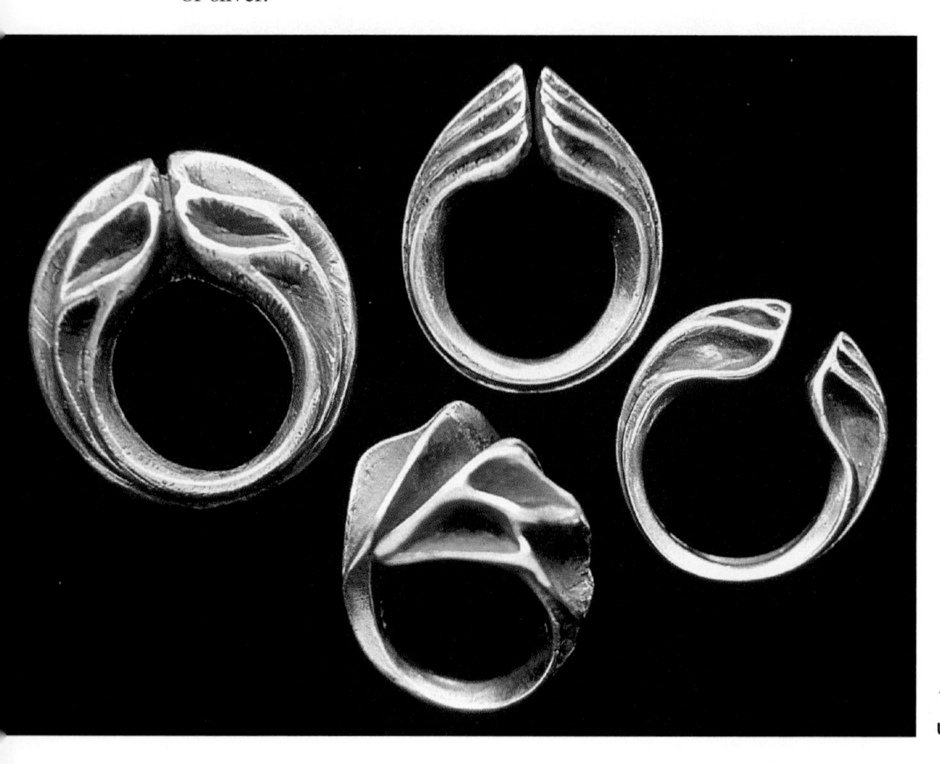

◀ **W. Gilbert, silver rings made using the lost wax method**

Bronze casting is also done using this ancient technique, known as the Cire Perdue or lost wax method. A mould is made from a model, then the inside of the mould is lined with wax to the required thickness. A core of suitable material, usually a composite based on sand, is then made by filling the inside of the mould. The wax is sandwiched between the mould and the core. The core is held in place with bronze pins and the wax melted out leaving a space into which molten bronze is poured. When cool, the mould and the core are broken away leaving a bronze cast. The cast usually needs cleaning up afterwards and is often patinated – a surface 'colour' is created by using acids and other patination media.

Casting in metals is potentially dangerous and requires a lot of expertise. It is not something you are likely to do at this stage of your career but it is important for you to understand the principles involved.

Sheets of wax suitable for making hollow forms can be created by pouring hot wax carefully onto cool water in a shallow tray. When the wax is cold it can be lifted from the surface of the water and shaped using your hands or a warm metal spatula.

Wax should always be melted using a double pan with the pan containing the wax set inside a larger one containing water. Never attempt to melt the wax in a pan which is in direct contact with heat.

Carving

The concept of carving is one of **subtraction** – cutting away material until the form you want to create is 'found'. There are different approaches to carving. Some sculptors like to work freely with a block of stone or wood, cutting away material until they 'find' the outer limits of part of a form they have imagined, or working from drawings or small, experimental models. They then continue to cut away material following the form as it gradually 'appears' to them. Some portrait artists work in a similar way in two dimensions – for example, they might draw an eye first and then extend the drawing from that point until it is finished.

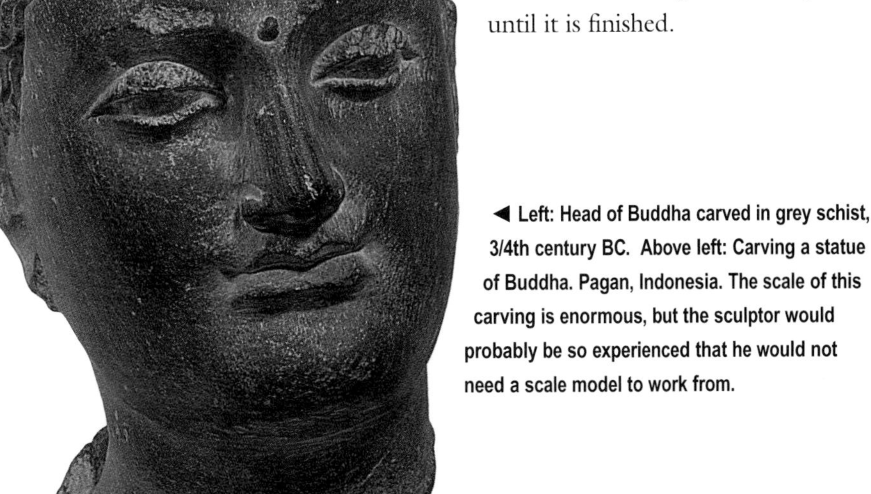

◀ Left: Head of Buddha carved in grey schist, 3/4th century BC. Above left: Carving a statue of Buddha. Pagan, Indonesia. The scale of this carving is enormous, but the sculptor would probably be so experienced that he would not need a scale model to work from.

Working from maquettes

Other sculptors prefer to work from a scale model – a maquette. A scale model or maquette is normally a reasonably detailed, small replica of the intended sculpture, scaled down to a given proportion. This enables the artist to work from measurements and to reproduce the form accurately. (**Scale** is listed as one of the 3D formal elements and this example will be useful when thinking about the use of scale in a piece of work – e.g. scaling up a model.)

► **Antonio Rossellino (1427-79), Italian, Florence – known as *'The Virgin with the laughing Child'*. This is an example of a terracotta maquette made for a larger sculpture.**

There are two kinds of three-dimensional sculpture – 'In the round' (or fully three-dimensional sculpture), and relief. Relief means that the image is made to stand out from a background by cutting away the surface of a flat piece of material. The sculpture is only partially three-dimensional – you can't see all round it – and usually relies on the effect of light falling on it to create the illusion of a fully three-dimensional form. Relief modelling is similar except that the image is built up from a flat surface.

► **This brass relief cast from Benin in West Africa shows an Oba, or ruler, holding a ceremonial staff, sixteenth century**

Construction

This concept is about **assembling** pieces of material in order to create a form. Assemblages can be fixed, when all the pieces would be joined to form a rigid structure, or they can be articulated, with joints which allow parts to move, creating a flexible structure. Automata are art or craft objects which have articulated parts.

► ***Paul Spooner, 'The Cat Drinking Someone Else's Milk'***

For many fine art students, assembling materials is often a cheap way of making art since they can use found objects or scrap materials. Craftspeople are also using scrap materials to make things such as jewellery and decorative pieces, although, like designers, they usually have to work with raw materials. This involves them in estimating quantities, preparing materials, cutting and shaping them, and assembling the pieces to create the final form. The range of constructed objects is very wide and includes objects made for pleasure, like those made from scrap, furniture, and articulated objects such as bracelets and toys. Most joining methods involve traditional techniques and processes and it is important to gain some experience of using them since their effectiveness will have been tried and tested over many years.

You need to explore a sensible mixture of experimental and traditional joining methods.

► ***Lucy Casson, 'Cormorants and Buoy', 1992 (recycled tin plate)***

A word of warning!
Exploring construction techniques can be fun, and using scrap materials is often an amusing way of finding out about different kinds of joining methods without the worry of wasting expensive raw material. However, using scrap material increases the risks to health and safety since it may be contaminated or may have been treated with finishes which can react to subsequent treatment, such as the application of paint or heat. It is, therefore, important to try to find out as much about the scrap as possible before starting to use it.

Exploring 3D formal elements

You can often combine an exploration of the formal elements with exploration of making techniques. If you simply experiment with different techniques without producing anything, it can be a waste of time. You could, for example, include a consideration of shape, structure, scale, and proportion in your technical exploration, so that your work would provide evidence of the two Performance criteria.

In many cases you will explore making techniques and formal elements as part of an assignment. For example, you may be given a 'brief' to produce possible models for small batch production of a series of items to be sold in a gift shop. You would then use both two and three-dimensional means to initiate and develop ideas, then explore a range of possible techniques and consider the formal qualities of the objects you intend to make. You would explore existing work of a similar nature to get information and you would produce drawings and scale models or maquettes which would involve issues of shape, scale, proportion and structure.

However, for the purposes of this section it will be better to consider the formal elements on their own initially.

Shape and form

You should refer to the section on Shape and form in Chapter 1, since it deals with similar concepts in the context of two-dimensions. For example, the paragraph on single shapes and forms suggests that it is useful to simplify them in order to understand their basic structure and illustrates the basic form of a head and shoulders portrait. Instead of doing a simplified drawing, you can make a three-dimensional model. The structure and form of a head can be explored by starting with a basic block of roughly the same proportions as a head, then by either modelling or carving, or both, begin to create a more detailed representational image. It is actually good practice to do both drawings and three-dimensional modelling – making a model helps you to understand the structure better and therefore enables you to draw it more convincingly.

Again, the basic forms are spheres (3D circles), cubes (3D squares), cylinders, triangles and 'pyramid' structures.

Unit structures

Again, as in Chapter 2, it can be very helpful to analyse a complex structure or group of forms in order to identify the basic shapes. Most forms of architecture are constructed from basic units and these often produce the main characteristics of a building. For example, materials such as brick and stone are used in different ways, both for creating strength and pattern, but the design of the building will depend on the material used. Many modern buildings are constructed from pre-cast concrete units designed both for structural functions and for aesthetic appeal. There are many interesting

Examples of experiments with 'units' to create decorative surfaces and structures

▲ These units were made by cutting and shaping wood within a square unit format then assembling them to create a surface pattern

experiments which you can do yourself by creating single units then combining them to create structures and patterns. For example, lengths of clay can be extruded through a die using a pugmill or wad box. The die can be adjusted to provide different sections and then the clay can be cut into small 'units' and assembled to create a surface pattern or a three-dimensional form. You can do similar experiments with blocks of wood prepared to a specific design. If you have access to woodworking machines, such as a bandsaw, cutting units of this kind can be partially mechanised. Wood can also be turned on a lathe to produce lengths with a round section. They can then be cut into short pieces just like the clay. Units can also be cast from moulds using plaster for small-scale experiments or cement and sand for larger-scale projects. Plastics can also be cast or shaped with a vacuum former to produce units from which experimental structures can be made.

▲ ▶ These units were cast in concrete using a wooden mould. They can be assembled in different ways to serve different purposes.

Structure

This is one of the most important formal elements, since almost every made or natural form has a structure. In Chapter 2, we discussed the structure of natural forms such as trees and people, referring to the structural characteristics of trunks and branches and the human skeleton. An essential characteristic of any structure is its strength, and you should explore different kinds of structures and the materials which are most suited to creating them. For example, some materials have great tensile strength, whilst others can withstand enormous compression. Stone is a material which has little tensile strength but is capable of supporting massive weight. A beam placed across two supports has to have both tensile strength and resistance to compression. At the centre of the beam the downward compression can result in failure unless its thickness, related to its length, has been calculated to withstand the forces to which it may be subjected. A comparison between an old building in which wooden beams were used and a modern one where steel is used will give you some idea of the different characteristics and strength of wood and steel.

You can explore the subject further by looking for ways in which architects and builders have solved structural problems by inventing new forms. For example, a simple post and beam structure can be extended to create a sloping roof support by creating a triangle with a king post through the centre. Similarly, the arch was designed to solve the problem of spanning a large space between vertical supports.

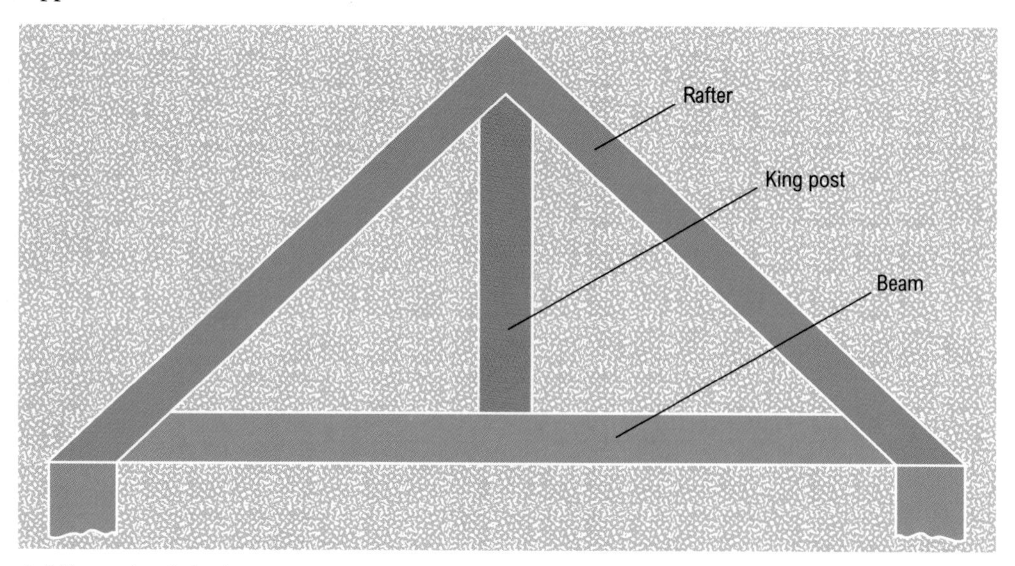

▲ **A king post roof structure**

In the thirteenth and fourteenth centuries in Northern Europe, the arch was extended into a pointed arch, allowing church builders to create higher and lighter structures, producing what is known as the Gothic period of church building. It was also extended three-dimensionally during the Renaissance to create domes which were capable of covering large circular spaces or drums (a dome is simply an arch rotated on its axis). The famous dome on the church of Santa Maria del Fiore in Florence, 'Il Duomo' , was finally built to designs by Brunelleschi (1337-1446) and it took him over 20 years to solve the problem of spanning a drum with a diameter of nearly 140 feet, 180 feet above the ground. Brunelleschi gained much of his understanding of such structures from his studies of the ruins of Classical Roman architecture in Rome.

▲ ***Brunelleschi (1377-1446), Cathedral of Santa Maria del Fiori, Florence***

A vault is also an extension of the arch, often used to create underground chambers and passageways which would support the weight above. The Victorians were expert in using brick vaulting in railway and canal tunnels using the same structural principles.

The most common building materials used before the twentieth century were wood, stone and brick, which limited what could be done structurally. Modern architects use materials such as steel, concrete and glass to create buildings which can be very high, light and airy, like skyscrapers; or spectacularly innovative, such as the Lloyds Building in London and the Pompidou Centre in Paris both by Sir Richard Rogers. Innovative design ideas are often dependent upon the development of new materials. Sometimes a new material will provide ideas for new kinds of structures, at other times it is the need to find a solution to a design problem which generates the search for an appropriate material.

▲ Skyscrapers in New York

▲ The Pompidou Centre in Paris

Try to find examples of both for your notebooks. An example might be the development of plastics which led to developments in their use, then, as the ideas began to outstrip the technology, new plastics were created to meet the need.

You can explore structures through practical experiments. Some can be purely for their own sake and not have any intended function, but you should also experiment with structures which are load-bearing or capable of great tensile strength. For example, look at bridge designs and experiment with different ways of bridging spans of various sizes.

You can also make experimental furniture, relating functional needs to a desire to create a fun object – design and make an 'experimental chair' perhaps.

► **An experimental chair**

Other ways of exploring structure might be to look at the sculpture of artists such as Naum Gabo, Jacob Lipchitz and work by the Russian Constructivists such as Tatlin.

Structures of natural forms can be analysed and re-presented as a combination of planes in space. Abstract artists like Anthony Caro create structures consisting mainly of lines and planes.

▲ *Anthony Caro, 'Prairie', 1967*

Scale

We have already considered scale in relation to models and maquettes, and it may be important for you to learn how to make accurate scale models, particularly if you intend to pursue a career in three-dimensional design. In two-dimensional work, scaling up or down involves working with surface area. In three-dimensional studies the same process involves volume which applies to the whole of a form (both its exterior and interior) and the space which it occupies. Architects and interior designers have to develop an awareness of volume, for example, in being able to visualise the three-dimensional space when making two-dimensional plans and working drawings. Scale models made from such drawings are a valuable means of seeing what the finished work might look like.

There are also important issues to do with the scale of objects in relation to human beings. Very large, imposing public buildings were often deliberately massive in scale in order to impress people and to emphasise the power and importance of the institution which they represented. Look at town halls, cathedrals, government buildings, and large country houses, for example.

The scale of sculpture is also an important consideration. A small domestic-sized figure has a very different 'presence' from one which is twice life-size. Look at the scale of monuments in our towns and cities. Not only are they usually larger than life-size they are mounted on pedestals to increase the sense of scale. The scale of sculpture depends to a large extent on where it is sited. Most public open spaces require large-scale works and their scale should be appropriate to the area and the scale of other built objects nearby. Henry Moore's sculptures sited in public spaces provide a model of carefully considered scale, but the ideas of Claes Oldenburg challenge our existing notions of scale.

▼ ***Claes Oldenburg, 'Lipsticks in Piccadilly Circus', 1966***

Proportion

The simple basics of proportion can be studied through single objects to begin with. The proportion of height to width and depth is a very important feature of anything you make. There are often functional considerations, such as those you would be concerned with when making furniture – the ergonomics of a chair for example. But there is also the way it looks – its aesthetic appeal. A badly proportioned object can be very unattractive. Look for examples of made objects which you think are well-proportioned and compare them with others which are badly-proportioned.

In two-dimensional work, the proportion of the height to width is important in relation to composition within the shape you intend to use. For example, the 'Golden Section' is considered to be an ideally proportioned format. The ratio of height to width is governed by a mathematical formula which produces a sense of harmony or rightness.

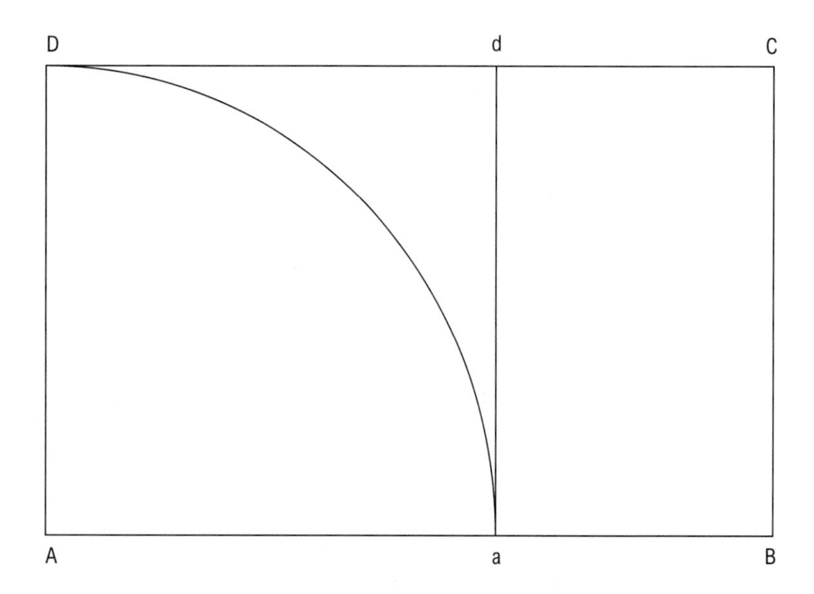

◀ **The Golden Section. The proportions of the rectangle – length (AB) compared to height (BC) – are the same as the division of the straight line (AC). Approximately 1.618...**

A simple way of remembering the proportions of height to width is:

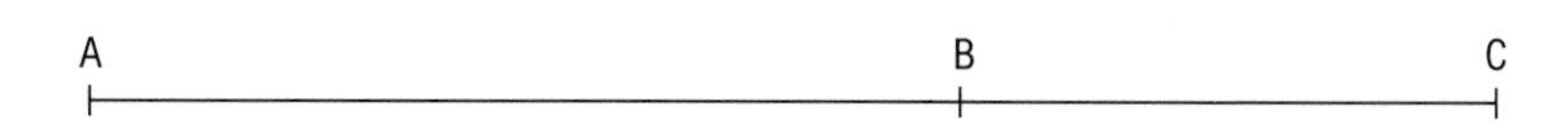

BC is to AB what AB is to AC

If you extend either of the two dimensions the proportions are altered and the oblong either looks too long or too high. This governing principle was used in the design and building of the Parthenon in Athens and is still used today by architects and designers. Le Corbusier, the French architect who was responsible for developing 'modular' building systems, had an idea that a whole complex of buildings could be built to one guiding mathematical formula. He suggested that decisions on the proportions of individual forms and their combinations could be made on this basis, and that the visual appearance of the product would therefore be harmonious.

Many designers use 'grid systems' as a basis for layout and composition, and the grids are based on mathematical formulae.

It is useful to remember that measurements related to made objects, such as buildings, originate from the human figure. The foot is a unit of measurement as are 'hands' and digits (fingers and toes). The importance of this lies in the physical relationship between things which are made and human beings who make and use them.

▲ ***Lever Building, New York, 1952.*** **This building set the fashion for glass walls cladding a steel structure and high rise construction which created public spaces on the ground. Its basic design is a grid or 'modular' system.**

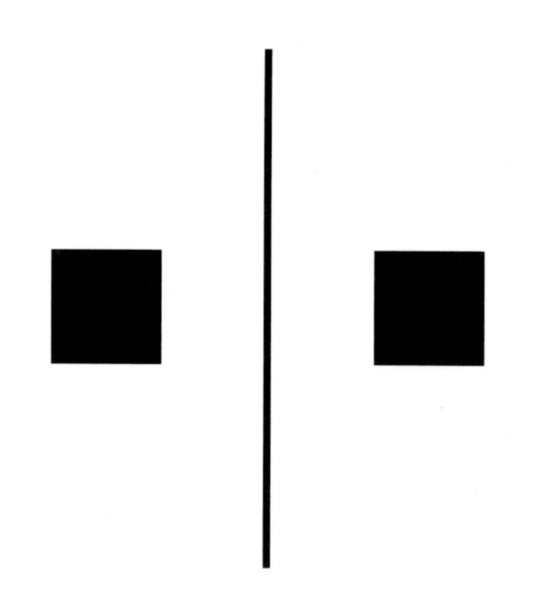

▲ Symmetrical balance between two squares of the same size and tone

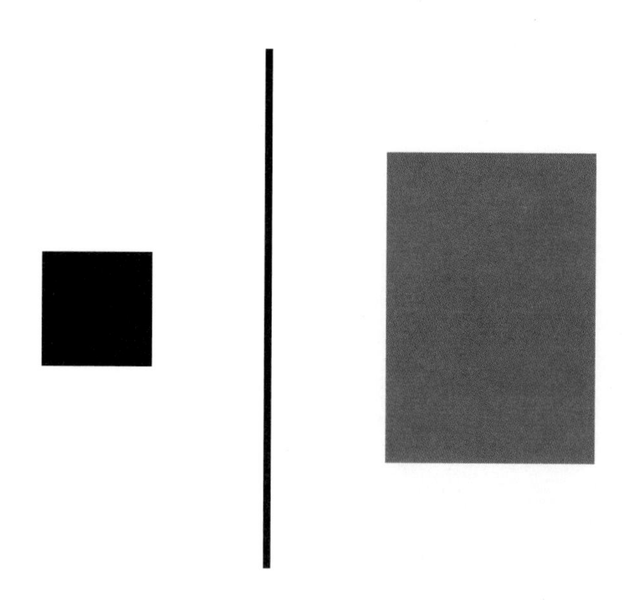

▲ A large grey rectangle balances the small dark square

Balance and Composition

Although balance is written into the Range specification on its own, it usually relates to composition – that is, the arrangement of things such as the formal elements to create a satisfying whole. This would involve you in composing elements which have different properties, such as weight and texture, in such a way that it looks balanced. In two-dimensional compositions there are no physical properties like weight, they would be purely visual, but in three-dimensional forms weight can be a real physical factor.

The simplest kind of balanced composition is one that is symmetrical – exactly the same arrangement either side of a centre line. However, as with a set of scales, balance can be achieved by balancing a small heavy object against a large lighter one. Visually, such a composition might be a small black square on one side of a centre line, balanced by a larger grey square on the other. This would no longer be symmetrical since the size of the shapes would be different but they could be said to balance each other. A sense of balance would be achieved within an asymmetrical composition.

This basic principle can be applied to all forms of composition. You can experiment with just visual elements then extend your experiments to include real three-dimensional forms which have physical properties such as weight and texture.

Since balance in terms of weight involves mathematics, the same is true of visual balance, and the grid systems mentioned earlier are examples of the way in which mathematical structures allow you to place elements of a composition within a frame to achieve a balanced whole.

There are other aspects of composition which involve balance, such as lines which create a sense of movement. You can balance linear movement in one direction with movement in the opposite direction. You can also counteract the effects of violent movement with areas or lines which appear static and stable. The theory of visual relationships between formal elements in a composition is known as 'visual dynamics'.

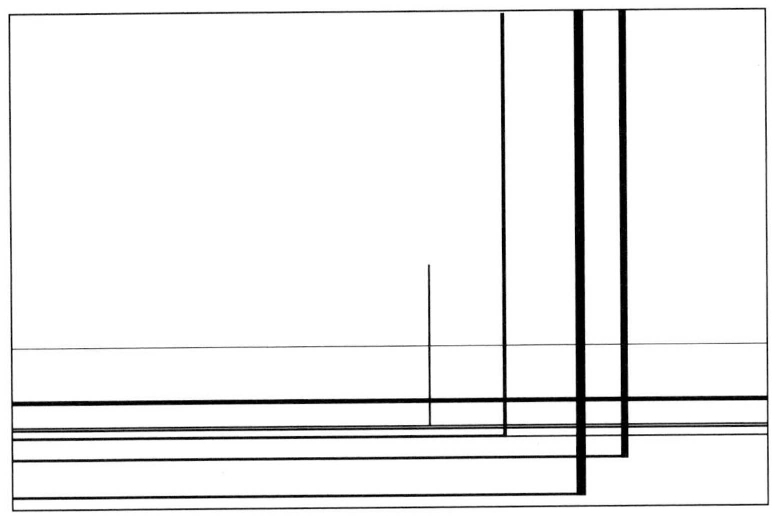

▲ Horizontal opposed by vertical lines create a sense of repose

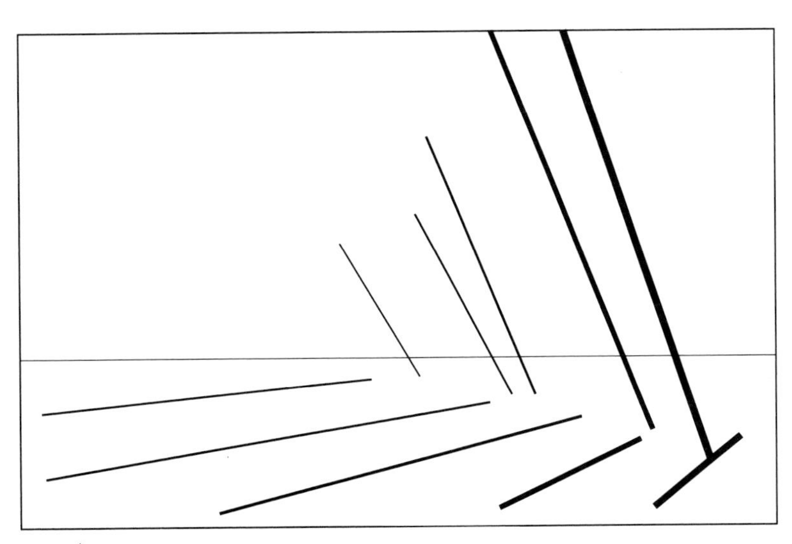

▲ Diagonal lines suggest movement which can be balanced through the use of opposing diagonals

You might begin to see how complex three-dimensional composition can be. Try this simple experiment. Starting with simple shapes and forms, such as cubes, make an arrangement of different sized shapes to create a balanced composition. They can be applied to a structure or simply arranged on a flat plane. As you move around them you will judge the composition from different angles and as you make adjustments to the composition from one angle it will affect how it looks from another. This simple experiment will demonstrate the potential complexity of any three-dimensional work – it should be composed so that it looks 'right' from any viewpoint.

If you then introduce other formal elements such as colour, pattern, line, and texture, you will be able to see the range of possibilities and complexity for yourself, particularly if you decide to use different shapes as well as all the other variations. It is, therefore, sensible to work systematically from simple to more complex arrangements in order to understand properly the formal aspects of balance and composition.

Information

Part of the exploration of visual language which you undertake in this Unit is the communication of information in three-dimensional form. We have covered some of this requirement in relation to the formal elements. As you use formal elements for particular purposes you are communicating your ideas about the appearance of an object to other people. This kind of work can be purely abstract, of course, and may simply be about your response to shape, form, line, and texture. Other kinds of information might be representational – that is, the object you make represents something else, such as a portrait of someone or a group of figures portraying a body of officials.

The kinds of information such work would be likely to contain might be about the subjects themselves, what they look like, what they are wearing, who they were, what they did, and what the purpose of the portrait is and so on. It, too, would include the use of formal elements of course.

A three-dimensional model or maquette, on the other hand, would have a specific purpose in containing the kinds of information which the artist, designer or builder would need in order to create a full-size replica. This information would have to be accurate in terms of scale, structure, and overall appearance. You can use models of buildings for trying out furniture layout, interior decoration, circulation routes, exterior layout of grounds, trees, pathways and so on. Similar models are used in theatre design where the designer often prepares a scale model so that the producer and the actors can experiment with the set to make decisions about movement and action sequences, colour, lighting, and the position of props.

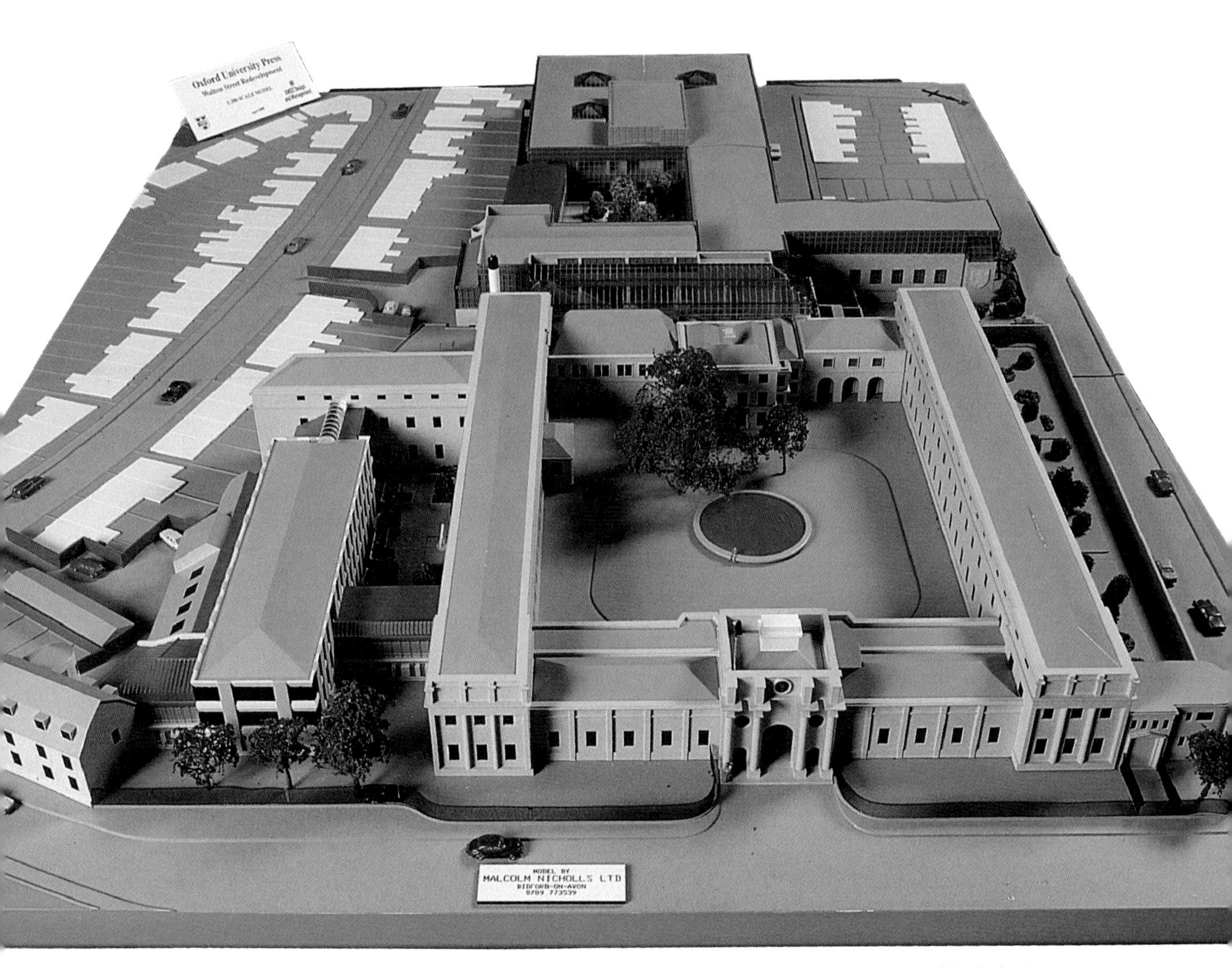

▲ **An architect's scale model showing the planned redevelopment of the Oxford University Press site**

Three-dimensional computer modelling

You are likely to have increasing access to computer-modelling software in the future. Although it is currently expensive and there may be limited equipment available in your Centre, such means of processing information and developing designs are commonly used in professional practice. Strictly speaking, the images produced are two-dimensional but, since they are about three-dimensional forms, it is appropriate to mention them in this context. Some systems allow you to design something directly on screen and, at the same time, are capable of producing detailed working drawings from the visual model. For example, some systems enable you to develop a visual representation of the object you are designing in perspective. You can see what it looks like from different viewpoints by turning the model around on the screen or by changing your position. The visual model contains accurate information about measurements and structure from which the working drawings are produced. This kind of work is known as Computer-Assisted Design or CAD.

Another form of computer system which controls the manufacture of objects is known as 'Computer-Assisted Manufacture' or CAM. If you put the two together and create a computerised system for both design and manufacture you have CAD/CAM.

Ideas and feelings

As well as exploring the processing of information by three-dimensional means, you are also expected to explore the communication of ideas and feelings. As in two-dimensional studies, ideas and feelings are often the most important basis for the work you do. They are usually the starting point for exploration, experiment, and creation of works of art and in all of the Units which require you to make something, there is a reference to stimulating ideas through responses to different stimuli. There is, however, another way in which ideas and feelings are important in your work and this often occurs during the process of making or exploring something. Many craftspeople, for instance, will develop their ideas directly in their chosen material and let it influence the direction which the work takes. Often, when you are making something, a better idea will occur to you and you will modify your planned approach accordingly. Sometimes, it is possible to simply start working with a material without any pre-conceived ideas about what you might make. Then as you manipulate it an idea becomes fixed and you go on to make it, or note it for future reference. **The main point is for you to recognise that ideas come from many different sources and at many different times during the creative process.** You should, therefore, avoid always working in the same way and explore different ways of generating and developing ideas.

3D Visual language in your own and other people's work

The last two Performance criteria in Element 2.1 require you to consider the effectiveness of the use of 3D visual language in your own work, but it may help you to do this if you look at the work of other artists, craftspeople, and designers. You are also required to show awareness of the potential of 3D visual language in the work you produce.

This will mainly be achieved by thinking about the use of formal elements in your work and the purposes which they serve. You have seen how any piece of artwork involves the formal elements and you therefore need to be able to show that you have used them consciously – that you have deliberately chosen to use certain combinations of formal elements to achieve what you intended.

However, quite often you will be making choices intuitively – you won't be thinking consciously at all. Your choices will be guided by your sense of what is 'right' or the most effective. This intuitive sense is very important for artists, craftspeople, and designers and it can be difficult, if not impossible, to explain in words what you have done and why you have done it. Remember that art is a visual language and if what you can express in art could be equally well said through words there would be little need for art. You should therefore develop confidence in your own judgements – your own aesthetic sense – and, as long as your work demonstrates that you have explored the potential of 3D visual language, you don't have to explain it all.

When you consider the work of others, however, you will mostly be involved in thinking about and discussing why certain formal elements and symbols were used and for what purpose. This is analytical thinking and it is different from the kind of thinking or intuitive processing that you engage in when you are creating art, craft and design objects. You will need an appropriate vocabulary, largely consisting of the kinds of words we have been using to describe the formal elements and visual dynamics associated with various kinds of composition. In Unit 3, the Performance criteria require you to discuss other people's work, and the reason is that by sharing your opinions and discoveries with others you will develop confidence in being able to talk convincingly about 3D visual language.

Examples of other people's work have been used to illustrate particular points in the text and you can see how important it is that you have some understanding of how things were created and how design problems were solved. It is also very important that you begin to understand why things were made or designed in particular ways. This usually depends on the context in which the work was done. Contexts can be historical, contemporary, cultural, social, economic and so on.

In the next chapter we shall talk about some of the different contexts in which art, craft, and design function, and how your increasing awareness of the contexts can play an important part in the development of your own work.

ELEMENT 2.2

USE 3D MATERIALS, TECHNOLOGY, PROCESSES, AND TECHNIQUES

Performance criteria

1. *develop skills in the use of* ***3D materials, technology, processes and techniques***
2. *explore working characteristics, potential, and limitations of materials*
3. *select and use* ***3D materials, technology, processes and techniques*** *creatively to meet* ***specified intentions***
4. *follow the 3D* ***health and safety procedures*** *associated with studio and workshop practice*
5. *discuss and review the effectiveness of own use of* ***3D materials, technology, processes and techniques***

Range

3D materials: card, clay, metal, plastics, textiles, wood

Technology, processes, and techniques associated with cutting, forming, and joining

Specified intentions: to communicate information, to express ideas and feelings; specified by the tutor, self-identified

Health and safety procedures: correct use of media, technology, processes, and techniques; elimination of risk to self and others (burns, cutting edges, chemicals, electric shock, fumes, lifting, sharp instruments, sharp tools)

Evidence indicators

Studies covering the 3D materials, technology, processes, and techniques ranged. Studies should be supported by records to show the student has:

- followed the 3D health and safety procedures required in studio and workshop practice
- discussed and reviewed the effectiveness of own use of materials, technology, processes, and techniques.

Two complex activities including developmental and final work. These activities should be set in at least two of the following contexts:

- art
- craft
- design.

You will see from the specification for this Element that it follows on from Element 2.1 – in the reference to materials, techniques, technology, and processes, for example. In Element 2.1 you were expected to explore making techniques and this involved handling and manipulating materials. Some of the references to making techniques also relate to the characteristics of materials – e.g. the different techniques required for cutting wood and metal.

Element 2.2 requires more sustained attention to making techniques and the technology involved as well as a more detailed analysis of the characteristics of different materials.

3D Materials, Technology, Processes, and Techniques

Working characteristics of materials

You will already have considered some of the working characteristics of materials but you now need to be more systematic about the way you identify and analyse them. Each material will have its own complex set of characteristics and there isn't space in this book to cover them all. Your tutors will introduce you to a range of different materials but it may be helpful to take just one example and consider its characteristics in some detail. Clay is likely to be one material you'll use quite often so let's look at clay.

Clay

Clay is a versatile material which is easy to shape, but you have to understand what clay is and what happens to it during its use in order to understand its characteristics. You can refer to pottery books for detailed information and you can explore the material through physical handling. All such work should be recorded to provide evidence of the range you have covered.

Clay is essentially specific kinds of earth mixed with water to create a consistency which allows you to shape it. Slip is a similar mixture to clay but with a much greater proportion of water. You should understand that the first change which will occur in all such mixtures is that of drying. As the water evaporates, the particles of earth become more closely inter-related and the shape you have made will shrink – it will have less volume. When the shape is dry you can no longer alter its shape, except by some kind of filing, which is potentially dangerous because of the fine dust created. You can, however, shape a 'leather-hard' clay object by fettling or turning. Fettling is shaving pieces off the form and turning is similar except that it is done on a wheel, rather like turning wood. The 'foot' of a pot is usually turned on the wheel with the pot upside down. The term leather-hard means that the clay has dried to the point where it is hard but still damp enough to cut and fettle.

Until clay has been fired it can be re-constituted by simply adding water. The clay reverts to a sludge and you then have to begin the process of drying it to a workable consistency and preparing it for use. The preparation includes wedging, where a lump of clay is cut into wedges which are then forced back together. The clay is then kneaded until it is ready for use. This process is designed to expel all air from the clay and to produce an even consistency.

Making your own clay

As an addition to your exploration of clay, you could try making your own. You could dig some clay from a suitable piece of ground and mix it with water to create a slurry. Then leave it for a few days for the clay to settle at the bottom of the container and siphon off or pour away the excess water. You should also remove any debris which you dug up with the clay. When the consistency is that of a sludge, spread it onto a plaster slab or other porous surface. The water will be absorbed by the slab and the clay will also dry in the air. When it is in a plastic state, wedge it and knead it before making some trial pots. You may find that the clay is 'short' and doesn't hold together very well, in which case you would need to add other substances, such as bentonite, to make the clay more plastic.

You could then try some firing tests to see what effect this has on the clay – what colour it is, what temperature is best and so on. Later, you could try experimenting with your own glazes, but this requires a lot of detailed preparation and more time than you could probably afford.

Firing

Changing dried clay objects into a permanent state is done by firing the clay in a kiln to a high temperature, which alters its chemical composition and it can no longer be re-constituted into its original state. The clay shrinks further during firing which is important when considering the final size you want and when applying glazes – a glaze must shrink at the same rate as the clay otherwise it will flake off.

Different kinds of clay can be fired to different temperatures to produce different end products. For example, earthenware is clay which has been fired to a temperature of around 1000 degrees centigrade. A characteristic of earthenware is that it retains its porosity when fired, and if you apply a glaze it remains on the surface, rather like a varnish applied to wood. Stoneware is clay fired to a higher temperature, around 1300 degrees centigrade, and if you've applied a glaze it will fuse with the clay. The clay also fuses and even when unglazed it will be impervious to water. Porcelain is a special clay, mainly 'China Clay', which is fired to an even higher temperature – up to 1500 degrees centigrade – it also fuses and becomes transluscent.

This example shows you the kind of things you need to learn about materials and the kind of information which you need to record in order to demonstrate that you have studied their characteristics.

1

Examples of different kinds of pottery:

1. **porcelain bowl**
2. **earthenware (terra-cotta) figures**
3. **stoneware vessel**

All other materials can be analysed in similar ways in order to understand their working characteristics. In some instances it will be helpful to learn about the chemical composition of a material, since its characteristics will depend on what it is made from. Plastics are a good example of this kind of material and you should find out as much as you can about how different kinds of plastic are made and the ways in which they behave when you cut, shape, and form them.

When exploring the working characteristics of wood, it will be helpful to understand how and where the tree from which it came grew, and how the pieces you are using were produced. The growth of a tree has important implications for the way that it can be used and manipulated. For example, there are important differences between hard and soft woods in their capacity to resist deterioration or water and in the way that the grain of the wood allows you to shape it. Close-grained woods such as boxwood and common trees like pear, can be carved or incised with a very high level of detail. Boxwood is used for wood-engraving because the grain is so tight that the finest lines can be engraved into the surface of the polished end-grain. Hardwoods, such as oak, are naturally resistant to weathering and to water, which is why so much was used for shipbuilding and house-building in the past. Weathered oak doors and windows can survive for hundreds of years and do not require any preservative treatment.

You should plan your explorations systematically so that you end up with a convincing record of the research and experimentation that you have conducted.

Discuss and review the effectiveness of own use of 3D materials, technology, processes and techniques

Finally, in this Element, you are expected to use your newly-gained knowledge of materials, technology, techniques, and processes creatively, and to discuss and review how effectively you have used them. You are most likely to do this within an assignment in which you would be expected to undertake a sequence of activities which leads to a final outcome. As we have said before, this will involve you in the whole creative process, but, for this Element, there is likely to be an emphasis on skills and control of materials. You can see that many of your other assignments will also have provided opportunities for the same range of work so you will have some understanding of what is expected of you.

Discussing your own skills and aptitudes is a similar process to the one described at the end of the section on Element 2.1. It is an analytical process in which you reflect upon the work which you have done and try to make critical judgements about it.

Understanding how others used similar techniques and processes can be very helpful in developing your own work. It is especially useful to be able to watch a professional at work. You may be able to visit studios and workshops or you may be lucky enough to work with an artist in residence organised by your Centre. If you don't have many organised visits you should really try to find contacts of your own so that you begin to learn what professional practitioners actually do. Remember that your teachers will also be professional artists, craftspeople or designers.

unit 3

Exploring others' art, craft, and design work

ELEMENT 3.1

EXPLORE HISTORICAL AND CONTEMPORARY CONTEXTUAL REFERENCES

ELEMENT 3.2

INVESTIGATE PROFESSIONAL PRACTICE

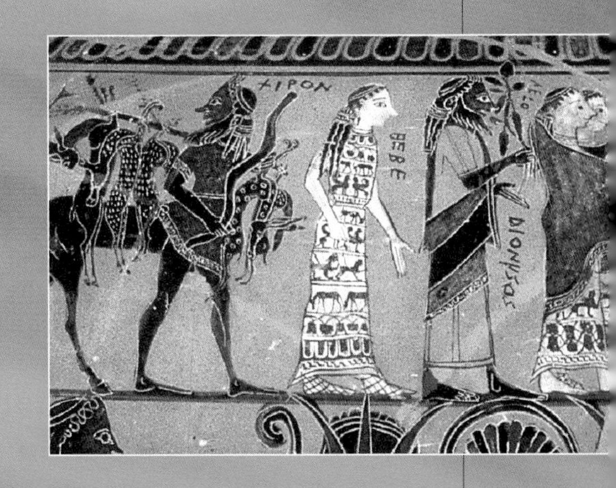
ΧΙΡΟΝ
ΗΕΒΕ
DIONVSOS

ELEMENT 3.1

EXPLORE HISTORICAL AND CONTEMPORARY CONTEXTUAL REFERENCES

Performance criteria

A student must:

1. *analyse the use of 2D and 3D visual language in* ***others' specified work***
2. *identify the use of media, materials, and technology in* ***others' specified work***
3. *explore* ***contexts*** *of, and references in,* ***others' specified work***
4. *organise visually stimulating* ***records*** *of findings*

Range

Others' specified work: historical, contemporary, western, non-western, 2D, 3D, art, craft, design, originals, reproductions

Contexts: commercial, social, cultural, scientific, contemporary, historical

Records: written, graphic, lens-based, samples

Evidence indicators

Notebooks recording the exploration of others' art, craft, and design work, covering the range for others' specified work.

Six case studies showing in-depth research into the practice of six recognised individuals (one case study for each person). The case studies should include findings on use of visual language; use of media, materials and technology; and contexts and references. At least one individual should be chosen from each of the following contexts:

- art
- craft
- design.

You should now be familiar with the way that the Unit Specification summarises what you are expected to do. This Element is concerned with the different ways in which **visual language, materials, techniques, and processes** have been used in the work of artists, craftspeople, and designers. It also requires you to explore the different **contexts** in which art, craft, and design function and some of the references that others have been influenced by.

The term 'references' means the range of styles, periods, movements which can provide ideas and information. It includes art, craft, and design from different cultures and different contexts.

You can see that there are **two basic requirements**.

The first is that you should study and make use of other people's work (meaning artists, craftspeople, and designers) in the majority of your studies. This is, therefore, a continuous process through which you form the habit of making reference to, and doing research into, other people's work as part of each assignment.

The second is that you should select six individuals to study from the range of art, craft, and design. This means that you can choose an artist, a craftsperson, and a designer as three and then concentrate on the area of your choice for the other three, or you could choose two from each area of practice.

There are good reasons for requiring you to undertake such a range of study. It is important for you to understand that your own work exists in the context of contemporary practice and in the context of what has gone before. Knowledge of both of these contexts will help you to develop your own work more effectively. For example, you can learn a lot about style and techniques by studying the ways in which others have tackled similar problems to the ones which you are trying to solve.

There are studies which will be **specific** to a range of work, such as existing solutions to graphic design problems, but others will be wider-ranging and will add to your **general knowledge** of art, craft, and design practices. Of course, as you undertake specific studies, your understanding of the whole range of practice also increases and this broad range of knowledge and understanding helps you to make choices from the range of possibilities which present themselves.

The Unit again consists of two Elements, **3.1 Explore historical and contemporary contextual references** and **3.2 Investigate professional practice** and it will be useful to look at each separately, although they obviously overlap to a considerable extent.

Historical and contemporary contextual references

This is an enormous topic for you to think about. It encompasses the whole of the history of art, craft, and design and the whole range of contemporary practice. Clearly it isn't possible for you to study anything but a small proportion of the body of knowledge that exists, and the first problem you face is selecting what to study.

You will have noticed that all of the other Units contain some reference to other people's work, particularly in obtaining information and ideas in preparation for doing work of your own. Such critical and contextual studies are, therefore, normally a part of the other work that you do. This is another important example of the way in which the Units are integrated and not studied separately.

In addition, you are likely to have timetabled lectures or seminars on broader aspects, such as historical studies.

The choices open to you are, therefore, narrowed by the context in which you are working. For example, you may have been given a brief to design promotional material for a fashion house which specialises in Far Eastern style clothing. Your historical and contemporary research might therefore be constrained largely to Chinese and Japanese sources. A ceramics brief might involve you in researching aspects of the history of some English pottery, Staffordshire or Wedgwood for instance, and a textiles brief may require research into the woollen industry.

On the other hand, a series of lectures on the history of art, crafts, and design will be decided by your teachers and will be chosen to give you some insight into important periods and movements. You will also learn about the significance of particular artists, craftspeople, and designers in both historical and contemporary contexts.

During the early part of your course, your choice of critical and contextual studies will mostly be restricted to the range suggested by your teachers. They will expect you to undertake assignments which contain a requirement to research a particular aspect of historical or contemporary practice. As you progress there will be an increasing emphasis on your ability to control the direction of your own work, and the briefs or assignments you are given will allow greater freedom in the range of research that you might do.

Remember that your ability to do research independently of your tutors can be important in assessing the grading of your work.

Research methods and recording research

The first important requirement is for you to learn how to access sources of information. You will probably be introduced to your Centre library and shown how to use the referencing system. This will enable you to locate the subjects you need, which can be in the form of books, resource collections, tapes, slides, photographs, videos and, increasingly, computerised materials.

All books on the history of art contain further references to sources, most of which would have been used by the author when writing the book. Other references may be to 'further reading' which indicates where you can get more information but which may not have been used by the author.

The references at the back of such books are usually in several forms. These may be:

- **Notes to the text:** These normally relate to 'footnotes' which you will see in the text next to the words to which they refer. e.g. a reference to Brunelleschi[4] means that further explanation is contained in note 4 of that chapter.

- **Bibliography:** This is a list of sources used in the writing of the book, particularly references to other publications.

- **List of illustrations:** A list of the illustrations used in the book containing information about the work illustrated – e.g. who it was by, its date, what it was made from, what size it is, where it can be seen, which source it was obtained from (perhaps another book) and who owns it.

- **Index:** A list of names or significant words and topics which tells you on which pages they can be found (more than one reference in the book is indicated by the appropriate page numbers).

You should get used to using the system by selecting some examples and following up the various references so that you get some idea of how it all works and the kinds of additional information there are.

NB. A useful habit to acquire is to look up the size of the original work used in an illustration. The size of a book illustration is dependent upon the designer's decisions, how much space there is and so on. It is often a complete surprise when you see the original for the first time when your knowledge of it only comes from the illustration. This is why it is always very important to try to visit as many galleries and museums as you can and look at the original work. Book illustrations and other forms of reproduction can never be a substitute for the real thing. You get no sense of scale and no sense of the actual qualities of an art object, such as the surface quality of paint or the texture of a particular material. Nor can you walk around a three-dimensional object. Colours can also be unreliable in reproductions, although the technology is now so well developed that usually colour reproductions are reasonably accurate.

George Seurat, 'Sunday Afternoon on the Island of La Grande Jatte', 1884-86, and 'detail'. **This painting is very large (2.02 x 2.75 m) but the illustration gives you no sense of scale.**

You also have to be able to look very closely in order to understand how Seurat used his 'pointillist' technique.

Although this section on research is mainly about using books and other published materials, as much of your research as possible should be from primary sources – real art, craft, and design work.

Making notes

It is very important that you also develop the habit of making notes when you research something. When you read a book it is important to note the key points for future reference and to help you to remember the information. A notebook or loose-leaf file containing all your notes will provide important evidence, for assessment purposes, of the research and reading that you have done. You can also include drawings, photographs and other reprographic materials alongside your notes (see page 23). Notebooks which contain a range of different kinds of recorded information are usually more interesting and informative than those which are restricted just to written notes. **You should note that Performance criterion 4 requires you to organise 'visually stimulating' records of your findings.** The use of a range of different recording media will help you to do this.

If a book belongs to you, it is useful to make notes in the margin, so that the next time you pick it up you have a reference system of your own to which you can refer. This is particularly important if the book is dealing with a progression of information because, as the narrative becomes more extended or complex, it can be difficult to remember what earlier sections were about.

An important habit to get into is to always note the title of the book you are using, the author, and the publisher. If you find a section particularly useful, note the page number and write a short description of the contents for future reference.

Another helpful working method is to prepare a **card index system**, or card file. Any stationer will have one in stock.

You could also create your own **cuttings file** for interesting articles, photographs and other references. Television, newspapers, and magazines are all sources of useful material and you should make notes of the appropriate reference. Videos of art, craft or design programmes on the television can also be collected to create a **video library** of your own.

As well as providing an invaluable and readily accessible personal resource and reference collection, all of these provide evidence of the research that you have done.

Visual research

This is the name given to working visually when you are researching something. In the first chapter we considered drawing as a means of investigating the appearance, form, and structure of things. Drawings can be straightforward records, providing information on what the thing looked like to you from a particular viewpoint or from several viewpoints. This is known as **objective drawing**.

The information contained in an objective drawing may be limited by the style, material, and techniques which you have employed, or because it only deals with one aspect of the object – an aspect of its visual appearance for example. A broad drawing in charcoal may only be meant to record the overall effect of light falling on an object and will not contain much detailed information on form, or structure, surface texture or pattern. It would contain little information on colour since you used only charcoal and you may not have included any information about its scale.

An **analytical drawing**, on the other hand, would be expected to contain detailed information about a range of aspects, such as form, structure, scale, colour, and surface texture. This kind of drawing could be in many different forms and could be spread over more than one sheet of paper. You could use different media to record different kinds of information, trying to find ones which were the most appropriate to the particular aspect you wished to record. It is also very useful to make notes alongside your drawings. Remember that before the advent of the camera and photographic technology, detailed analytical drawing was the only way to record and convey accurate visual information of this kind. Think of botanical and zoological drawings from the great voyages of discovery and the anatomical drawings of Renaissance artists such as Leonardo da Vinci and Michelangelo.

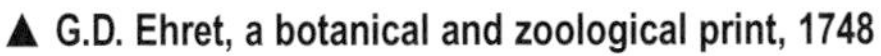

▲ G.D. Ehret, a botanical and zoological print, 1748

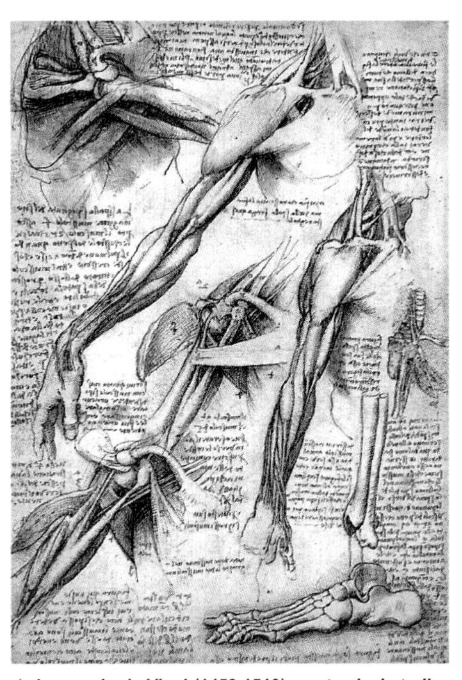

▲ Leonardo da Vinci (1452-1519), anatomical studies

Making drawings and analytical notes of real objects is very important but you can also analyse reproductions and photographs – secondary sources.

Merely copying a reproduction is unlikely to tell you much – you must try to analyse its 'visual language'.

These are useful examples of the way in which the context and purpose of a piece of work influences decisions on the choice of materials and techniques and of how you can often interpret others' work by identifying the reasons why materials and techniques might have been chosen. In the first example of an objective charcoal drawing, the purpose was to record a particular effect of light on an object. Since this could be achieved by using mainly tone and would probably need to be drawn fairly quickly, the choice of charcoal is sensible. If you were looking at another person's charcoal drawing you could probably deduce similar intentions and you would be engaged in analysing and interpreting a work of art – engaged in critical study.

The term 'critical studies' simply means that you are analysing an art object and making critical judgements about its qualities and purpose.

In the second example, the choice of materials and techniques was related to the different kinds of information which needed to be analysed and recorded. Each material would be chosen to suit the intention. For example, the use of water-colour in an analysis of the colour properties of an object might be your chosen medium because it provides a quickly accessible and portable means of recording information (you might be working outside where the colour varied with the differences in sunlight and having to carry your equipment). You might choose a fine pen and ink to record an analysis of structural and surface details, and you might choose pastels to record textural qualities. The range of work and the way that it would be spread over successive sheets of paper, suggests that you were not trying to create a 'finished' drawing or composition but were simply concerned to get down all the information you could in the time you had available.

As in the first example, you would probably be able to deduce another artist's intentions by analysing the evidence provided in the studies.

◀ ***Robert Hills, 'Studies of Country Children', c.1815***

It would be useful for you to go to a museum and look at artists' notebooks or sketchbooks to try to deduce their intentions by means of this kind of analysis. You can see how much you might be helped in attempting this by first doing similar work yourself, or conversely, how much your own visual research methods might be improved by an understanding of how other artists have tackled them.

It is worth noting here that all art materials and technical equipment have been created for a particular purpose. You should learn to use specialised materials and equipment in the way that they were intended to be used.

This does not mean that you should not experiment with new ways of using them, but in general it is important to develop a proper respect for materials and equipment. Well organised and maintained working environments are actually very important in developing an efficient professional practice.

Photography

If you study the Impressionists, you will discover that they made use of the new medium of photography to analyse and record the visual appearance of things (the term **visual phenomena** is often used to describe such properties). Since the invention of photography was one of the reasons for the development of the style of painting known as Impressionism, it is appropriate that the camera

▲ P. H. Emerson, 'Setting the bow net', 1886 (photograph)

▶ Thomas F Goodall, 'The bow net', 1886 (oil painting)

became a useful tool to record the kinds of information which they needed for reference. The Impressionists were concerned to record particular effects of light at particular times and were, therefore, involved in making records of their immediate impressions. They often worked in the open air, directly from nature, and the materials they used were also newly developed (oil paints in tubes and stretched canvas on portable frames) enabled them to work 'on location' and to work quickly. But they also recorded outdoor scenes and the effects of light by photographing them.

Photography also began to be used extensively to record people and events which led to a reduction in the use of artists as illustrators and portrait painters.

Contemporary photography has many different and important functions in addition to simply recording things. It can be used in relation to text to illustrate stories or news reports. It can be used to explore situations by taking multiple photographs which produce a visual record of things seen by the photographer over a period of time. These kinds of photography are a form of expression since they tell of things from the point of view of the photographer. It can be an art form in its own right – there is an interesting debate about whether or not photography is actually an art form or mainly a means of recording information and illustrating things. It can tell stories without supporting text, through sequences of images deliberately constructed to create a narrative.

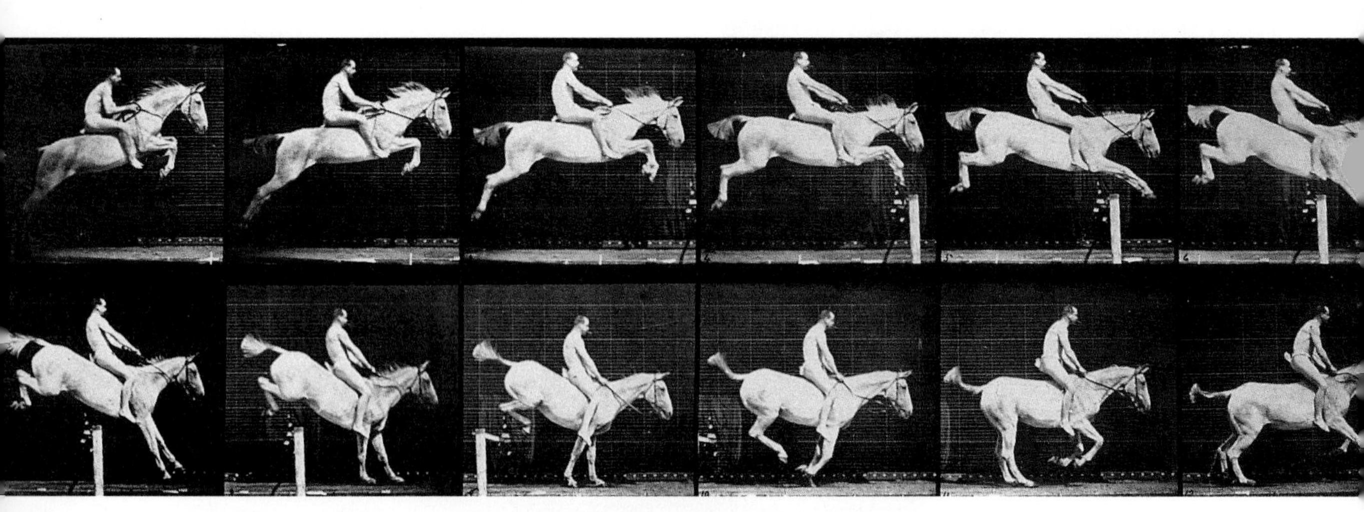

▲ ***Eadweard Muybridge, 'Animal locomotion', 1887.*** **Sequences of still photographs such as these exploring movement by Muybridge were the forerunners of film and animation.**

▲ *Dave Sowerby, 'Shuffle and Skip'*

So, not only can you use photography as a means of recording information as part of visual research, you also have to analyse and interpret photographs in similar ways to those you use in relation to other art objects and images.

A structure for critical appraisal

This brings us to another important aspect of the process of researching art objects. You can see that it is helpful to have some method which helps you to analyse things and extract information. In the examples we've considered you would be identifying the intentions of the artist by making deductions about the choice of techniques and materials used. But there are many other aspects which can be analysed and interpreted to achieve a greater understanding of the purposes of art objects.

A structure for critical appraisal can be a simple list of basic questions. For example, **'What is it?'**, **'How was it made?'**, **'When and where was it made?'**, questions can be a basis for understanding **'Why?'** an art, craft or design object was created. Or, if you know why it was made, perhaps the other questions add to the information you can acquire from simply looking at it.

What is it?

A sensible starting point for critical appraisal of an art, craft or design object is to ask **'What is it?'**. For example, if you are looking at a painting, simply try to **describe** what you see.

There will be the **physical form** of the work, its shape, size, and proportion; what materials have been used (oil paint, water-colour, gouache, acrylic); what it's painted on (paper, canvas, board, wood); and how it is framed or presented.

There will be its **composition,** what formal elements have been used and for what purpose – the 'visual dynamics' of the work.

There will also be the **content**. If it is a narrative painting, its content will be concerned with telling a story of some kind which may involve images of people who can be identified. When you know who is included in the painting you might begin to understand some of the reasons why it was painted. You will probably have to do more research to find out about the story. For example, if it is a narrative painting depicting a myth or a legend you can find references to the traditional story in books such as *Hall's Dictionary of Subjects and Symbols in Art* [1] or *The Oxford Companion to Art* [2]. You need to get used to pursuing the search for further information until you have enough to understand what the content of a work is about.

▲ **Detail, Right-hand panel from the reliquary *'The martyrdom of St Ursula'***

◀ ***Hans Memling, 'The reliquary of St Ursula', 1489***

The reliquary tells the story of the martyrdom of St Ursula. She had been on a pilgrimage to Rome with a group of virgin attendants. When they called at Cologne, the virgins were all killed by the Huns. Ursula was killed by an arrow when she refused to marry the barbarian leader. She was martyred for her religious beliefs.

▲ ***'The Marriage of Rama and Sita', Mithila ceremonial painting.*** **This ceremonial painting from Bihar State in Northern India is totally different in style from the Northern European example, but it also has a narrative content – the great epic of the Ramayana. Only women paint these traditional scenes which are for family ceremonies, such as weddings. The scenes decorate the walls of marriage chambers, the wrapping of gifts and the letters with which unmarried Mithila girls propose marriage to the man of their choice.**

As we said right at the beginning of this book, much of art, craft, and design is concerned with **symbolism**. The content of a work may consist of objects which have symbolic meaning and you must try to understand its symbolism in order to understand what the work is about. Again, you can refer to books such as *Hall's Dictionary of Subjects and Symbols in Art* but there are many other sources which you need to identify.

In the illustration of *The Arnolfini Marriage* by Jan van Eyck, the symbolism is the main point. The painting is of the wedding of Giovanni Arnolfini, an Italian merchant living in Bruges, to Giovanna Cenami, daughter of a Luchese silk merchant. It is much more than a

▲ *Jan van Eyck, 'The Arnolfini Marriage', 1434*

recording of the event. The painting is about the two main virtues of marriage – fertility and fidelity. The green of the bride's robe is a symbol of fidelity and the dog also stands for faithfulness. The single candle in the candelabrum tells us that God is present and the couple have removed their shoes, showing us that this is holy ground. The Latin inscription on the wall above the mirror says that 'Jan van Eyck was here in 1434' and he has painted himself behind the couple in the reflection in the mirror, showing that he is a witness to the wedding.

In abstract work, there may be no content in the sense of subject matter – it may not be about anything other than an arrangement of formal elements to create a new image. On the other hand, colours can be symbolic and you would need to be sure of your ground before deciding that there was indeed no content in a particular work.

Your critical enquiry would then focus on the formal qualities rather than the content.

▲ ***Barbara Hepworth, 'Three Forms', 1935***

◄ Total Design, Signs in Schipol Airport, Amsterdam, 1967

Designers often use symbols to process information. The simplest symbols are those such as direction and identification signs – directional arrows in airports and male and female lavatory signs. Other images are less obvious and attempt to encapsulate or 'symbolise' in a general sense the feelings which arise from a

▲ A modern London Underground poster

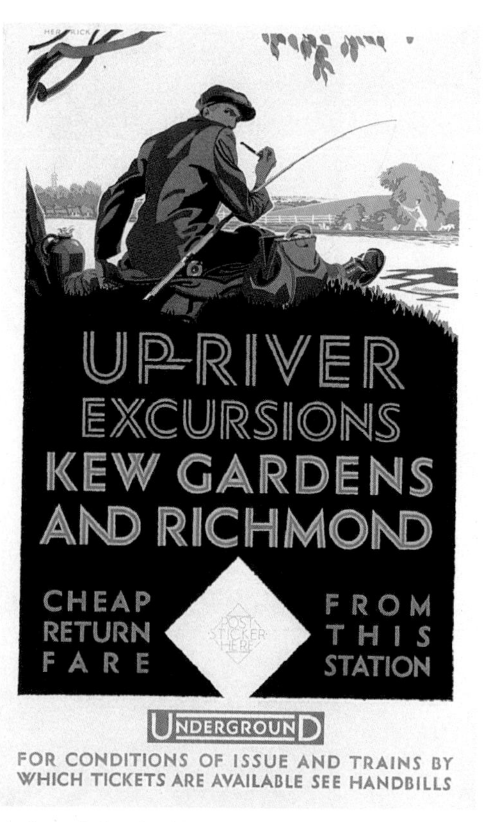

▲ An early London Underground poster

particular place or event. The two London Underground posters show how the designers have attempted to do this. The style is influenced by the period in which they were produced.

Finally, you might ask the question **'What is it about?'**. You will see that, starting from a simple description of the work, you begin to analyse it and deduce its purposes – you begin to understand 'Why' it was made. This will be easier to do in relation to work which has content, but often much more difficult in relation to abstract or 'new' forms of contemporary art, such as installations or conceptual art. In such cases you may have to research other work by the artist or refer to written material which explains the ideas in which the artist is interested; exhibition catalogues can be a useful source of information, for example. Sometimes there will be no satisfactory explanation, you will be left to make up your own mind about the work and its possible purposes. Or the artist may simply have intended you to accept it as it is without analysis – to like or dislike it as an unexplained image – in which case you will be free to express your personal opinion without further research.

▲ ***Calum Colvin, 'Sloth', 1993,* from the series *'The seven deadly sins'***

When you are analysing and describing work other than 'Fine Art' there is usually more precise information available. For example, if you are considering a design solution you may be able to gain access to the original brief and to some record or commentary on the work itself. Similarly, in product design 'What it is' can often be self-evident – a teapot is a teapot – but there will be all kinds of interesting information available about its design, how it was made and for what market.

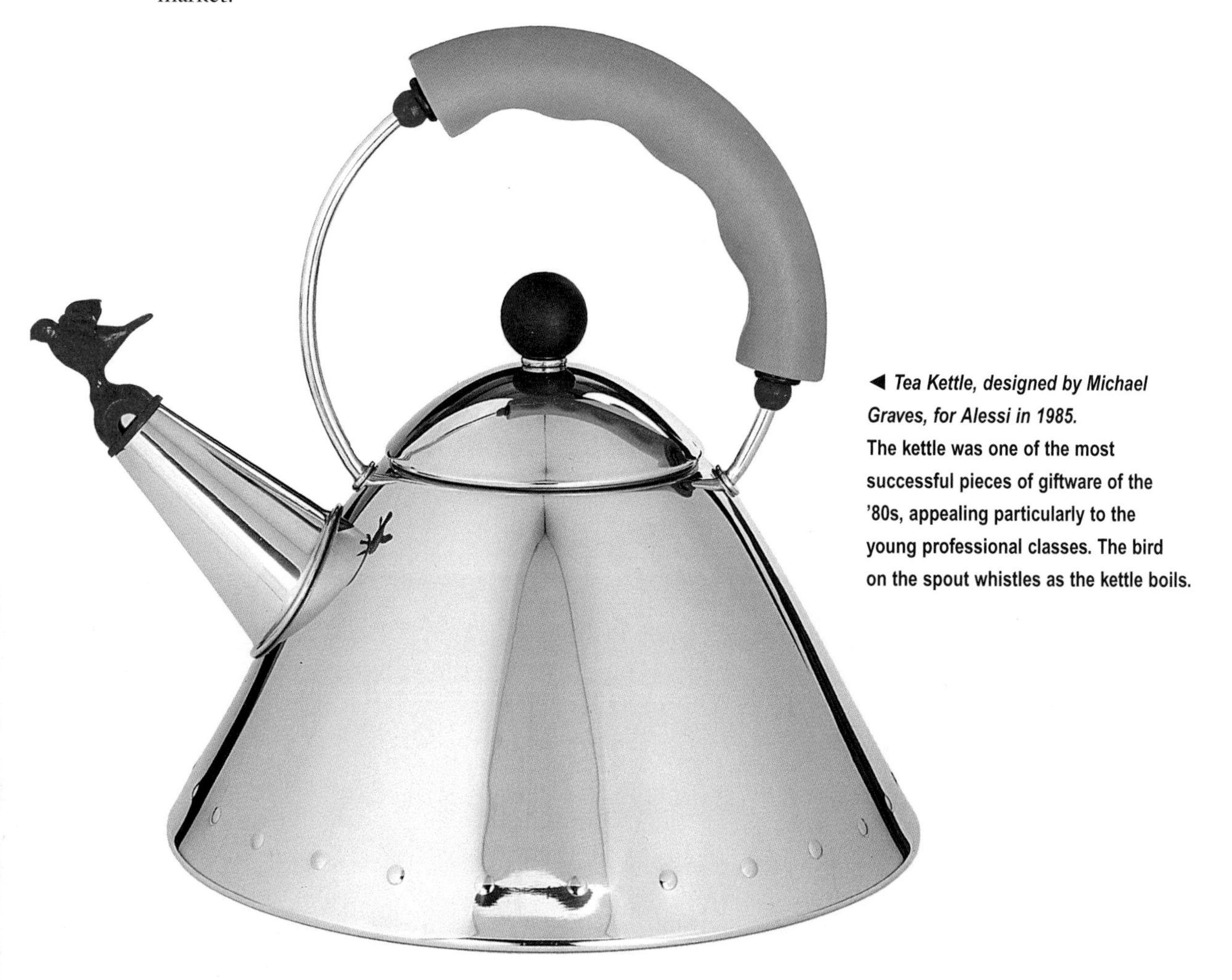

◀ *Tea Kettle, designed by Michael Graves, for Alessi in 1985.*
The kettle was one of the most successful pieces of giftware of the '80s, appealing particularly to the young professional classes. The bird on the spout whistles as the kettle boils.

How was it made?

The second question might be to ask **'How was it made?'** This relates to the use of materials, technology, processes, and techniques. (You will be familiar with these terms from the Unit Specifications).

Analysing the use of materials

The choice of materials is an important consideration and you could begin by thinking about why the artist, craftsperson or designer chose to use particular materials. You have already seen from the earlier examples how the choice of materials relates to what you need to do (water-colours for outdoor work which requires a quick responses for instance). You can often see something of what the artist's intentions were from thinking about the chosen materials. If you think about designing something, you'd probably use materials which were easy and quick to use for sketching out initial ideas – felt-tipped marker pens, colour pens, and crayons perhaps. Then you'd use another range of materials and media for developing your ideas and doing research. Finally, you'd use materials appropriate to the form of the presentation you wish to make to clients. The use of computer-assisted design programmes often shortcuts the need for this range of material and it might not be until the final presentation that the work appears on paper at all. You can begin to see how analysing others' use and choice of materials can be helpful to you in your own work.

▲ **Student's 'roughs' in pencil and crayon for a college information booklet**

Analysing techniques

Analysing **techniques** can be just as helpful. You can often see from a finished work what techniques were used. The most obvious are the marks made by the artist or craftsperson during the making of the work. In painting, the way that oils are applied is usually easy to see, water-colours usually show whether the artist worked quickly or very deliberately, and a sculptor may leave a piece unpolished, showing the marks made by the carving tools. Potters usually leave some evidence of the way that they made the pot. Simple hand-built pots will normally show the results of coiling, throwing, slab-building and so on. Surface textures, deliberately applied, provide clues to how it was done – combing, fettling, burnishing and so on. In textiles, weaving techniques can be fairly easy to identify and so can processes such as tie and dye, batik, and screen-printed surface treatments. Designer's techniques may be less obvious but it is usually easy to recognise when techniques such as air-brush and photo-montage have been used.

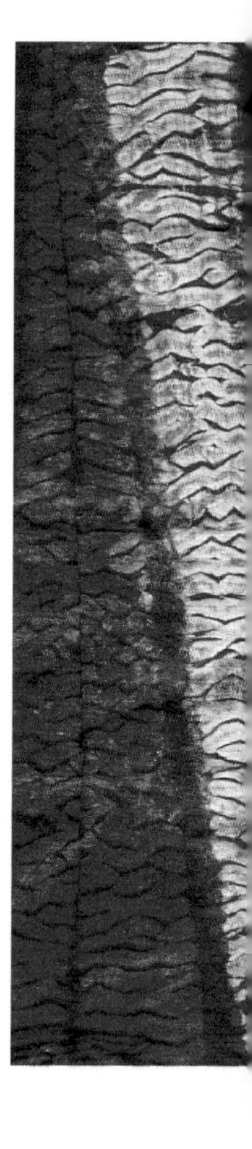

◄ **Oil painting using palette knife technique**

▼ **Detail – direct use of watercolour to create 3D effects**

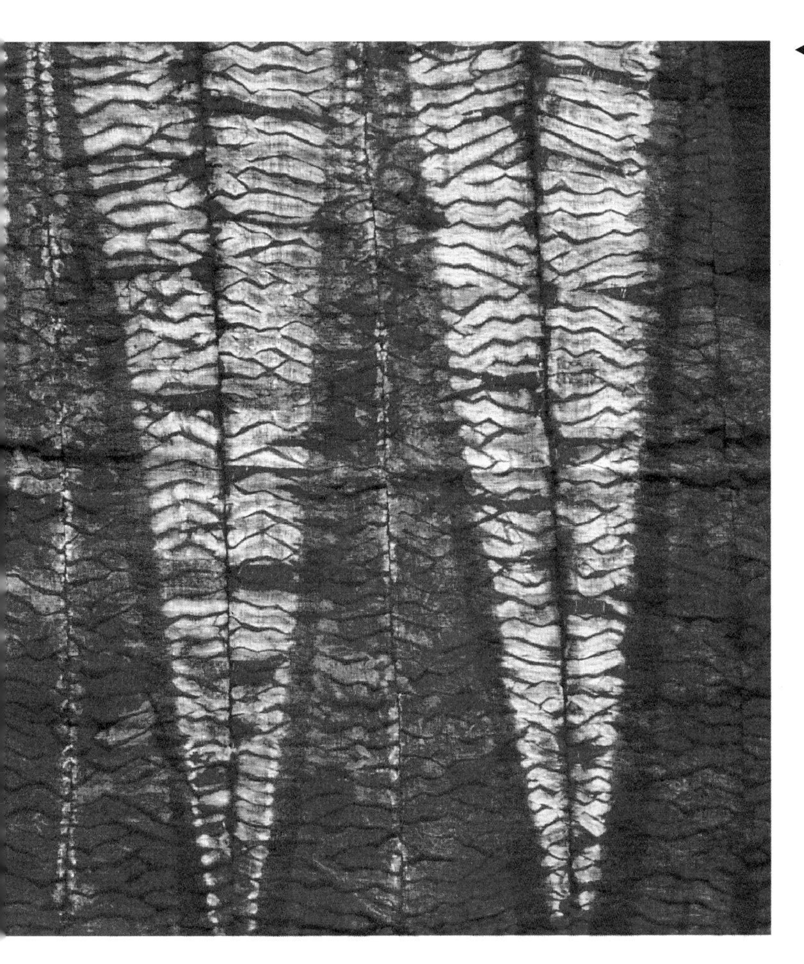

◀ Tie and dye technique to create pattern

▲ Detail – use of watercolour in portraiture

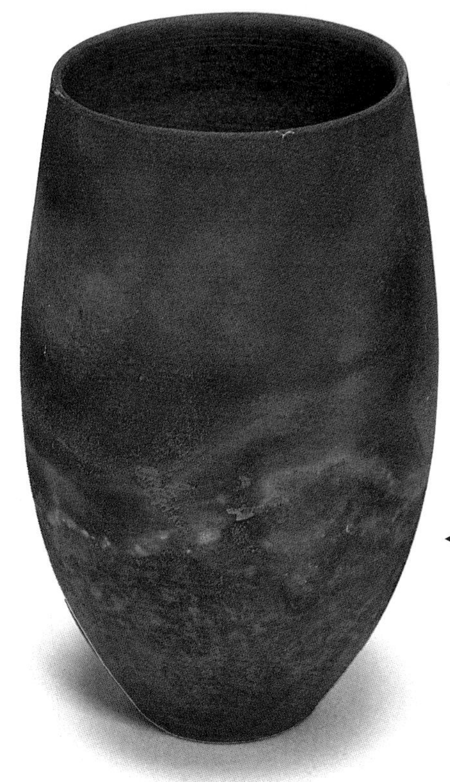

◀ Raku technique to create colour and pattern effect

In printmaking, the three categories of intaglio, relief and screen printing can normally be identified fairly easily but subtle differences between say, drypoint engraving and etching may require you to have a greater knowledge of the techniques involved. An interesting exercise is to collect examples from a range of different printmaking processes and then compare them. For example, etching, drypoint engraving, lithography, wood engraving, wood cuts, lino-cuts, photo-lithography, screenprinting and so on.

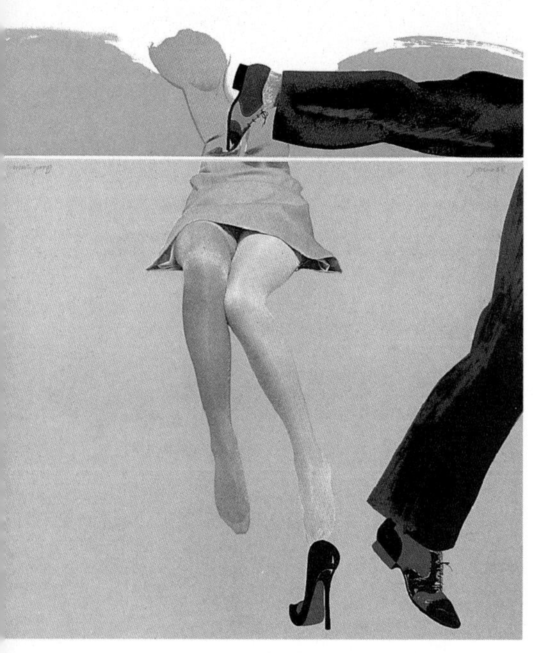

Both of these prints use photography as a means of transferring the image on to the plate

▲ Allen Jones, No. 2 from the series 'Life Class', 1968 (litho and photo-litho)

► Victor Pasmore, 'When the Lute is Broken', 1974 (etching and aquatint)

It will obviously be much easier for you to recognise the use of different techniques if you are familiar with them yourself. If you have no idea how batik works, or how to do tie and dye, you clearly won't understand what the visual evidence means. However, this range of critical study can help you to acquire a broad range of technical competence of your own and it is one of the reasons why the study of other people's work as an integral part of your own creative work is so important.

Analysing technology

Technology and technique are obviously closely related since the use of any technology involves specific techniques. The range of technological equipment available to you will vary, depending on your Centre's resources and it may, therefore, be difficult for you to gain an understanding of some technologies if you have no experience of using them yourself. This means that identifying the uses of technology in others' work will be more difficult than identifying techniques.

However, many creative activities require very little technology and, if you are studying work from an industrially under-developed country, the technology available will often be low-cost and probably unsophisticated. An example might be in ceramics where sophisticated power wheels, pugmills, blungers, turning lathes and so on are used extensively in developed countries but in under-developed areas simple kick wheels may be the only technology available. It would be a mistake, however, to assume that just because the technology was unsophisticated the ceramics ware was 'primitive'. Many cultures produce high-quality, refined work with very limited resources. Sometimes, too much technology can get in

▲ The use of a stick wheel in Indian pottery

◀ The Whychford Pottery, Warwickshire

In these illustrations the process is much the same but the technology available is different. Compare the simple stick wheel in the Indian pottery with a modern electrically-powered wheel.

the way of producing refined products and important basic hand-skills can be lost. In this country, hand-made objects can be of very high-quality and greatly prized. For example, some hand-made furniture is collected as an investment, whereas most furniture manufactured in quantity depreciates in value.

◀ **Traditional cloth weaving, Sylhet, Bangladesh. Compare hand-weaving on simple looms, such as the one illustrated, with examples of modern computer-controlled weaving technology.**

A very important, fundamental question for you to consider is whether the perceived value of hand-made objects compared to mass-produced items is justified. Why can't a mass-produced object be of similar quality to one which is hand-made? This is part of an interesting and important debate about the value of the crafts in a modern technological society. What place do they have? Are they just quaint hangovers from the past or do they contribute to innovation and the development of new products in the manufacturing industries? What influence does a craftsperson who makes high-quality furniture have on developments or innovation in the furniture industry? What is the relationship between the glass industry and craftspeople who work in glass? – and so on.

The debate can be widened to include a broad consideration of the relationship between design and manufacture. How important are designers to a manufacturing industry? What contribution do they make? Are they sufficiently regarded by manufacturers?

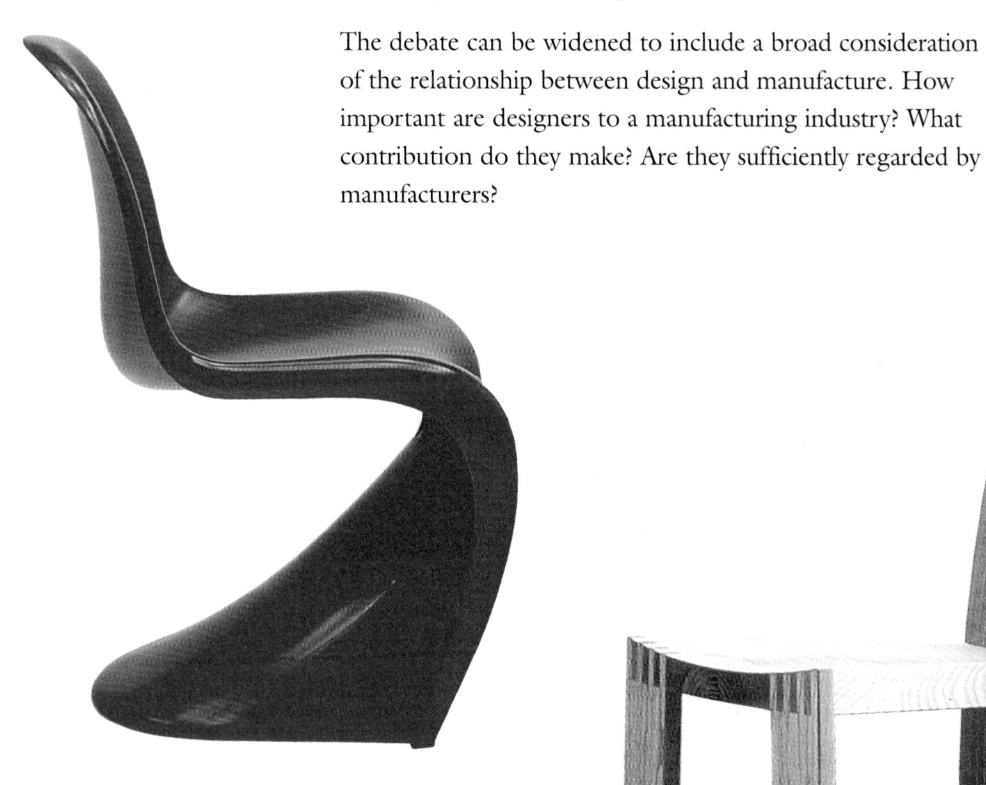

▲ ***Plastic stacking chair, 1960***

► ***Split Plank Back Chair, Pearl Dot Workshops***

Think of the different purposes these two chairs were made to serve. One is a one-off hand made piece, the other is designed for mass production.

These are very broad issues, but they do focus on technology. Technological change, since the beginning of the Industrial Revolution, has been dramatic and it is interesting to speculate about whether the concentration on technological development has resulted in poorer quality products. If there was a time when this was true,

has the current insistence upon quality control re-established a proper balance between the means of manufacture and the product? What is it that establishes the quality of a product – its function, its form, the means of manufacture, the attitudes and tastes of the makers, or all of these?

Would there be any point in making a lemon squeezer by hand? In the example of Starck's design for a lemon squeezer, what was he trying to achieve? A lemon squeezer is a lemon squeezer – did it need re-designing?

◀ ***Phillipe Starck, design for a lemon squeezer, 1990***

Analysing processes

Again these relate closely to techniques and technologies, but they are different in the sense that they can be methods of working which do not involve technology. We talk about 'the creative process' as if there were only one, but the term is meant to include all aspects of the making of things from the first glimmer of an idea to the finished product. Within this broad category there are more specific ones which are referred to in the Unit Specifications. For example, 'the making process' refers to the means of manufacture, and 'the design process' refers to the different ways in which an idea can be developed without necessarily making anything. Lower down the scale there are even more specific processes – the dyeing process in textiles, the firing process in ceramics, the welding process in metalwork and so on.

It may help you to think of a structure – a hierarchy of processes:

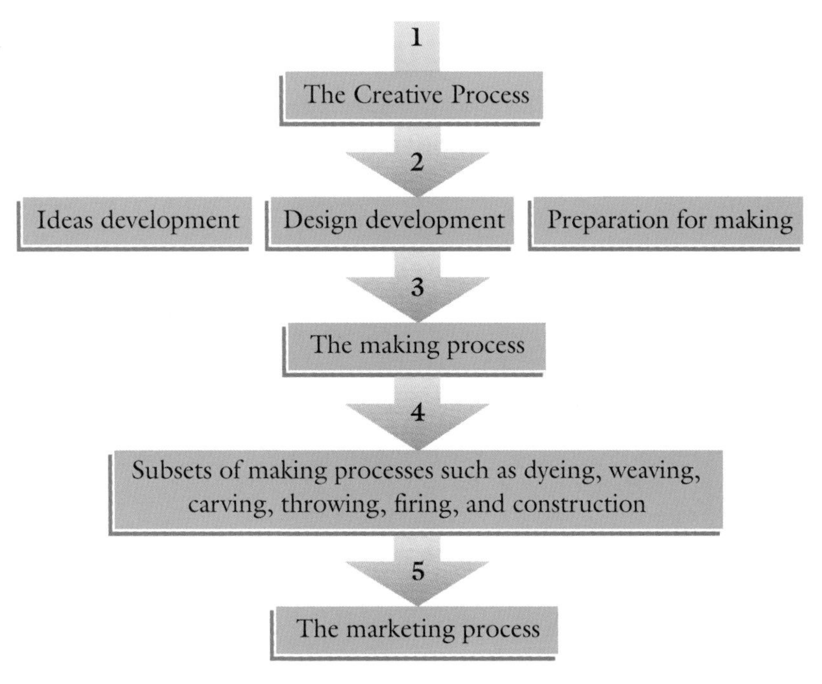

You can see from the diagram how it works and you might find this a useful concept to bear in mind when you are considering others' work. You could use it as a structure for analysing the making of an object for instance.

You could start by identifying the lower categories in the making process and work your way up the scale until you'd achieved a reasonable understanding of the whole creative process.

For example, you are looking at a chair with turned legs and curved back. You could start by thinking about the turning process, how each piece was made. Then you could look at the shaping or forming process – how the back rails and seat were made. Next you would consider the construction process – how the pieces were joined. Finally you could think about how the maker developed this particular model and for what market – the design and marketing processes. You would then have a good idea of the whole process of manufacture.

Historical and contemporary contexts

When was it made?

The third question **'When was it made?'** introduces the concept of historical and contemporary contexts. As we have said, all art, craft, and design, exists in some context or other, and the context influences both form and function – how it looks and what it's for. For example, *The Arnolfini Marriage* illustrated on page 152 is something which we would associate with the fifteenth century in Northern Europe, perhaps more specifically with the Netherlands and even more specifically with the kind of work done in Bruges at the time. But what is it about the work which produces characteristics which enable us to identify its location so precisely and what influences are responsible?

You know how to analyse an art object in terms of its form, its function and how it was made. Part of the answer to the question lies in these aspects – what it is, its style, what it was made from and how it was made. All of these things are influenced by the circumstances in which it was produced. For example, something made in the context of an industrialised society would probably have involved the use of technology, whilst a similar object made in an under-developed country would probably have been made by hand. These characteristics are about 'How it was made' but there are other, more important, influences which determine form and function.

For example, in societies where there is a strong narrative tradition, many objects would be likely to include story-telling as part of their decoration. Greek pottery was often decorated with stories of the gods, of popular myths, and with records of ceremonies and events.

► ***Heracles breaking off one of the antlers of the Kerynesian deer, Athens, c.540 BC***

◀ ***Guests arriving for the Wedding of Peleus and Thetis, Greek Pot, 570BC***

The Arpillera from Peru (below) is an appliqué wall-hanging made by a group of women who use this means to tell the story of their working life. They are depicted picking prickly pears and using cochineal insects for dyeing. You can tell from the content that it was made in the context of a rural economy in which much of the tedious labour was done by women. The women weren't trained artists, they were workers who had been encouraged to use this means to tell of their own experiences. Further research would reveal more of the prevailing social conditions and you could find other examples from the same area which would tell you more about traditional narrative styles of image-making.

▶ **An Arpillera from Peru (appliqué)**

Contemporary contexts are considered in the next section on professional practice, but you should try to develop some understanding of the relationship between a contemporary object and the history which lies behind it. Most things are not completely new, they are re-designed and made to suit changing circumstances and to take advantage of developments in the use of materials and technology.

In this century, the emphasis in fine art has been on challenging established ideas and values. Also, the quest for originality sometimes produces art, craft, and design which can be very difficult for you to accept as such. However, the vast majority of contemporary artists are expressing very seriously-held views on contemporary society, their own feelings about things and speculations about the future. You can't expect to have the reasons why they make their art explained to you in detail. If art could be expressed in words there would be no need for visual images at all. You, therefore, need to see as much contemporary work as possible. You need to visit exhibitions, read the catalogues and try to understand what the artist is trying to do or say.

Cultural contexts and cultural relativity

This introduces the fourth question **'Where was it made?'** The place, or circumstances, in which an object is made can have an effect on the way it looks and how it is made. For example, the way buildings are designed depends on the materials which are available. Timber framed houses were built largely because of the relative scarcity of alternatives such as brick and stone. In places like the Yorkshire Dales and the Cotswolds, stone was the most readily accessible building material and in the Midlands and the London Basin, there was plenty of clay from which to make bricks. If you know something about geology you can also tell from the composition of stone (and even brick) where it comes from. The Potteries became the centre for large-scale ceramics manufacture because of the availability of the right kind of clay and the means of processing it, such as facilities for firing. The area south west of the Potteries around Ironbridge in Shropshire was the birthplace of the Industrial Revolution. Iron was first smelted in quantity in this area, since there were materials such as iron ore, coal and limestone, and there was a river suitable for transportation of raw materials and products. Names like Ironbridge, related to the famous cast-iron bridge built by Abraham Darby, and Coalport, resonant of china pottery, provide clues to the nature of manufacturing industry along the banks of the Severn.

People's beliefs or values affect objects they make. Some decorative styles or uses of visual language have different meaning in different cultures. The dragon symbolised good in Chinese culture whereas the dragon in early Christian times symbolised evil. As illustrated in the Introduction, the myth of St George and the Dragon in Western culture symbolises the triumph of good over evil, of Christianity over Paganism.

Dragon Robe with Twelve Imperial Symbols, Chinese nineteenth century

It is important for you to recognise that beliefs, values, traditions, and conventions vary between cultures. Remember that Britain has never had a single common culture – it has always been a rich mixture of regional, racial and class differences. Living as we do in a multi-cultural society, we are surrounded by images which illustrate cultural relativity. Something which has significance in one culture may have no meaning at all in another. The Mosque is particularly significant to the Muslim community but may have little meaning for Christians. If you have little knowledge of the history of Christianity or of the Bible, you will have difficulty in understanding the content of most Western European medieval imagery. You will also need some understanding of Greek and Roman civilisations in order to understand the Renaissance.

The point is that you have to learn something about a particular culture before you can properly appreciate its art forms; and you also need to have some general historical knowledge in order to place the history of art, craft, and design into appropriate contexts.

In a more general sense, an understanding and respect for other people's cultures is very important in terms of racial harmony. It is arrogant and erroneous to think that only Western cultures are capable of producing highly sophisticated objects of quality, or that the working classes are incapable of appreciating and creating 'high art'.

ELEMENT 3.2

INVESTIGATE PROFESSIONAL PRACTICE

Performance criteria

A student must:

1. *identify and give examples of* ***clients*** *of artists, craftspeople, and designers*
2. *identify and give examples of* ***responsibilities*** *of art, craft, and design professionals*
3. *describe* ***business functions*** *carried out in art, craft, and design*
4. *describe how areas of* ***legislation*** *affect artists, craftspeople, and designers*
5. *explore and identify potential* ***progression routes****.*

Range

Clients: audience, end-user, individuals, groups

Responsibilities: ethical, business, own, to others

Business functions: planning, production, research and development, selling, teamwork practice

Legislation: environmental, health and safety, consumer protection, copyright

Progression routes: opportunities for study, opportunities for training, opportunities for employment, art, crafts, design.

Evidence indicators

Two case studies drawn from research into art, craft, and design professional practice. The case studies should be based on:

- one example of commercial practice
- one example of a public service or voluntary business

The case studies should include details of clients, responsibilities, legislation and business functions. If the two case studies do not cover all the requirements of the range, supplementary evidence in the form of notes may need to be provided.

A file containing information on opportunities for study, training, and employment in art, craft, and design.

Professional Practice

Element 3.2 requires you to investigate professional practice. Again this can be a tall order – you can imagine how professional practitioners might react if they were bombarded with requests for interviews and visits from all the students doing Art and Design GNVQ! However, there are less obtrusive ways of getting some insight into how art, craft, and design businesses work.

Magazines and periodicals

There are periodicals which cater for professional groups and these are likely to be available in your library or in the Art and Design department. Magazines, such as *Crafts*, *Design*, and *Art Review* are monthly publications which contain up-to-date information on current events, exhibitions, and examples of professional craftspeople and designers at work. You can gain a lot of information by making sure that you refer to them on a regular basis. One of your responsibilities in planning your own working schedule should be to note which published materials you need to see each month and when they become available.

Exhibitions

There are, of course, many exhibitions of contemporary work, particularly in art and craft, and you can often meet the artists or craftspeople at an exhibition, especially the smaller local ones. Again, your planning should include details of which exhibitions are on and when you can visit them. One of your tasks might be to make a list of the sources of information about exhibitions and other events. It is very difficult for your teachers to organise a lot of visits and their planning may only involve a few trips to exhibitions each year. This is not really enough for you to gain a reasonable level of understanding of what's going on in the art, craft, and design world, so you should make additional visits yourself.

Retail outlets

Another source of information about professional practice is the small art or craft shop and shows at which practitioners sell their work. There are many small retail outlets which will bring you into direct contact with makers. In some parts of the country, there are organised groups or societies, which regularly promote the work of their members. For example, the Devon Guild of Craftsmen has a centre at Bovey Tracey which holds regular exhibitions and also sells work. These organisations will have lists of members and it is often possible to visit their studios and workshops since they also sell work there. Such organisations exist in all parts of the country and you can go to your local library for details.

Freelance designers

Designers are perhaps more difficult to contact. They usually work in private premises and are involved in providing a service to clients rather than making things to sell. The retail outlet is therefore not a point of contact. However, there are many designers working wherever there is a need for their services and they can be contacted if you are sensitive to their particular circumstances. These are freelance designers – they work for themselves.

Employed designers

Designers who work for other people, or as part of a practice, are not free to do what they want. They are constrained by the kind of business they work in or the contracts to which a partnership is committed. Most large manufacturing industries will employ specialist designers who work only on the firm's products. For example, as a product designer working for a firm of sanitary ware manufacturers, you might only be engaged in designing lavatories, baths, and wash basins.

When you consider the range of work and responsibilities of professional practitioners you need to bear this in mind, since what they are responsible for will vary according to whether they are self-employed or employed by someone else.

Jill Howarth

Owner of the SILK TOP HAT GALLERY, Ludlow

I was always interested in art. My mother painted, my father painted, my brother's a sculptor, so we've got the art background without a doubt.

I don't think I set out with the firm intention of running a gallery. I didn't do A Level Art at school. I went to Sussex University to do French. After two terms one had the option of changing and I decided to change to English. There was a queue for English but Art History was a new subject and there wasn't a queue for that so that's what I did. So I came out of Sussex with a degree in Art History and thought what will I do with this? I decided the kind of environment I wanted to work in was in an art college so I applied for a few jobs which fortunately I didn't get so thought what else can I do – librarianship – Wolverhampton Faculty of Art and Design offered me a job and I worked there for nine months or so.

I then did a one year post-graduate course in librarianship at University College, London. And having done that, I was told about somebody who was looking for someone to run St Mary's, Lambeth as an arts resource centre. This never happened but it led to a job running the Institute of Contemporary Prints which became the basis of the Tate Gallery's Print Collection. I was there, at the Tate, for about five years but during all that time wanted to move back to the country and eventually ended up here. I didn't plan a career route for opening a gallery.

I was also deeply influenced by Pauline Norton who had a gallery when I was at school in Bridgnorth. She exhibited contemporary artists who I got to know and meet occasionally. Without that it would never have occurred to me as a job somebody could do because in the rest of my career I didn't come across a provincial, commercial gallery. I think it's quite relevant that you tend to be influenced about what can be done by what's being done around you.

I started by renting a room in Dinham House (then a local arts/crafts centre). I manned it myself but selling paintings from one room doesn't make money so to support it I went out and got a job for a couple of days a week. In the room next to me was a man selling hand made furniture. You tend to chat to the person in the next room and we discovered that if I took one of his very nice chairs and put it in a corner surrounded by my paintings it would get attention from customers and when I took some of my paintings and put them on a wall by his table the same would happen. Basically we swopped stock between the two rooms but kept our separate identity.

After a year the property in Quality Square, for rent and renovated, came on the market and we took on the rental of it between the two of us. I remember looking up at the three floors and thinking how on earth are we going to fill it! However, after five years there was no room to move and the furniture maker moved out to another property at the same time as this building came up for sale and I bought it. This meant the outgoings quadrupled overnight. It was a scary time. But in retrospect paying a mortgage rather than rent has made the whole enterprise much more viable. A shop sort of grew to fill the ground floor and it now has a stock of cards, art materials and gifts.

The one thing I've never had is a shortage of artists. There are a lot of artists – very good ones in my opinion – in the area. Perhaps my opening of the gallery coincided with the time when a lot of artists became somewhat disillusioned with the London/city scene and moved out to a more rural background. I'd already picked up on people who were at Dinham House and there was also a very good little booklet that West Midlands Arts did of artists and craftspeople in the area and I picked out the names from that of artists and some of them named other artists and so it went on.

One of my reasons for opening an art gallery was to exhibit my family's work but also I wanted to support the work of other contemporary artists. I started off with 2 dimensional work – paintings, drawings and original prints – which is bound to be my hobby horse because of my background at the Tate. The works of art that I have are ones that I think fit into a domestic setting. I display them in room-sized rooms. I'm not interested in 'museum' art. I do display large paintings but they are large things that would go into a house. It's only in the last three or four years that I've acquired two display cabinets where I can display craft work better than I could.

If you were to ask me what sort of work do I look for I'd find it very difficult to say. I just react to work that I like. I think aesthetic judgements aren't that easy to make. I have now added a restriction to the work of the artists I exhibit which is not only must I like the work but I must like the artist as well. I find it far too difficult to deal with the ones I don't like. If I have faith in an artist's work I like to stick with them. One artist I can think of came here years ago; he looked round the gallery and then he wrote and said he was interested in the gallery showing his work. He wrote the letter, he made the appointment, he brought the work – and I exhibited his work. I've stuck with him over the years. He's gone through all sorts of different phases. We've had wildly successful exhibitions and total flops but I like him and I like his work and I'll stick with him. If I just exhibited the work that I knew would sell I'd

cont ☛

find the whole undertaking boring. I would love to have control of an artist's annual production, however, I accept that I wouldn't be able to sell enough for them to make an annual income; most of them have to have a supplementary income through teaching or other part-time work. I couldn't possibly compete with a West End gallery.

Pricing work is problematic wherever you are. In my case I say to the artist 'what do you want this to go for?'. My commission is a third of the selling price which is fairly standard. I prefer that artists think in terms of selling price rather than their price so I stress to them that they get two thirds of the selling price. If I think the work is too highly priced or underpriced I tell them. Amongst the artists I exhibit I go from one extreme to the other – from those just starting out to artists who are established and have a contact with a West End gallery. I don't work as the artist's agent going forth and spreading their work about the world but I do consider myself as their agent in so far as it's my job to promote and sell their work to the best of my ability.

I only learnt to drive five years ago so I didn't get into the habit of travelling much. Mostly artists come to me. If I was giving advice to someone opening a gallery I'd advise them to go out and meet artists more than I do. I'd advise them to go to Degree Shows to catch artists just starting out. And to start out with a lot of money! I'd love to be able to say to artists whose work I like I'll buy that from you unframed and sell it framed. But, I still don't have the money to be able to do that. I still take everything on sale and return.

My core customers have been established over the past thirteen years. I think I've worked really hard at establishing that core. Rather than just saying 'thank you very much for your cheque, here's your painting, goodbye' I take their name and address; I established a Friends of the Gallery and I now have about a hundred and fifty people. I produce three Newsletters a year which gives all the background of the artists, what's coming off in the next few months, and gives a 10% discount on gallery purchases and artists' materials in the shop. I have a mailing list where I put down names of people who specify an interest in a particular artist so next time that artist is on show those people will be invited. It's a lot of labour.

There's also the day-to-day running of the gallery. Each work that comes into the gallery is entered on a stock receipt pad which is filled in with the price, title, medium, artist, date, etc. There's a typed catalogue list for the work in exhibition which has to be duplicated and put out to customers. If I have a Private View, there's a whole series of other things to do – the invitations, the drinks, refreshments, the clearing up. I write the Newsletters - the last one was ten pages of A4 with a calendar of events on the back. I generate vast quantities of paper!

I spend five days a week in the gallery. I very rarely have holidays; in recent years I've had one holiday that lasted more than a week. I often work here on Sunday mornings as well as staying late in the evenings. If I was looking for a business to invest in I wouldn't invest in me! But I have supported myself – albeit just adequately – and that's fine with me. It wouldn't suit most people. If you want to go for the lifestyle that goes for the microwave, the colour TV, the video, foreign holidays, then my way of life wouldn't suit you because I don't have any of those things. I don't miss them; I don't want them and they don't come with the package.

But the job satisfaction is total. I love it. There are good bits, bad bits, scary bits – and I love it all. ¶

Employment in Art, Craft, and Design

What do Artists Do?

You may find it useful, at this stage, to think about some of the ways in which artists, craftspeople, and designers make their living. Perhaps you have only a vague idea of what they actually do? You may have a notion that 'artists' are rather eccentric people who live exotic lives and behave differently from ordinary people. Of course some are, but most artists live normal lives and do a day's 'work' just as they would if they had a 'normal' job. They have to be disciplined and to organise their time so that they are productive – they can't make a living just sitting around waiting for inspiration.

Artists, unlike designers and craftspeople, normally make things which are not meant to be 'used' in the functional sense. Their work can be very personal, about the artist's feelings and views; or they can be for other people's needs, for example a commissioned painting or a portrait. Artists usually have only themselves to rely upon for generating ideas and deciding what kind of work to do.

The range of 'media' which an artist can use is very wide, from paint and pencils to objects which are assembled to create an installation, and some even use themselves as part of 'performance' art.

Most artists actually work for a particular purpose. They might have an agent who expects them to create sufficient new work to stage regular exhibitions through which they sell their work. Since artists are usually known for the kind of works they produce, they experience some constraints if they wish to change their style. If you have ever been to a Private View of an exhibition you might get the impression that it is just an excuse for a party, but there is a very serious intention which is to attract as many people as possible who might buy the work and to create a contact list.

▲ **A group of students at a Private View at the Serpentine Gallery, London**

The exhibition is the artist's market place and they have to provide for that market just as much as if they had set up a fruit and vegetable stall in the local market. You may have the impression that the 'art market' is a place where prices are astronomical and you have to be a millionaire to shop there, but in reality most artists sell their work for quite modest prices. There are hundreds of small galleries which sell artists' work for sums as low as £100 – £200, depending upon what the work is and how successful the artist is. For example, if an artist is a printmaker, the work is usually produced in limited editions. This means that there is a specific number of prints made from the original and then the printing plate is destroyed.

◀ ***Eileen Hogan, 'Man in a hat', 1980, limited edition of 70***

The prints are signed by the artist individually, and if you buy one you may find that it increases in value because only a limited number were produced and the artist is becoming more popular. So the value of a work of art depends on many different factors including scarcity, the type of work it is, and how popular or famous the artist becomes. Most prints are quite cheap compared to paintings or sculptures, which are normally one-offs although some sculptures can be cast from an original and also sold as limited editions.

The majority of artists probably work to commissions. That means that they are asked to paint or model something for a client, just like an architect designing a house for someone. The most common example is portrait painting and modelling and many artists make a good living from it. In this case, artists have to become 'established' and to use the same methods for publicising their work as any other person who makes things to sell. The market has to be researched – the artists have to find out the kinds of work which might be attractive to buyers, how to publicise their product, maintain contact lists, exhibit work in order to show others how good they are and so on.

There has been an increase in recent years of artists working in and for the community. They organise art-making activities and you may well have seen a mural done by such an artist. Sometimes they become artists-in-residence where they are paid to spend some time producing work in everyday situations. You might have been in contact with an artist-in-residence at your school or college. There are also special projects such as those where artists come together to create a sculpture trail or create an 'environment' for the public.

Some artists also simply use the landscape as a means of producing art. For example, Richard Long's work often consists of pieces of natural material found in the landscape, re-arranged to make an art form.

◀ ***Richard Long, 'A line in Ireland', 1974***

In all of these situations artists have to be business-like and organise themselves to be as efficient as possible. In reality, artists do many kinds of work which their skills equip them for and the distinctions between artists, designers, and craftspeople are rather artificial. Designers paint pictures and illustrate books and artists design things. Craftspeople are often artists and designers as well, since their work involves designing, making and decorating an object. So it is important to recognise that although you will choose an area of specialisation you are also likely to be able to do many other kinds of artistic work.

The skills and knowledge you acquire are transferable.

As an artist you should be able to:

- initiate a range of work relating to different purposes – e.g. for personal reasons, for someone else, or for an identified 'market'
- develop your work in your own way to create a distinctive personal style
- develop and maintain practical skills, keeping up to date with new technologies
- modify your work as it progresses, responding as much to intuition and feeling as to intellectual concerns in order to create new forms of expression
- evaluate and be critical of the results of your work for future reference and development
- prepare work for public exposure – exhibitions, presentations or showing to clients
- maintain a list of contacts through which you can promote and sell your work
- be efficient in administering your business – keeping records, accounts and setting up an office system, for example

– Artist

I'd known from a very early age that I wanted to pursue art as a career – from the age of ten or twelve. It was a burning ambition, no matter what, that was what I wanted to do. I know when I went to art college for an interview they scoffed at it – having that kind of feeling towards it – but I did. I never wavered.

I went to school in Sussex and had quite an academic background in the sciences – I took A level biology, chemistry – and art – for which I was constantly the butt of jokes in the chemistry department! The academic side was good on paper but after that it didn't really mean a lot to me. After school I did a two year Foundation Course at Worthing – a two year Foundation because I didn't really know what areas of art I wanted to pursue – I was very vague – 'I love art but I don't really know, on a practical level, what to do with it'. So a two year Foundation seemed sensible. I had much longer to try out all the different areas – theatre, photography, graphics – it was so wide. It was wonderful. I had the time of my life trying everything and having the time to try everything.

After a year and a half on Foundation I still couldn't make up my mind. I was very drawn to theatre and fashion and fine art – I'm very much a maker. Then a lecturer in textiles from Goldsmiths' College visited and everything just seemed to click

cont ☛

– that was what I wanted to do: it combined the fine art with the practical making aspect. I applied to Goldsmiths' for a textiles degree and got in. It was like winning the pools! The course was very much textiles as fine art rather than commercial textiles – there's a great deal of difference. A commercial textiles course is very much geared to people wanting to go into the industry. They work with fabric manufacturers and on printing designs and the actual making of the fabrics. Whereas in fine art textiles there's so much freedom. It's not assumed that you're going to make fabric into clothing – or that you're even going to make fabric. You're working with ideas. We had to learn to knit, to weave, very basic embroidery, and printing, but beyond that we could apply them however we wished. It was very much a development of our own creativity and self-expression.

So three years later I had a degree and was terribly confused not knowing what to do. We had had very little business advice or preparation for what it would be like outside. I had the degree but no business skills – nothing about how to approach bookkeeping or galleries or anything like that, which are really important. The college advised me to do an MA but I'd had enough of student poverty. So, I moved down to Brighton and worked in a polytechnic library to pay off my debts. The job was so full and demanding I didn't have time to do my own work. I really wanted to be doing my own work but had such a huge overdraft I had to rid myself of that before I could think of leaving full time work and becoming self-employed.

Then I was offered the chance of exhibiting with some quite well-known painters – The Brotherhood of Ruralists – I share quite a lot of their ideals. It was a huge ego boost to have my work shown with painters - acknowledging it as fine art. I didn't have enough work so to get things ready I left the job and leapt into the void. It was very frightening. I moved back with Mum and spent four or five months producing five pieces of work. It was very difficult. Would it be good enough? What sort of reaction would I get? How much was I going to charge? I can laugh at it now but they put two of my works in at £50 each – and they both sold. I was shocked. It seemed incredibly excessive. I didn't make a profit out of that exhibition but it gave me the self-confidence to carry on. It was a beginning.

After that I applied for the Enterprise Allowance. It was a weekly amount you could use towards your business. I had to do a two week business course. It was helpful but wasn't really geared to the art world. The grant lasted for about six months. On top of that I applied to The Prince's Youth Business Trust for a materials grant of £1000. I got that too and that was a great help. I bought a very expensive sewing machine. I had to have a detailed business plan, show my work, go for a couple of interviews, do some market research, and approach my bank. I took some of my work to the bank and the manager went into the bank and asked two or three people if they would buy my work – and they said 'yes'. Myself and my mother went round two or three galleries – that was a gentler way of doing it – and I discussed with the owners if they thought my work was commercially attractive – even if they wanted to show the work – and I had a good response.

I took my work to Convent Garden, to Telford, and to various craft fairs. I also took it to the Ideal Home Exhibition which was quite an eye opener. For the first two days I didn't sell anything – as the hours went by the depression set in. Luckily I had two very good days as well but the first two days were awful knowing I'd spent so much time and money to be there and not selling anything.

There was also a range of local events that provided enough work to keep me going and also had the effect of getting my name known which is very important as I'm not very good at selling myself and it's just so important to get the work out there to as many people as possible – even if they don't buy – just to get the work seen. I managed to get my work into an embroidery magazine and then I started to approach the local galleries and, on the whole, they were keen to exhibit me. I had one or two rejections and that's very hard to deal with because you want everyone to like your work. But, not everyone will and it's important not to be disheartened. Actually I ended up letting my mother take my work – the coward's way out – so thank you, Mum. And the work really took off about a year and a half ago. I've built up a firm foundation of about half a dozen galleries and from there I've generated more work through commissions.

My work is very much about my joy and love of the countryside and my very deep feelings towards that. It hadn't really developed into anything beyond that to start with – just the landscape – and that's what I worked with throughout my degree and into the first year of self-employment. As I've grown and developed and matured other more important things have developed. I think the very deep feelings towards Nature were already verging on the spiritual – it was more than just going for a walk in a pretty wood – it was something very fundamental. Over the past two or three years I've become very interested in a lot of spiritual teaching, particularly those of Native Americans and I'm also finding out a lot about Buddhist teaching. They have meant a lot to my life as well. My work is very much an expression of where I am in my life and the work is just a natural expression – it's wanting to share what I experience. Art is communication. It's sharing the joy of life, the joy of being, the wonderful things that are around us. So many times in our daily lives we walk past things and just give them a cursory glance – we don't let them touch us – so that's what I'm trying to do. It's something that's very difficult to verbalise – that's why I use images.

My approach to the work hasn't changed a great deal. The technique has improved. I still embroider on my machine. I don't have the time to hand embroider. I wouldn't be able to charge for the amount of time I'd spend on that. It's very intense – many, many stitches, colours built up in layers. It's worked on a basic calico background with cottons and rayon thread with beading and mirrors and tassels and what have you.

I have to do quite a few commissions – and maybe not all of them to my taste. They're instantly recognisable as my work but they're not necessarily what I'd choose to do. But, I have to earn my living and they're my bread and butter. I can't expect to have the freedom to produce the work that I want to produce all the time. I try to bring a bit of humour into it. It's nice to be light about one's work from time to time and not be too intense and precious. People enjoy the work and maybe that's the bottom line. Beyond that I have something I want to communicate but I can't do that all the time. It wouldn't be commercially viable.

I'm still learning – even now – and very much learning by my mistakes. You glean things from other people and other people's experience. There's a whole gamut of things I still need to learn. ¶

What do Designers Do?

A designer's job usually involves creating new products or improving existing ones. Sometimes the work will include an involvement in the whole process of design and production, from the initial ideas through production to the point at which the objects are promoted and sold. There is an enormous range of different kinds of work undertaken by designers. The largest occupation is in graphic design which encompasses all aspects of the organisation and presentation of image and text, mainly in two-dimensions. Product designers work specifically within their chosen manufacturing range which might be as wide as from designing cars to toothbrushes. The textiles, fashion, ceramics, and furniture industries all have specialist designers for their products and there is a large group of designers who work on the design and layout of interiors of buildings.

One of the biggest areas of employment for designers is the media. If you think about the range of possible design work involved in the communications industry you will realise how diverse this field can be. Graphic design work on paper to create an image or to organise text is still common, but most designers now work on computers and, increasingly, use multi-media. This can involve them in manipulating video images, still photographs, drawn images, sound and text in one product. As an increasing amount of information is transmitted in visual form, through sign-systems for example, the greater is the need for good graphic design in presenting and processing the information. There is also an increasing need for design education so that the general public are able to 'read' visual information.

Because of the nature of their work – designing, or re-designing things for other people to use – designers (like architects) have to have a sense of values which is much wider than a concern for their products. They have to be aware of environmental factors, ethical and moral concerns, and of public opinion. Designing something which creates adverse public reaction can be counter-productive. They have to develop a sense of responsibility to the society which they serve.

As a designer you should be able to:

- talk to clients and respond to their needs

- analyse the problem you have been set and plan ways in which you might go about resolving it

- research the field to discover any existing products which you need to know about and make early decisions about the kind of designs you may want to develop
- initiate the first set of ideas using relevant sources of information for reference and talk to clients and colleagues about them
- develop the ideas into a set of possible solutions, probably in collaboration with others
- work collaboratively with other people in a design team and from other areas of specialism which you may need to use
- develop and maintain practical skills, keeping up to date with new technologies
- select and prepare your proposed solution(s) for presentation to the client and decide on a preferred solution
- when required, supervise or instruct the makers of the product
- deliver the product on time and within the costs agreed
- perhaps become involved in the promotion and marketing of the product
- evaluate and record the results for future reference and for your portfolio.

Mostly, however, you would only be involved in some of these processes and, probably, as a young designer, be only one of a team led by a senior designer. It is, therefore, very important that you learn how to work as a member of a team and develop good communication skills. These are even more important when dealing with clients and you must be able to communicate effectively both in conversation and in writing (this is one of the reasons why the Core Skills in the GNVQ are so important).

You will have to be familiar with a wide range of materials and equipment, particularly the use of computers both for information processing and for computer-assisted design (CAD), and the way that a design practice operates. An important part of a GNVQ course is to gain experience and understanding of professional practice and you should take every opportunity to visit designers and find out how their businesses work.

Julian Gregory

Graphic Designer – Oxford University Press

I think as far back as I can remember I've been interested in art and design – right back to primary school. It's what people told me I was good at, and what I've always wanted to do.

I did O level Art at school – we didn't have Art and Design as a subject – most of it was painting and drawing, there wasn't a lot of design involved. Then I did A levels – Art, English and Maths. I have to say I've found having a mathematical knowledge extremely useful because (surprisingly perhaps) there is a lot of maths in graphic design – particularly geometry. But it also gives you a way of thinking – a logical approach to problems. And there is written communication involved, particularly with my job – heading a team of designers – I'm having to communicate by letter and memo, as well as verbally, all the time. So in that sense the English is a help too.

After school I did a year's Foundation Course, which is a stepping stone to a degree, and I'd read up on the sort of area of art I might specialise in. I suppose at that stage I sort of knew what I *didn't* want to go into rather than what I did. I knew that I wasn't a Fine Artist – I hadn't got concepts in my mind that I wanted to present to the world. I wanted to design or illustrate for a purpose.

At the start of my degree I still thought I was going to be an illustrator and then half way through the first year I started to experiment with type, and page layout, and actually using the photographs and illustrations of other students to create designs. And it was at that point that I knew I wanted to be a graphic designer, and began to specialise in page design. In my third year I was lucky enough to be asked to co-design a poetry anthology for the Welsh Anti-Apartheid

Movement with a fellow student, which was a great learning experience. It was the real world. I had to liaise with printers and typesetters – it was my real introduction to book design.

Six months after my degree I got my first job as a designer here at OUP. I didn't actually apply for an advertised position. I just wrote on the off-chance that there might be a position going. Because book design has extended periods of time when one works on a project, my interviewers wanted to find out if I had the staying power to stick with a project for quite lengthy periods of time – rather than the sort of thing you might find in a design agency when you're designing things from day to day, or week to week – but having worked on the poetry anthology at college I did know that already. We talked about my portfolio and discussed the work that I'd done. Now, I've subsequently been an interviewer and I've found that, although one does use the portfolio as a basis for an interview, it's also necessary to ask pertinent questions to find out a candidate's personality and skills over and above their design talents. It isn't just the portfolio that counts. All designers have to be able to justify or 'sell' their ideas.

As graphic designers here we're involved in producing concept designs and specimen pages for a particular project. We're given manuscript material and we have a briefing meeting with the Editor where basically we discuss what sort of book or project we're actually trying to produce – the sort of 'look' that is wanted for any particular project – an authoritative tome or something upbeat and fashionable, say. The Editor is usually the expert on the market. In taking the briefing, I have to be able to extract the information, and establish what sort of finished product is wanted. It's my job to visually interpret that. Then with a specimen manuscript and a specimen art brief we put together pages to simulate what the actual book might ultimately look like – the format, what goes on the page, the way the photographs and illustrations are used, the typographic treatment... Basically the way the thing is put across to be motivating for the reader.

We work on Apple Macs, so we can make the thing look like the finished product if necessary. Many designers who are graduating now work straight on to screen, others will start out by sketching ideas with a pencil and paper and then, at a certain point during a design, go on to screen, which becomes just another tool. It's a very useful way of producing something quickly, inexpensively, and to the degree of finish that otherwise would be extremely laborious and time-consuming.

We usually work on two or three projects at any one time, so after the specimen design there's usually a gap while the Editor and the Author put the manuscript together. Then it comes back to us and we actually implement the page layouts, commission illustrators, art direct photographers, and then put everthing together ready for reproduction.

As a Designer I get my ideas and inspiration in the form of magazines, posters, packaging, TV, etc., as well as from art and design history. I look at everything partly in terms of its visual presentation and I'm constantly looking out for ideas. It can often be quite sub-conscious: just part of everyday life. At other times I might take a photo or make a sketch of something – I normally carry a pen and paper with me. Very occasionally I might wake in the middle of the night filled with inspiration and quickly scribble something down.

Now, as a Design Manager, I run a team of five Designers. I think that many Designers find that

cont ☛

career development involves an increase in management, and it's a bit of a dilemma because time spent managing is time not spent designing. But I think to whatever job you've got in art and design there's a business side, and for me this is it – the planning, the coaching, the working-out of schedules, the purchasing, the budgeting. And there are, of course, advantages to being involved in these areas. Also there's great satisfaction in identifying and nurturing the talent of other Designers.

This is an 'in-house' business, involving lots of teamwork. Each project has its own team – Designer, Editor, Picture Editor. I also have weekly meetings with two other team leaders and the department manager to discuss any purchasing decisions, or policy, or anything to do with the running of the department as a whole. I liaise with Managing Editors who give me an initial briefing on each project and I will then decide which Designer is most appropriate. I spend quite a bit of time scheduling projects and Designers' time: there are definitely peaks and troughs in a Designer's schedule and part of my job is to dovetail projects so there aren't awful clashes of time. I have to prioritise and if necessary get in freelance support. So I am involved in lots of meetings and memo writing: verbal communication is as important a part of the job as the visual communication.

Technology is developing all the time. There are training courses initially for new software, but I think the best way of learning is to actually use it on a real project. Also working in a large organisation and in an open-plan studio gives us all the opportunity to share each other's knowledge. New Designers come through with new skills. We go to shows and exhibitions and get MacUser, Creative Review, and Design Week which are circulated round the department. To be competitive we have to keep up with what's going on.

Graphic design is now a subject in schools, so there must be more awareness of what it involves than there used to be. We do take on work experience people here every so often, which is, I think, quite a useful way for students to find out exactly what is involved with the job, because it isn't an obvious thing – it isn't drawing.

The nice thing about books is that, although after a number of years they may get tatty, they're not just a leaflet that gets thrown away in the bin. They are semi-permanent objects that are used; they have a life. Also, working in this field one feels, to a certain extent, worthy because there is a purpose to all this: there is a function behind it, we're not just selling, we're educating. Hopefully we translate the Author's bare text into something which is readable and digestible; and that digestion is aided as best it can be by what we, the Designers, do. ¶

What do Craftspeople Do?

Craftswork usually involves making things for particular purposes, most of which are 'functional' – they are made to be used. However, there has been an increase in recent years in crafts objects which are not functional in the utilitarian sense, they are decorative objects and the distinction between the work of an artist and a craftsperson is blurred.

In many ways, the work of a craftsperson is also similar to that of a designer but the difference is that the main process of making is, normally, fully in the hands of the craftsperson. Design is only a part of the whole process of producing things, and creative ideas, which are very important to an individual craftsperson, often come from working directly with the materials being used. Craftswork normally involves making things by hand rather than by industrial processes where much of the process of manufacture is done by machines. Craft objects are usually made for a particular market and for particular uses, for example domestic pottery, furniture, and clothing.

Many craftspeople work alone or have only small businesses and they are, therefore, responsible for every aspect of making and selling their wares. They have to organise their working life so that all the materials and equipment they need are available, their workshops are efficient, their sales outlets are created and satisfied and that their business affairs are properly administered. Perhaps, above all, they have to maintain the quality of their work and be creative in originating and developing new ideas and products.

In the early part of their careers, many craftspeople work with an experienced person in an established business to gain experience and improve their skills. There are now **New Apprenticeships** available, during which it is expected that apprentices will be able to gain professional qualifications such as NVQs.

As a craftsperson you should be able to:

- develop a particular preference for materials and ways of working to create articles in your own personal style
- research the market for the kinds of objects you wish to produce or in response to a client's needs
- initiate and develop ideas
- develop a suitable range of products for the identified market
- make successful products to a high standard, controlling the whole process from ideas to completion and marketing
- develop and maintain appropriate practical skills, keeping up to date with new techniques and technologies
- promote and market your work
- evaluate your work and prepare ideas for future products
- maintain a portfolio of your work for future references and showing to potential clients
- maintain an efficient administrative system, including accounts, files and business records.

The following extract from a publication on careers in the crafts by the Crafts Council may help you to understand what it's like to be a self-employed craftsperson.

Careers in the Crafts – Professional Profiles. Crafts Council, 44a Pentonville Road, Islington, London N1 9BY.

Kate Malone – Ceramicist

BEGINNINGS

I've always loved just making things – I was terrible at drawing but I could always make things – and when I went to secondary school I used to look through the mucky windows of the pottery room. You could just about see through it because it was covered in clay. And I used to see all these things on the shelf and used to say to myself one day I'm going to know what all those things do. I knew it was like a vocation.

TRAINING

After A levels I did a one year Foundation Course, then a three year ceramics degree at Bristol Polytechnic followed by a three year MA course at the Royal College in London.

THE WORK

I always wanted to have the largest kiln in town and to build a big studio where several craftspeople could work together and I've been very

lucky because I've got both those things. My partner built me the studio at the bottom of our garden. I work a full day and it's very varied because I'm interacting with the other artists in the studio which is very exciting and although I'm a potter I don't just make pots. I have photographs taken of my work; I'm on the phone organising commissions and exhibitions; and I teach. One of the brilliant things about ceramics is it's making functional things – a factory ringing up and saying could I design an egg cup, or it can be a town council ringing up asking me to make a centre piece for a roundabout, or a Japanese architect saying he's got £20,000 to spend decorating a hotel dining room and what ideas have I got. It's very, very varied. So you are making things that are used by people as well as things that are purely aesthetic and that's very exciting – it's technical at one end of the spectrum and completely sculptural and inspired at the other end. I work a five and a half day week at about twelve and a half hours a day. I really believe in the uplifting power of art – the quality of life is enhanced by the things we encounter.

THE IDEAS

I get my ideas from observing and looking at things but it's nature that really does inspire me. It's exactly the wonder of nature. Like finding a beautiful and perfect shell on a beach just grown through nature itself. I just constantly, constantly wonder at it – putting a seed in the ground, giving it water and this huge thing grows out of it. And that's like the transformation of clay that goes from this soft stuff to something completely different. And the glazes go through being raw, powdered, not-very-nice materials to being this shiny glass. It's a transformation in the kiln that I have control over. It's this material of soft mud through to finished pot that's as magical a transformation as from seed to flower, from polyps to growing coral. It's very much a time thing – the time it takes to grow. Some ceramics pieces take over three or four months. They grow in the same way. And I find that magical – inspiring – because I've got a bit of control over it.

GETTING STARTED PROFESSIONALLY

When I first left the Royal College the Arts Council allowed me to use a studio, rent free – nine feet by nine feet and damp – under the arches on the South Bank. I had an Enterprise Allowance and I had some teaching. So I had some income and was in a luxurious position where I could make what I wanted and didn't have to rely on the sale of my pots. Then I had a lucky break which was a double page spread in one of the Sunday supplements so I began to get known. But even now I send off maybe ten folders of slides and photographs of my work each week to people who might be interested and maybe one or two will pay off.

THE BUSINESS SIDE

So many people – businessmen, town councillors – think artists are a complete waste of time. I take pleasure in proving them wrong. You've got to be business-minded and it's not difficult. It's like learning to drive. It's difficult once you're learning but once you're on top of it it's automatic. It's just a simple set of basic rules that once learnt become habit.

I'm really lucky in that I have an appetite for work. I can't wait to get out to work in the morning. I want to work. Life's too short to work at something you don't enjoy. One can take the long hours and working really late into the night and having a slight financial worry at times because all that's outweighed by wanting to work and getting so much pleasure from it: it's priceless. ¶

[Look again at the table of craft occupations in the Introduction to see how wide the range of work can be.]

Other kinds of employment in art, craft, and design

There are other kinds of work which do not fit easily into the three categories above, for example, the whole field of photography, film, TV, video, audio, and tape-slide production. This is commonly known as the area of 'lens media' and whilst training in art, craft, and design is important, there are many other aspects which are specific to the specialism you may choose, particularly those involving technical processes.

In further and higher education, lens media courses are usually included in the range offered under art and design and media studies, either in their own right or as supporting areas of study in other courses. It is a very important field and the media expansion which has been brought about largely through new technologies provides an increasingly wide range of employment.

Photography

This is one of the biggest areas of employment in this field. It ranges from the photography shop and film processing service in the high street to highly-specialised fields of work such as under-water photography and medical photography. We have mentioned the range of functions served by photography, so you will have some idea of the different kinds of work involved. Although it can be quite expensive, photography is something which is comparatively easy for you to do without a lot of equipment. Often, all you'll need is a good single-lens reflex camera. This will enable you to experiment with different ways of using it and explore the different functions of photography. The local processing service will provide ready access to processed images. However, if you want to do more than explore the use of the camera in these ways you will need to expand your range of camera accessories and possibly buy some lighting equipment. You will also need to gain access to a darkroom.

[1] *Hall's Dictionary of Subjects and Symbols in Art. James Hall. 1974 John Murray. London*

[2] *The Oxford Companion to Art. Edited by Harold Osborne. 1970. Oxford University Press. Oxford.*

Range

The Range for Elements 3.1 and 3.2 is listed in the Unit Specification. It includes the following:

Others' specified work

This means art, craft, and design work from different periods of history and from contemporary practitioners, work from different cultures, work in two- and three-dimensions, and either original work or reproductions.

Contexts

These can be commercial, social, cultural, scientific, contemporary and historical.

Clients

This term means the range of people who buy, commission or use works of art, craft, and design. They are described in the Range as – audience, end-user, individuals, groups.

Responsibilities

These relate to professional practice and include: ethical considerations, business needs, the designer/craftsperson/artist's needs, and their responsibilities to others such as the general public and their clients.

Business functions

These include: Planning work, production sequences, research and development, selling work, and teamwork practice.

Legislation

This covers environmental issues, health and safety law, consumer protection law, and copyright.

Progression routes

These are the different ways in which you can go on to further education or employment in art, craft, and design.

Evidence indicators

You should look carefully at the requirements listed in the Evidence indicators for each Element to see what evidence you must provide. They are self-explanatory but if you have any doubts discuss them with your tutor.

[unit 4]

Applying the creative process

ELEMENT 4.1

CLARIFY THE BRIEF AND CARRY OUT RESEARCH

ELEMENT 4.2

ORIGINATE AND DEVELOP IDEAS

ELEMENT 4.3

PRODUCE FINAL WORK

ELEMENT 4.4

EVALUATE AND PRESENT WORK

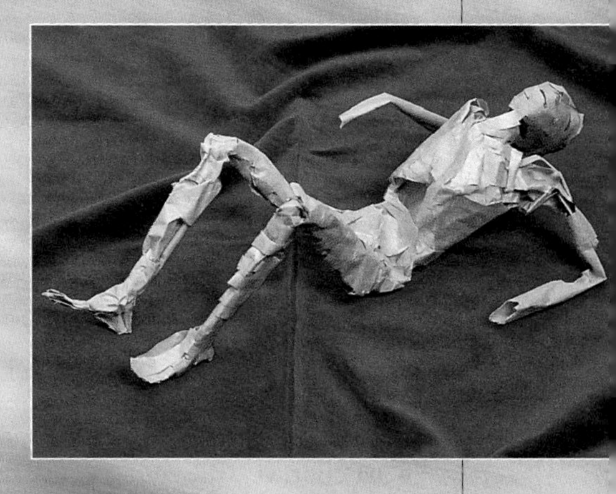

This Unit requires you to use **all four** of the Mandatory Units in the development, completion, and presentation of projects. It, therefore, acts as a means of integrating all of the other skills, knowledge, and understanding that you have acquired.

So, if we look back on the other three Units, Units 1 and 2 were concerned with developing an understanding of visual language in two- and three- dimensions. You were engaged in exploring the use of visual language through practical work, involving the development of particular skills and techniques. You were also expected to use visual language creatively and to develop your own ideas.

In Unit 3, you will have explored others' work, including the use of visual language, materials, techniques, technologies, and processes, and incorporated your knowledge and understanding of these factors into your own work. You will also have gained some understanding of professional practice and this should influence your own work too.

Unit 4 is designed to allow you to demonstrate the understanding and skills gained from all of these aspects of study in one complete project or assignment. You will see that it adds some new things as well, such as planning a whole project and presenting the outcomes.

You will see from the Evidence indicators that you must do at least two major projects from the contexts of art, craft, and design. You cannot do two projects from only one of these contexts.

The main differences between work in an art context, a craft context, and a design context are:

- **art context** – the emphasis will be on making a personal response. This means that you would probably not have to work to a given brief but could choose the subject of the project yourself. However, it is quite likely that a general theme will be set by your teachers and you will be expected to make a personal response to it. The direction of your work will be determined mainly by your own personal ideas, feelings, and intuition.

- **craft context** – the emphasis will be on designing and making things. You will be responsible for the whole creative process, from initiating ideas to presenting a final product. You will probably be given a set brief to work to but, again, there is the opportunity to choose the focus of the work yourself.

- **design context** – the emphasis will be on responding to a set brief and preparing design solutions. The degree to which you have freedom of choice will depend upon the nature of the brief. It may be a highly restrictive one which requires you to work within closely defined limits, or it may be more open-ended and capable of wider interpretation. The first requirement – to clarify and confirm the brief – is intended to ensure that you understand the constraints clearly before you begin any design work.

Contexts such as photography, film, and video are subsumed under the terms art, craft, and design.

The main focus of this chapter will be on the following:

- **How to begin work on a set project or assignment.** Initially you will be expected to clarify the brief and to undertake appropriate research.

- **Originating and developing your ideas.** As discussed in previous chapters, this process should not follow one particular method – the design process for example – it should be appropriate to the set task and can take many different forms. The emphasis is on innovation and creative development.

- **Producing successful outcomes.** This requires you to complete the project to a proper level of 'finish'. In many of your other studies, producing finished work will not have been a major objective – the emphasis may have been on exploration and experimentation. Now the emphasis has moved to one in which the degree of finish is very important. It is your main chance to show that you can produce carefully considered and refined work which has involved you in sustained attention to completing the task properly. You will be demonstrating qualities such as perseverance and patience – in creative work where you have to take 'risks', things often go wrong and you have to be persistent and determined if you want to succeed.

- **Evaluating and presenting work effectively.** This requires you to think about, and to make critical judgements of, the work you have produced. You should record your evaluation in any suitable form – written notes, photographs, tape recordings etc. Finally, you are expected to make an effective presentation of your work. This can involve you in display and exhibition techniques, and assembling your work in attractive folders, portfolios or other portable forms of presentation.

ELEMENT 4.1

CLARIFY THE BRIEF AND CARRY OUT RESEARCH

Performance criteria

A student must:

1. ***discuss briefs*** *and agree* ***objectives***
2. *record* ***objectives*** *for final work*
3. *identify research needs*
4. *carry out research and select* ***relevant information***
5. *organise visually stimulating* ***records*** *of findings*

Range

Discuss: with peers, with tutor, with client

Briefs: key objectives, available resources, time

Objectives: related to practical constraints, related to creative intentions, established by self, given by tutor/assessor, suggested by others

Relevant information: that provides ideas, that leads to an understanding of the brief

Records: written, graphic, lens-based, samples

Evidence indicators

Evidence of two projects set in more than one of the following contexts:

- art
- craft
- design.

Notes on the student's discussion and interpretation of the briefs for the two projects in more than one of the following contexts:

- art
- craft
- design

including a summary of agreed project objectives.

Records of research findings.

How to begin work on a set project or assignment

The most important thing to do first is to **make sure that you thoroughly understand what the brief requires you to do**, or, if you are choosing your own theme, what its potential and limits might be.

Let's consider a set design or craft brief first.

Discussion

There can be different circumstances in which a brief is presented to you. For example, your tutor may take the part of a client requiring a particular job to be done or you might even be faced with a real client. Discussions with clients might then consist mainly of a set of questions which help to clarify what they want – or what they think they want. Many clients will not have thought about what they want in detail, they may only have a vague idea of the kind of product which would suit their needs and they will expect you to help them clarify the requirements and suggest possibilities. You can see that a discussion in these circumstances would be different from one in which the client had a clear idea of what was required and had worked out in some detail how much could be spent and what the other constraints were. **Importantly, your role as a designer would change according to the circumstances.**

Your first task is to sort out these issues and to get to a point where you have a clear idea of the needs and the possibilities. This would then enable you either to decide on the **objectives** yourself, if you had sufficient freedom of choice, or to agree a set of objectives with the client.

Secondly, you may not have to work to a set brief at all, particularly if you are working in the context of art. A good deal of fine art is self-generated where the artist works to his or her own ideas, needs and responses. Many craftspeople also work to self generated briefs and therefore the process is similar.

.However you will still need to clarify your ideas (clarify the brief) do research and plan your work, taking account of any constraints. So much of the process described is common to all three contexts of art, craft, and design.

Very often, discussions with clients will involve you in making suggestions for possible outcomes in the form of drawings, sketches or other fairly rapid means of illustrating your ideas. If you've had the chance to think about the brief before you meet the client you could have already prepared some visual materials to illustrate your first ideas.

It is worth noting that a presentation, even at this stage, needs to be carefully thought about. Presenting ideas at different stages of the creative process is very much part of a designer's pattern of working. It will often involve presenting ideas to your colleagues if you're working in a team, and can form the basis for discussion and 'brainstorming'.

You can also discuss the brief and any ideas you may have with other people – your friends for example. If you've made good contacts with some professional practitioners you can even discuss the brief with them, but remember that the whole purpose of Unit 4 is to allow you to demonstrate your own ability to produce and develop ideas. Be careful not to allow others to influence you too much.

Since you are expected to show evidence of such discussions for assessment purposes, you should keep notes, drawings and any other recorded material that may be useful for this purpose.

Constraints

Another important part of the clarification of the brief is to determine what the constraints are – what limits there are to the kind of work you might do.

These will involve questions about the form of the possible outcome – what it might look like, its size, shape and so on. Then there will be its functions – what it's required to do or be used for. When these considerations are clearer you will probably be faced with constraints in the choice of materials, technology or techniques. For example, it is quite common for the number of colours in a print run to be limited because of costs. The paper will have to go through the press each time you want a different colour added which will increase the time the printer needs to charge for. The technology required might be screenprinting which may affect the way that you can use colour.

Constraints to do with function – the purposes for which the work is intended – could include considerations of the customers or audience, environmental issues, and health and safety concerns.

Time may be another important constraint. The product might be needed urgently and you would probably have to limit the range of processes involved in order to complete the project on time.

Time will also be a factor in meeting the deadlines that you have been given for completion of the project. **Managing your time is one of the most important aspects of your planning.**

Research needs

You will have to do research to find out the things you need to know for the work in hand. There are many kinds of information which you might need. Perhaps the most important will be the need to identify sources of ideas and inspiration. Where to go to see examples of similar design solutions or to find references to a range of resources which provide information on possible styles, techniques, use of different materials and so on.

These resources can be in many forms. They can be original works – such as those found in museums, galleries and collections, or they can be photographs, book and magazine illustrations, reproductions, and exhibition catalogues.

► Students working from primary sources

There is, of course, the whole environment, both natural and constructed. Many of the sources of ideas and information you could use are all around you, which is why you are expected to keep a sketchbook and use things such as a camera to record what you see and experience. Your own sketchbooks and reference collections should be a valuable source of ideas and information.

Other kinds of information will be required as your ideas develop.

• Information about the kinds of people who are likely to use, buy or respond to your product.

• Information on materials, ways of making something (particular techniques and processes for example), and the range of technology available.

• How long something might take to make or do.

• Information about what already exists in a similar, competitive form to the things you might produce – market research.

• Information on health and safety factors which may be involved.

• Information on whether you can do something by yourself or whether you'll need to involve others.

You should now begin to see how the work you have done in the other units will be the basis for much of the work you'll do in Unit 4 – using 2D and 3D visual language and referring to the work of others, including professional artists, craftspeople, and designers.

ELEMENT 4.2

ORIGINATE AND DEVELOP IDEAS

Performance criteria

A student must:

1 *explore and originate ideas to meet project briefs*

2 *combine and develop ideas to meet project briefs*

3 *review alternative ideas against the project* ***objectives***

4 *select the idea which best meets the project* ***objectives***

5 *organise visually stimulating* ***records*** *of the development of ideas*

Range

Objectives: related to practical constraints, related to creative intentions

Records: written, graphic, lens-based, samples

Evidence indicators

Developmental work related to two projects chosen to cover the range in:

- art
- craft
- design.

Notes of the review of ideas, including the reasons for selecting the most appropriate.

Records of the origination and development of ideas.

Originate and develop ideas

This element specifies the things you have to do to originate and develop ideas for solutions to the problems you have been set in the brief or for those you have set yourself. You'll see that it follows on naturally from Element 4.1 in that you will already have clarified the brief, identified objectives, and collected a lot of information.

The main problem in following such a sequence is that it tends to become too rigid and can prevent you from experiencing the flashes of insight and inspiration which are truly creative. **You should, therefore, always be alert to the possibility of ideas arising at any stage – don't leave it until the next stage just because you aren't supposed to be originating ideas in the one you're working on.** If ideas occur to you and you can't spend time developing them much further at a particular stage, make sure that you note the idea, preferably with some visual information such as sketches or other visual reminders.

You should get used to the idea that a **framework**, such as the one provided in the Unit Specification, is only a guide to what you have to do and that you can alter the sequence if it suits you. It isn't a Syllabus which you have to follow slavishly in a particular sequence – it's a list of things that you must do at some time in order to complete the Unit. We've already talked about some of the ways in which professional practitioners develop their ideas. **Remember that, sometimes, simply experimenting with materials will generate ideas and that research isn't something you do only at the beginning of a project – you'll probably need to do research at all stages of development.** How tightly you follow the sequence is dependent upon the amount of time that you have available. Some people need to leave a period of time for ideas to 'gel'. If you have the time, and you get stuck with a problem, sleep on it – you'll be surprised at how often the problem is solved when you wake up.

It might help you to understand what is required if we summarise the requirements of this Element.

You need to think of ideas in any way possible, and explore them by experimenting and trying out alternatives. Then you need to develop them further by trying out different ways of combining them, or combining parts of one idea with another, refining and modifying the original idea as you go on. You then 'review' what you have done and see which ideas might best suit the objectives you have identified. The next stage will be for you to select the idea which seems to offer the best solution.

In doing this kind of work, you will be expected to keep examples of each stage of development and to organise these records in a visually stimulating way. In other words, use your design skills and understanding of visual language to make an interesting and attractive presentation.

Examples of students' developmental studies and design ideas

Generating ideas

The process of originating, or generating, ideas is one of the most difficult but exciting things you'll do in art, craft or design. We've mentioned a few of the ways in which ideas come to you but you really do need to think very hard about the full range of possibilities that you can explore.

The emphasis in the Specification might seem to be on generating ideas from a range of things such as art, craft or design objects, books and other second-hand sources. These can be thought of as **'visual resources'** – things you look at, observe and touch in order to extract ideas and information. But **ideas often come from experiences, from our imagination, and from our memory**. Some arise sub-consciously and can be intuitive rather than reasoned ideas. You need to develop your ability to use all of these means. For example, suppose that you have just experienced something which affected you deeply – a musical experience, a transient scene of great beauty or an emotional parting. If you do nothing about it, it may be only partially committed to your memory. You may be able to retrieve the memory of it when you wish or, more probably, the experience will in time become only a vague recollection. If, however, you make some immediate response, such as exploring your feelings about the experience through painting or drawing, you will increase your ability to remember it.

◀ ▲ Examples of pages from Ann Carrington's sketchbooks

You will have something extra to add to your memory and something which acts as a visible personal record to help you to remember it more accurately. The artist Ann Carrington has a collection of 'sketchbooks' which she has kept since she was a child. They are not just books of sketches though, they consist of all kinds of items stuck onto the pages, which remind her of things she has seen and experienced – bus and train tickets saved from a memorable journey, found objects from places she has visited and so on. Some of the material also consists of jottings and half-developed ideas which came to her at the time of the experience. Think of the value of such a collection which constantly enriches and supports her memory.

The point is that memory and imagination can be enhanced by the constant practice of putting on paper things which happen to you and occur to you. Artists should always be alert to the possibilities suggested by experiences. They should be inquisitive, curious, and open-minded.

Developing ideas

Once you have a range of ideas which you want to take further, you'll be involved in the process of developing them. Development can take many forms and, again, you shouldn't get the notion that there is only one process. A more or less standard method is to develop ideas systematically, working through a particular sequence of activities. An example might be in the use of colour in one of your ideas; where you could start with a basic colour scheme and then work through a sequence of alternative combinations until you have enough to be able to choose the one which you like the best. Or, you could start by drawing your idea in pencil, then try another image in pen and ink, then another one in colour, then one where you modified the shape and another where you modified its form and so on. The main idea of a sequence is that you work on a **succession** of **separate** images until the idea is developed. In these examples you would have a sequence of studies as a record of the process of development.

1

TRANSPORT OF DELIGHT

Project

If previous attempts are anything to go by, you might be forgiven for believing that part of the brief for an ecologically sound form of transport is 'make it as dull and unappealing as possible'. The truth is that 'consumer appeal' is still the primary driving force behind any new product. If it does not make you desire it in the first place, you are less likely to want to buy it. How can you combine the very real, pragmatic, technical requirements of a new form of transport with its requirement to excite and attract the purchaser of the future?

The brief is simple. create a new form of urban transport (for 1-4 people, it's up to you) which is ecologically-sound, uses only technologies available today, and 'blows the socks off the jury'. The vehicle must be capable of being manufactured today, the more straightforward the technical solution the better.

Submission

1. Maximum of six A2 boards showing all aspects of the design.
2. Typewritten description of the reasoning behind the design (up to four sheets of A4).

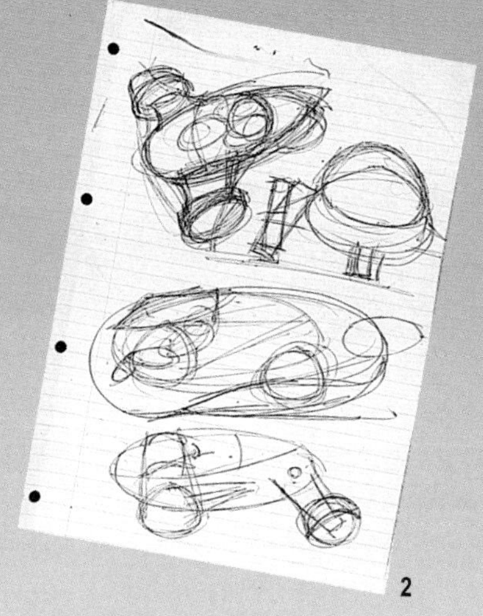

2

3

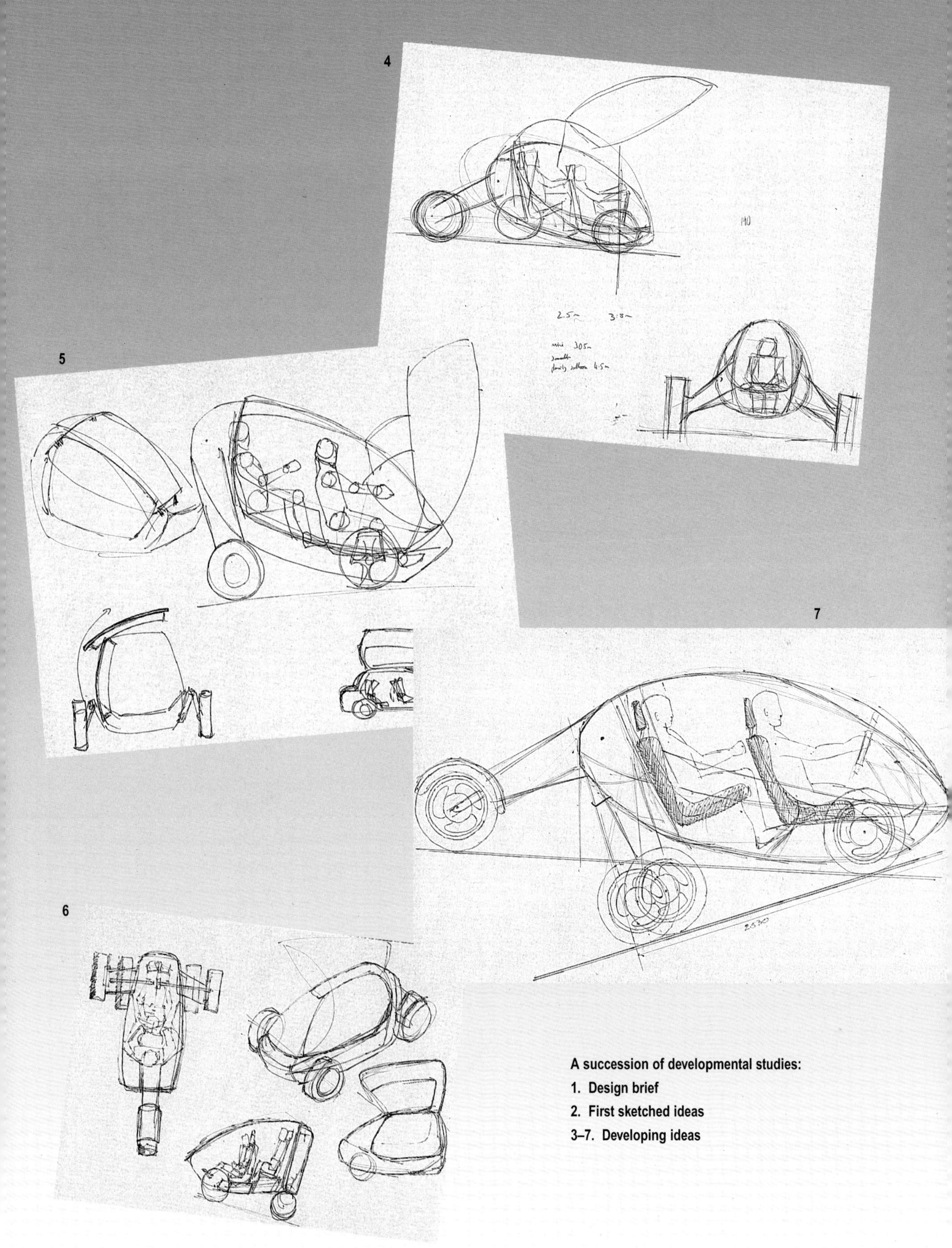

A succession of developmental studies:

1. **Design brief**
2. **First sketched ideas**

3–7. **Developing ideas**

PROJECT TITLE
DRAWING TITLE
ORTHOGRAPHIC PROJECTION
SCALE
DATE
DRAWN BY
DRAWING No

8

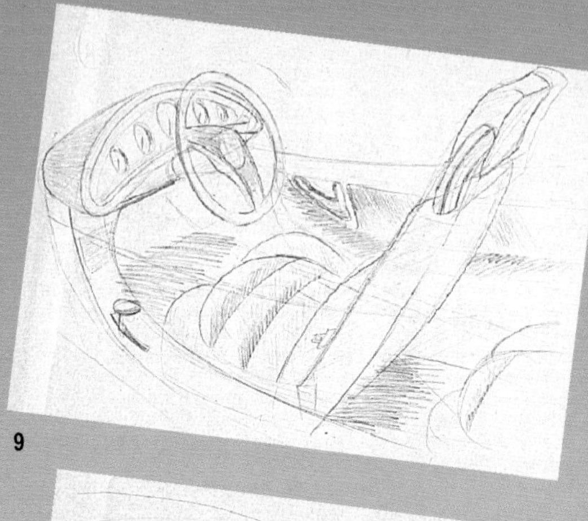

9

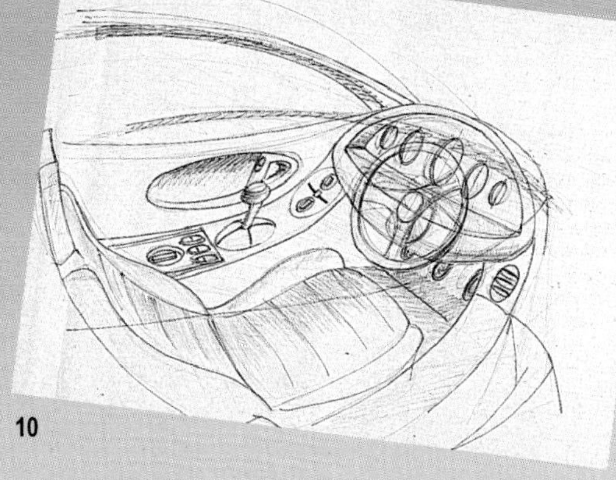

10

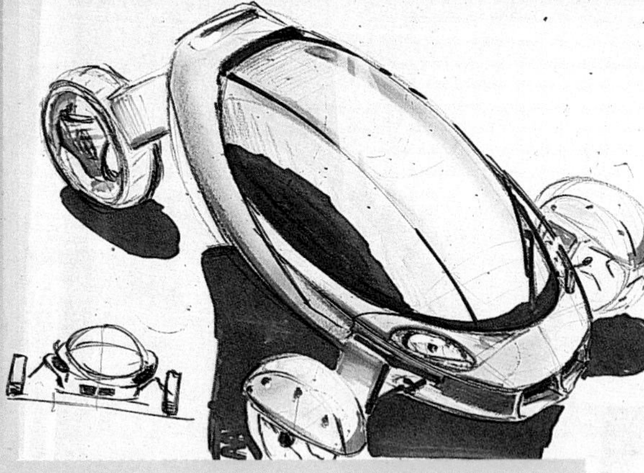

11

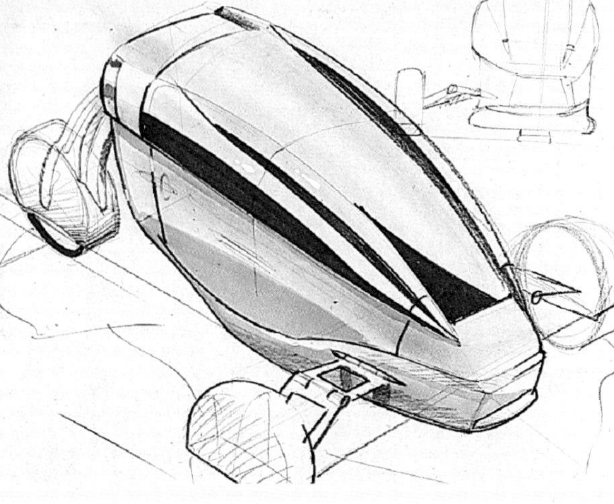

12

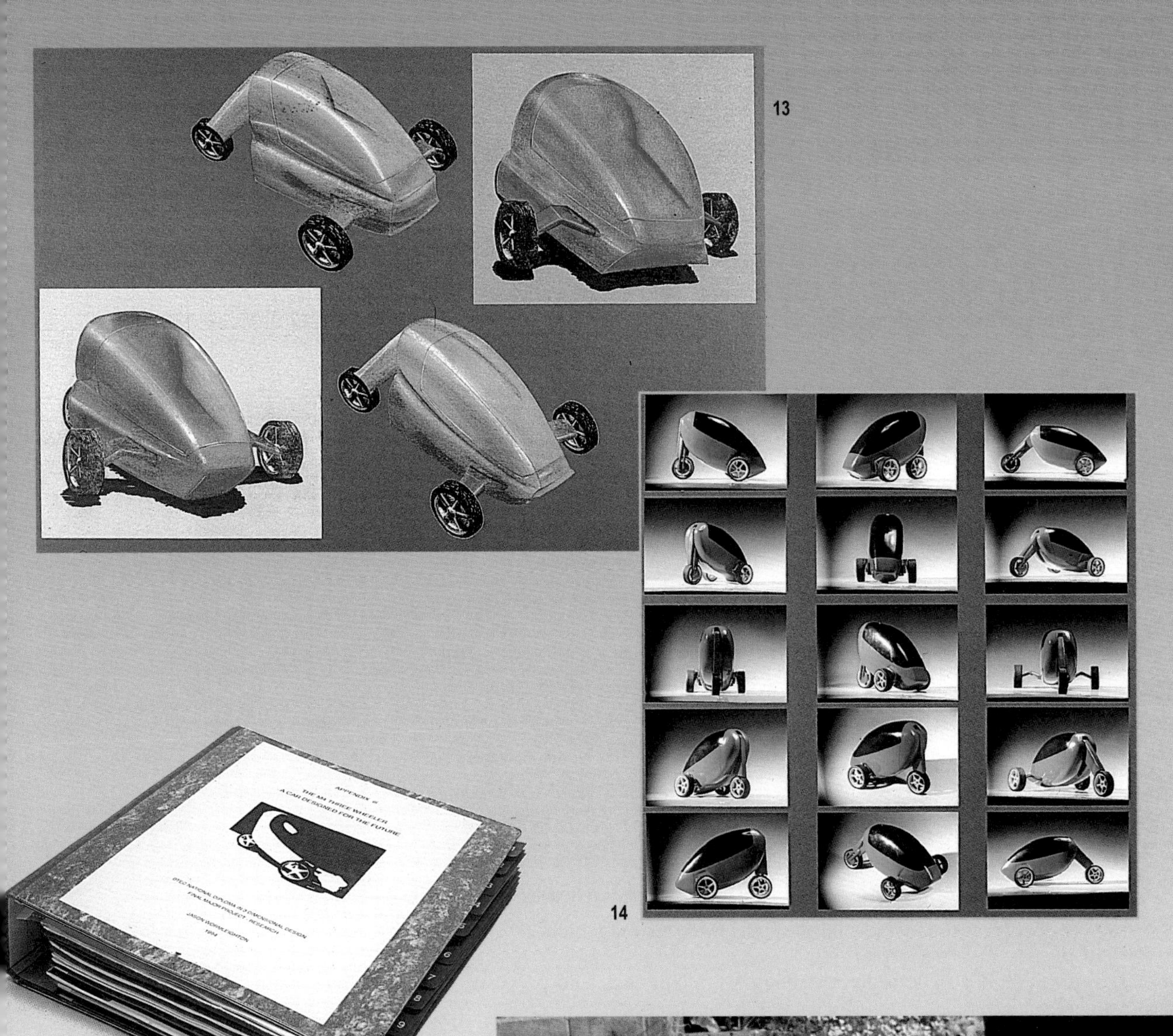

13

14

15

8. Engineering drawing
9 and 10. Designs for interior of vehicle
11–12. Introducing colour with rapid markers
13. Computer modelling of finished design
14. Photographs of scale model
15. Research folder
16. Prototype of vehicle without the fibre-glass shell

16

However, if you were working on a computer, or on a painting, where you often modify and refine the **same** image until you reach some conclusion, you wouldn't have a record of each successive stage. This makes it much more difficult to provide evidence of the creative process for assessment purposes. You could photograph a painting or your computer screen at appropriate stages of development which would provide some evidence, but you also need to make notes.

A sequence of modifications to a computer image could be 'saved' and stored under appropriate file names at each important stage. You should remember the need to provide such evidence when you are working on your ideas.

Reviewing and selecting alternative ideas

Once you are satisfied that you have done enough exploration and development of your ideas, you will need to review them. The purpose is to reflect upon the process and to make some judgements about which ones are the most suitable for further progression. The **criteria** (the qualities and characteristics which are used to help you to judge) for selecting ideas will be those which come from your **objectives**. For example, if an objective was to produce a design intended to suggest *colour* and *excitement* – how well your ideas meet these two criteria would be the basis for your judgement.

You would also consider the materials, techniques, and processes which would best enable you to complete the assignment – meeting the objective of producing a satisfactory result on time. If your project was about preparing a model or maquette for a full-scale production process, materials, techniques, processes, and technology would also have to be considered in the further context of production. In other words, you might choose certain materials and techniques to make the model, but they might not be same as those used for producing the real thing.

You can now see how important it is to determine and agree the objectives. In most instances, your client would certainly be involved at this stage of selection and would have to be considering the same objectives as you.

▲ An architectural scale model

◀ An example of a maquette for a sculpture

Refining and modifying ideas

Part of the process of reviewing your ideas may involve refining and modifying them to achieve a better solution. Improvements to prototypes and constant modification of ideas are characteristics of an effective creative process. It is often not until you can see a thing in something like its final form that you can see possibilities for improvement. You should allow time in your planning to put such improvements into your design and be prepared to make improvements right up to the last minute. This will often make the difference between a high-quality product and one which is only satisfactory.

ELEMENT 4.3

PRODUCE FINAL WORK

Performance criteria

A student must:

*1 produce final work which meets the project **objectives***

2 select and use appropriate realisation techniques

3 produce final work of appropriate quality

4 produce final work that expresses an individual approach

*5 use **resources** appropriately and effectively*

6 seek support and advice to overcome unforeseen problems

Range

Objectives: related to practical constraints, related to creative intentions

Resources: media, materials, technology, time

Evidence indicators

Final work for two projects set in more than one of the following contexts:

- art
- craft
- design.

Records of observation by assessor of student using appropriate realisation techniques and using resources appropriately and effectively

Notes on the use of resources and any problems encountered, and actions taken to overcome them.

Produce final work

This Element should be reasonably self-explanatory – it is about producing a 'finished' piece of work which meets the requirements of the brief.

The main problem might be in deciding what 'finished' or 'final' work actually means. The interpretation can differ depending on what the brief requires. For example, if the brief requires you to design and make a textile print to something like 'production standards', you would have to take it to a degree of finish which was similar to the product as it might appear in a fabric showroom. This kind of requirement would be unlikely at Intermediate level but, nonetheless, you should be prepared to work to very high standards of finish.

If, on the other hand, the brief requires you to produce four designs for printed fabric from which a client could make a choice for production, you may not even have to print it at all – your presentation could be in the form of hand-painted designs or computer-generated designs. These would be 'finished' as far as the presentation stage required but not in the sense of replicating the finish of a production run.

In some cases, the final work required might be a series of 'unfinished' designs. For example, you might have been asked to produce ideas in the form of maquettes for a sculpture competition.

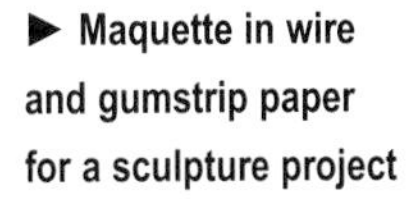

▶ Maquette in wire and gumstrip paper for a sculpture project

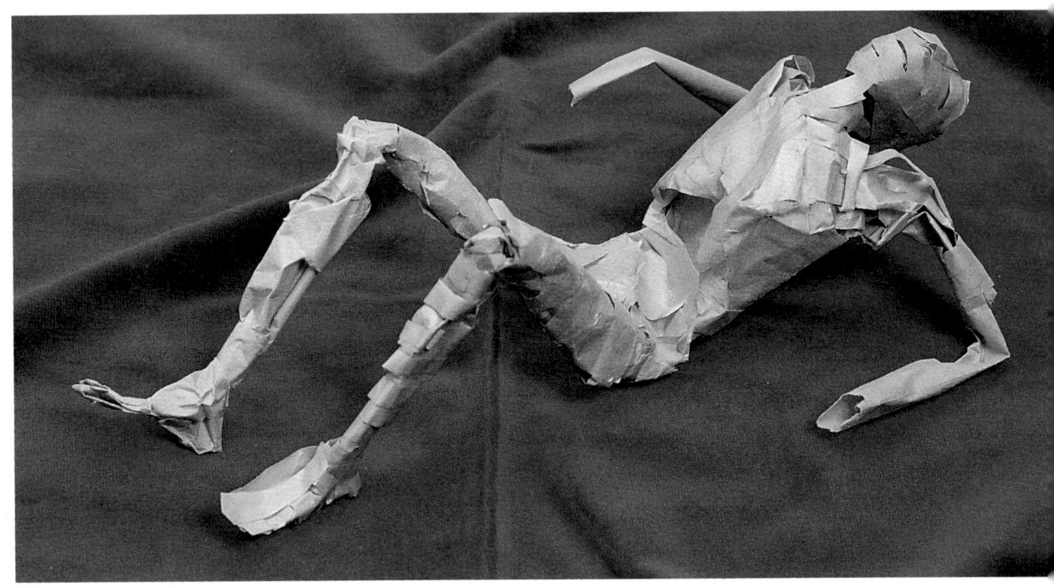

The maquettes would be accurately scaled-down versions of the suggested sculpture but would not be finished to the extent that they included information on the surface quality or other details of the final sculpture.

You must decide what 'final work' means when you are planning your work.

The term **'realisation'** refers to the end product and the process of producing it. In other words, it simply means what the element title suggests – producing finished work using all the appropriate making processes.

You are also expected to show that you have used resources **appropriately and effectively.** These can be useful terms when you are evaluating your work. **Resources** will include time, workshop facilities, other people, and materials – all of the things you need in order to complete the project.

The other significant aspect of this element is **planning**. You will need to prepare thoroughly to ensure that the resources you need are available and in the right condition. It's no good beginning a finished piece of ceramics if there isn't enough clay prepared to complete the task – you'd waste a lot of time stopping work to get more ready.

Time is an important factor in planning, and with the best will in the world, we all get it wrong sometimes. At your stage, your planning should allow extra time during each stage of the project to deal with difficulties which arise or problems which you hadn't foreseen. You should also be prepared to ask for help in such circumstances and not try to solve every problem by yourself.

The final thing to remember is that your work is expected to be **individual**. This means that the whole project, from the initial ideas to the final piece and presentation, should mainly be the result of your own work. It is expected that other people will help and advise you, since you are required to discuss the project with your friends, tutors or other professionals. However, you must be selective about advice and use what you can adapt to your own approach. This doesn't mean trying to be original for its own sake (very few ideas are truly original), it means what the word suggests – the final work should reflect your own ideas, personality, and particular ways of working.

ELEMENT 4.4

EVALUATE AND PRESENT WORK

Performance criteria

A student must:

1 *discuss and **review working methods** used to produce final work, and identify possible improvements*
2 *discuss and **evaluate** developmental and final work, and identify any possible improvements*
3 *clarify and agree **aims of the presentation***
4 *select **presentation methods** to meet the aims of the **presentation** and to suit the **selected work***
5 *present and explain the **selected work** effectively*
6 *receive feedback constructively*

Range

Review working methods in terms of: use of technology, processes and techniques; use of media and materials; planning

Evaluate: strengths, weaknesses, quality

Aims of the presentation: for assessment (by self, by peers, by tutor), for audience

Presentation methods: display, audio-visual

Presentation: formal, informal

Selected work: initial ideas, work in progress, final work

Evidence indicators

Evaluation report that covers the range and comments on working methods, and developmental and final work, and records possible improvements of two projects set in more than one of the following contexts:

- art
- craft
- design.

Record of observation by the assessor of the students giving presentations, one formal and one informal.

Notes on the presentation aims and methods selected, and how these meet aims of the presentation and suit the work. Records of feedback received.

Evaluate and present work

This is the last stage of Unit 4, *Applying the creative process.* It involves you in reviewing all of the work that you've done, making judgements about how well you've done it, and how good you think the final outcome is. This is the **evaluation and review** stage included in the Performance criteria.

You then have to think about how best to present your work and who your presentation is for. This should lead you to deciding and agreeing (perhaps with your tutor) the **aims of the presentation**.

Next you have to decide on the most suitable **methods** of presenting your work. This includes presenting evidence of the development process as well as the 'finished' results.

Once you have decided on the methods of presentation, and you get on and do it, you will see that you should be prepared to **explain** the presentation to others, particularly your tutor and the assessor.

Finally, you are expected to **respond positively to criticism**. The term *receive feedback constructively* means that you should accept criticism in good grace and use it to good effect in future work – you really mustn't throw a tantrum, assault the assessor or storm out of the interview if you think your work has been unfairly criticised! Defend your own point of view by all means, but do it sensibly.

How do you react to criticism?

Let's now look in a little more depth at some of the requirements:

Formal and informal presentation

Formal presentations are those which you might make to a client who had given you the brief in the first place, to a professional practitioner who had been invited to visit the course, or to your tutor making an assessment of your work. **You can see that the form of presentation will vary according to these different circumstances**. The client will want to see your final ideas, and some of the development stages perhaps. There may be a need to consider alternatives which you had discarded and you would, therefore, need to have available examples of the full range of ideas which you considered. A visitor might be more interested in the process of development than in the final piece, and your tutor will need to see everything you've done, including notes, records, evidence of research, development of ideas, your own evaluation and so on.

The work should be carefully selected and properly displayed or mounted – the appearance of your presentation is very important in these contexts. The whole presentation should be designed to be 'visually stimulating'.

The form of such presentations can be as an exhibition or a display of 3D products, supported by studies in portfolios, folders and notebooks. It might be a less extensive display of selected examples which show off the final work to best advantage, such as a series of draped fabric prints for a textiles brief or a 'mock-up' for a graphics or typography project. **This is why you need to clarify the aims of the presentation thoroughly.**

Informal presentations are those that you will have experienced as part of your course – for example, discussions of your work with other students in a seminar group and tutorials. In these situations you would probably not go to a lot of trouble to create an exhibition or display, you might show your work by spreading it around on tables or on the floor and by using display surfaces to hang work just for the discussion.

Preparing for career progression

One of the most important reasons for this Unit is to help you to prepare for progression to further and higher education or into work. Whatever you choose to do after you have successfully completed the Intermediate level you are likely to be interviewed. Most interviews will involve you in talking about a selection of work which you have taken with you. You may be interviewed by more than one person and have to engage in a discussion of your work and what you hope to do in the future.

You can see that constant practice in discussing, reviewing and evaluating your work will be very helpful in preparing you for such interviews. You can also see why it is important to select your work carefully and make sure that it is presented as well as possible. There is nothing worse for an interviewer than to be faced with a student who has brought far too much work stuffed into a tatty folder or plastic bags and who can't talk sensibly about it. Some students, in their enthusiasm, simply can't stop talking in an interview and that can also be irritating and waste valuable time.

It is crucial for you to understand, and gain experience of, the process of interviewing and being interviewed, which is why group discussions, seminars, tutorials, assessment sessions and group critiques are so important. If your course doesn't provide enough opportunities for you to become confident in such situations, you should try to get your friends, your family or professional acquaintances to talk with you about your work.

If you've worked hard, assembled a good portfolio, and feel confident of talking about it, you have every chance of a successful transition to the next stage of your career.

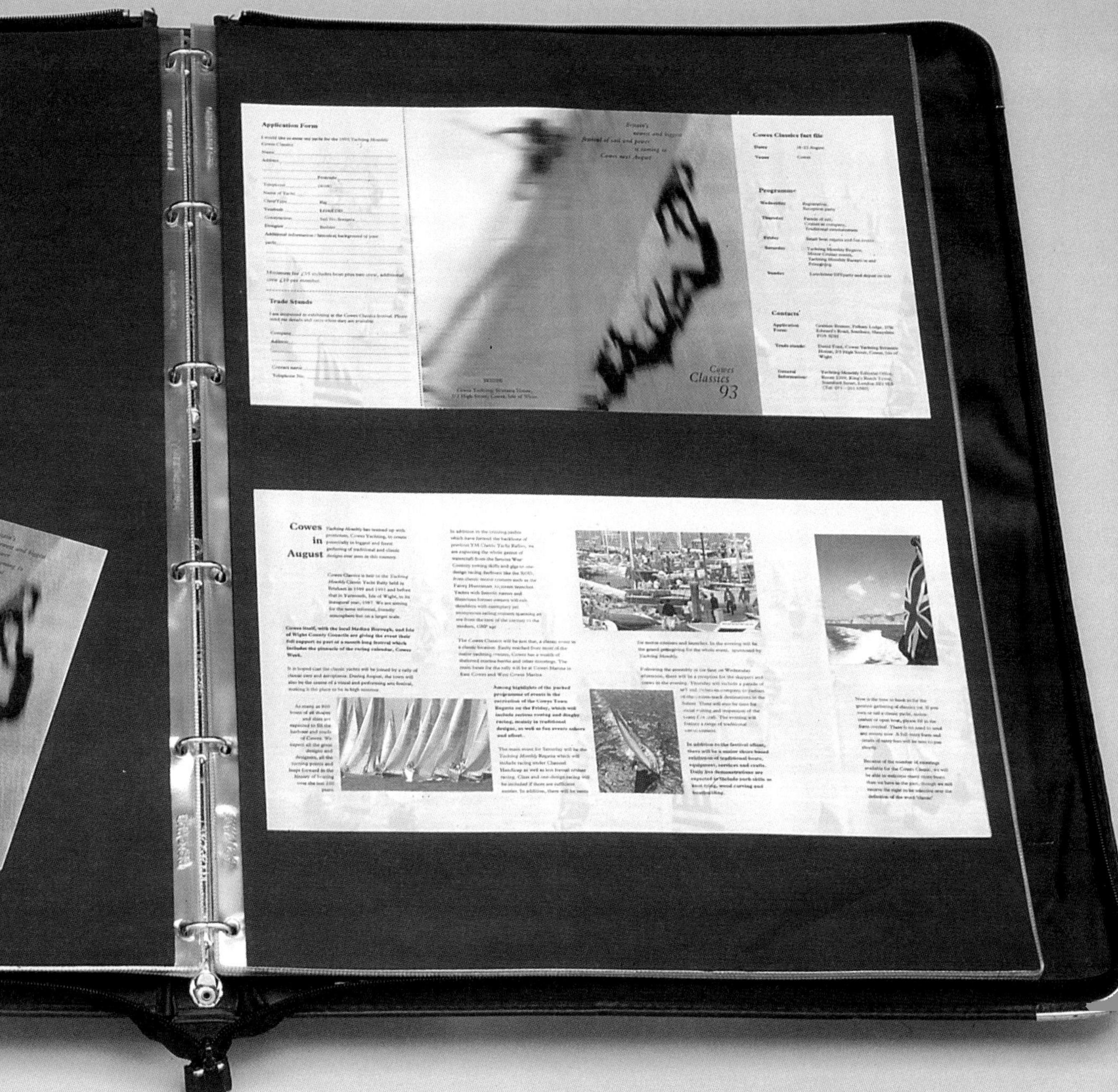

The following pages contain examples of project work which show the creative process from initial ideas to realisation.

They are self-explanatory and include a summary of the brief and examples of the process of development. They have been deliberately chosen from *Advanced* GNVQ studies in order to give you an idea of the exciting range and quality of work you will work towards as you progress in your career.

FINE ART 3D PROJECT: CLOCK DESIGN

Aims

To produce a clock design and flat pack which is professional and marketable based on your study of a C20th art movement.

Brief

You have been commissioned to design a clock based on a twentieth century art movement. The clock is to be retailed as an educational toy in the form of a flat pack, produced from card and aimed at a young adult market. You should examine your chosen art movement carefully, and attempt to interpret the ideas and style of the movement in an exciting and innovative way. DO NOT COPY ANY EXISTING IMAGES. Your designs may be figurative or abstract, and your clock must be made up of at least 4 seperate parts. You are limited to card, acetate and paper for this assignment. Your clock may be reproduced as a 3D design or in relief format.

Schedule

Start date: 6th January

Deadline: 3rd March

1

3

4

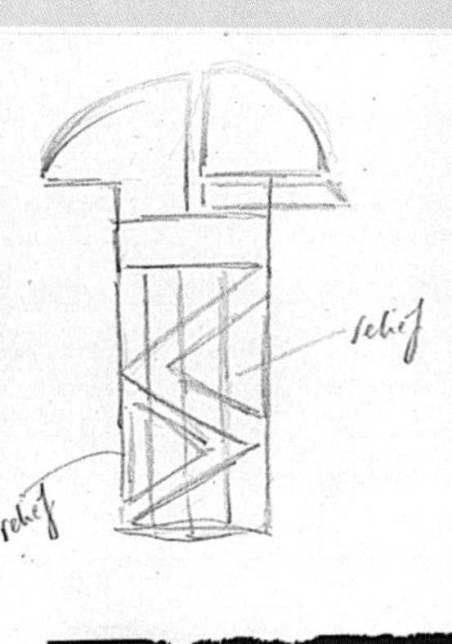

2

5

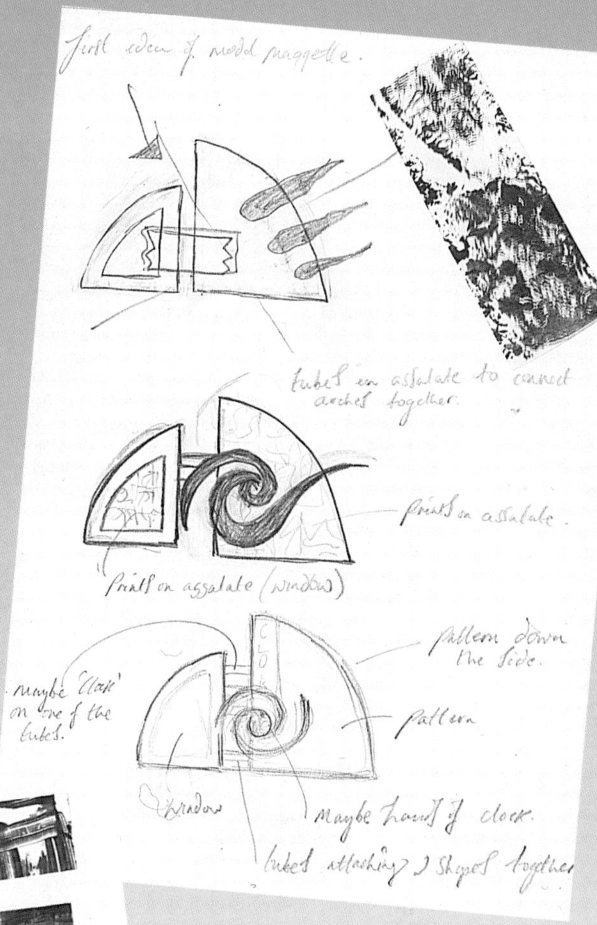

7

6

8

1. **Brief**
2. **Sketchbook**

3–6. Developing ideas through research and investigation

7 and 8. Trying out ideas for detail and the final form of the model

9–11. Development of ideas for final structure and surface decoration

9

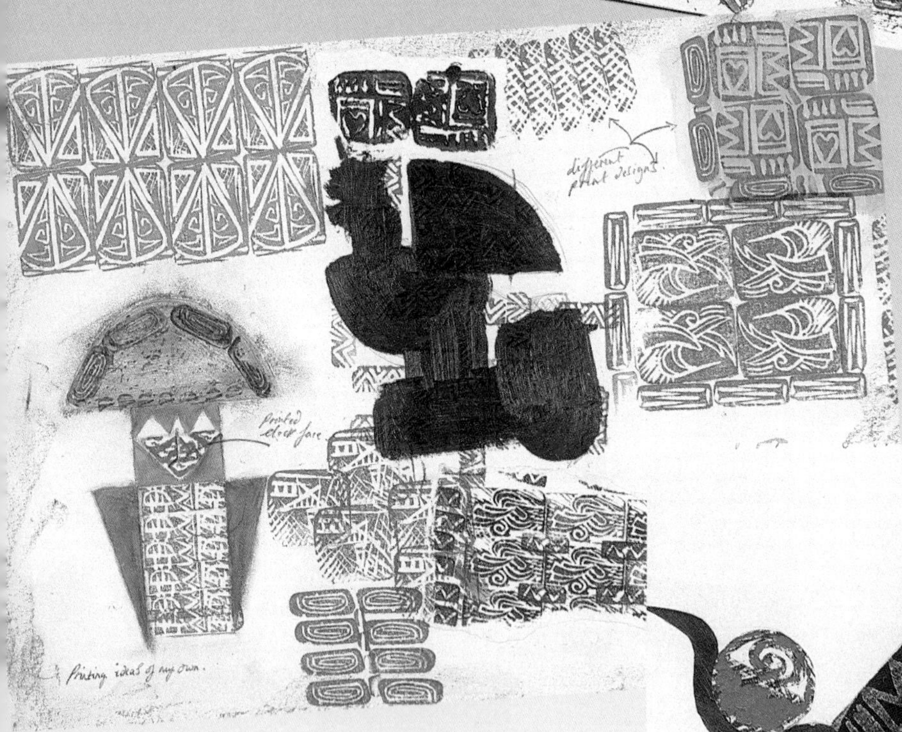

11

10

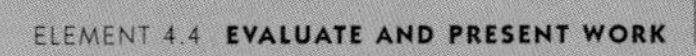

12. Cover for project record
13. Final design
14. Finished model

12

13

14

Graphics project brief

MOTOR SKILLS

Choose a motor skill and illustrate it with either words, pictures, or both, ensuring that people can understand it.

The project is in two parts:
1) a simple comprehensible design
2) a design which is different to anything you have done before. Make it WILD!

Project duration: 2 weeks

1

Part 1. A simple comprehensible design

1. Graphics project brief
2. Spider chart exploring ideas
3. Clarifying the sequence of instructions

4, 5, 6 and 7. Experimenting with different layouts and details of illustrations

8. The final instruction sheet

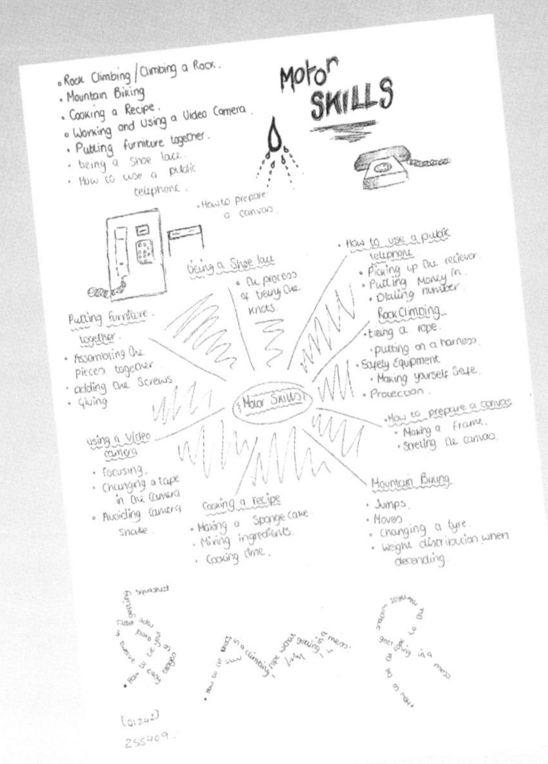

2

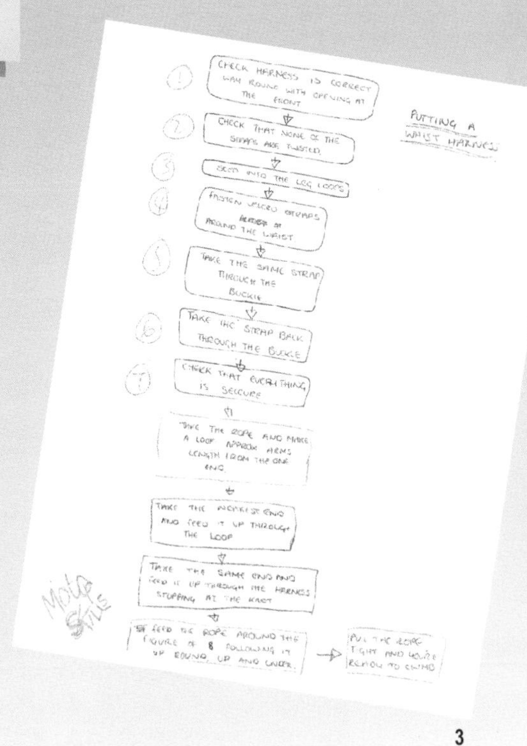

3

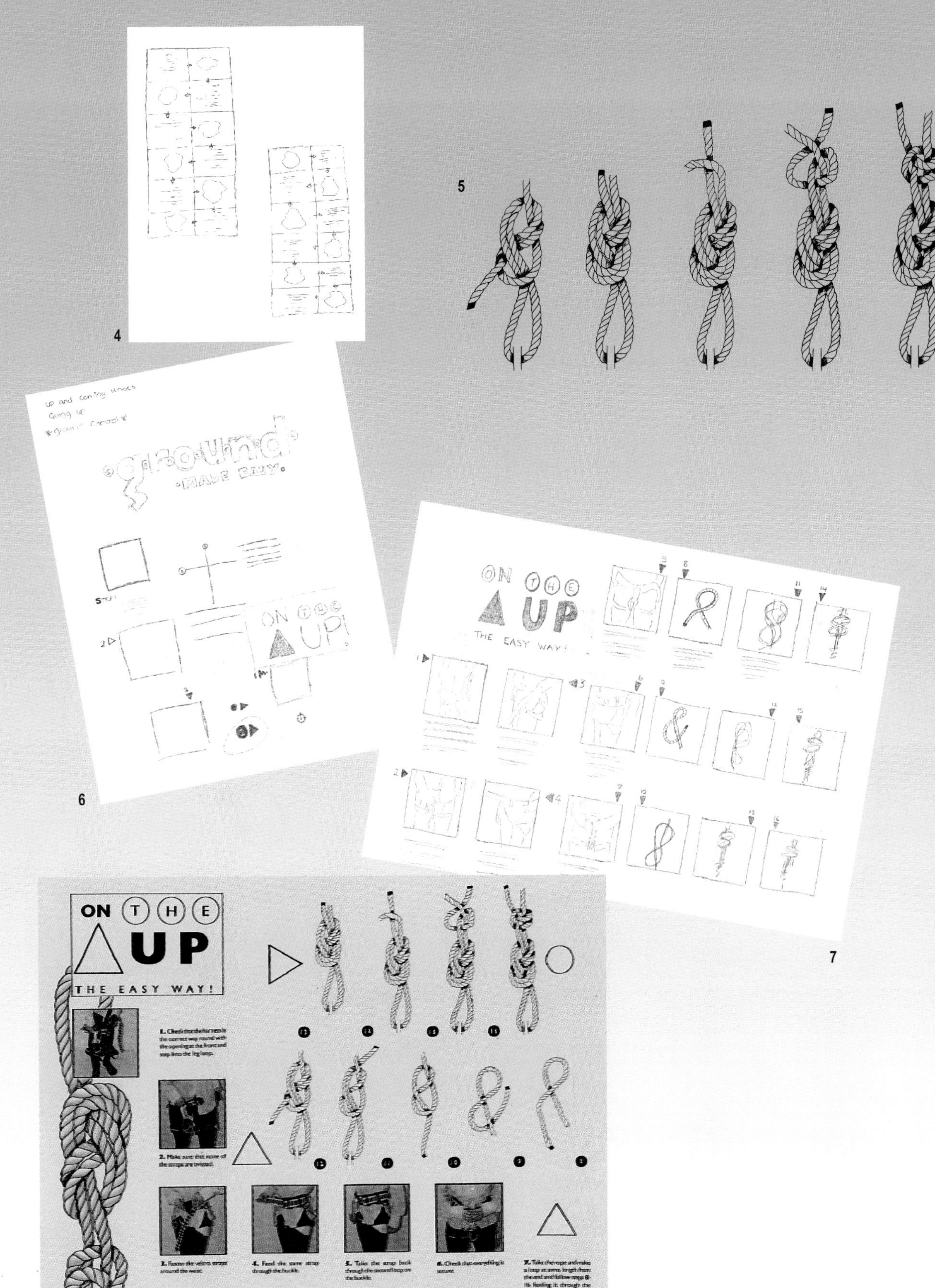
4
5
6
ground
MADE EASY
ON THE
UP
THE EASY WAY!
7
ON THE
UP
THE EASY WAY!
8
ON THE
UP
THE EASY WAY!
1. Check that the harness is the correct way round with the openings at the front and step into the leg loop.
2. Make sure that none of the straps are twisted.
3. Fasten the velcro straps around the waist.
4. Feed the same strap through the buckle.
5. Take the strap back through the second loop on the buckle.
6. Check that everything is secure.
7. Take the rope and make a loop at arms length from the end and follow steps 8-16 feeding it through the harness on step 11.

9

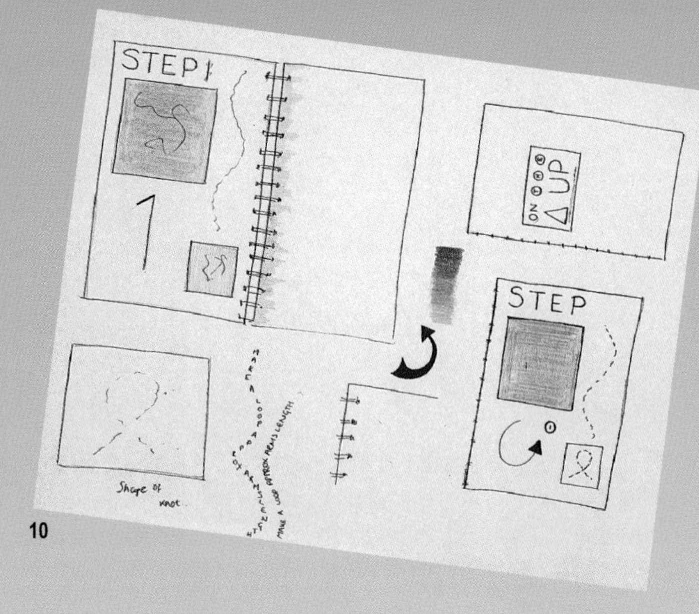

10

Part 2. A completely different approach

9, 10, 11 and 12. Developing the idea of a spiral-bound instructional booklet

13 and 14. Refining the format

15. Roughs for page layouts

16. The finished booklet

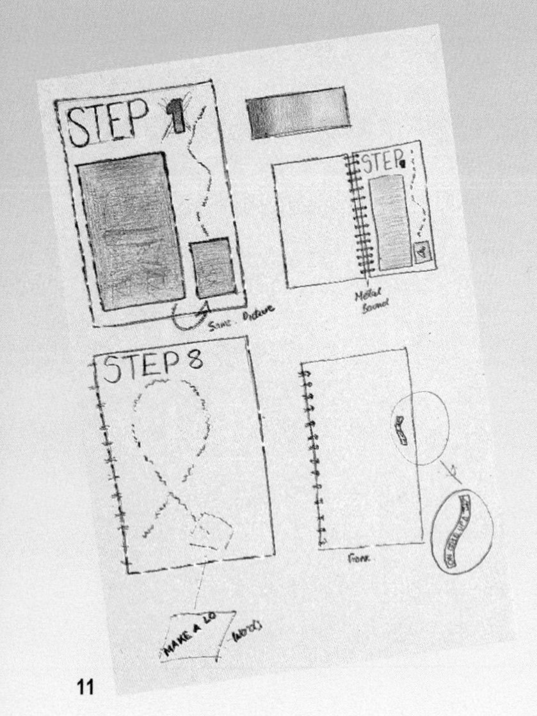

11

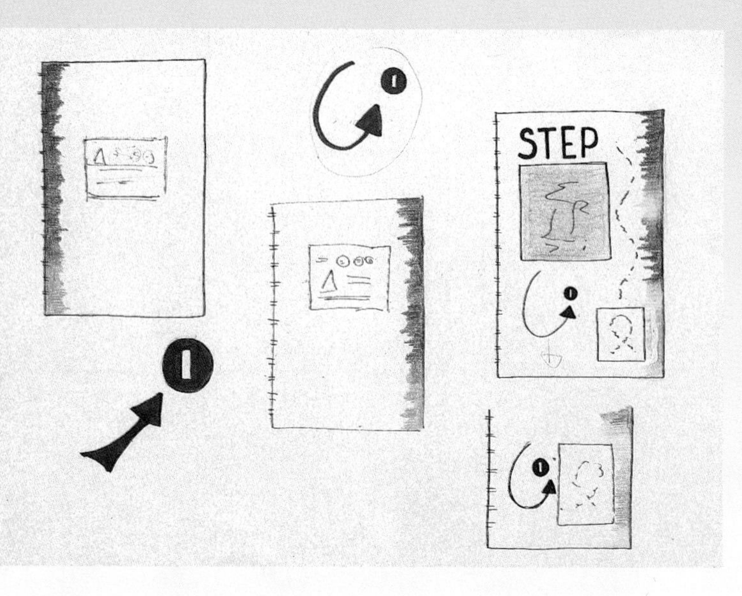

12

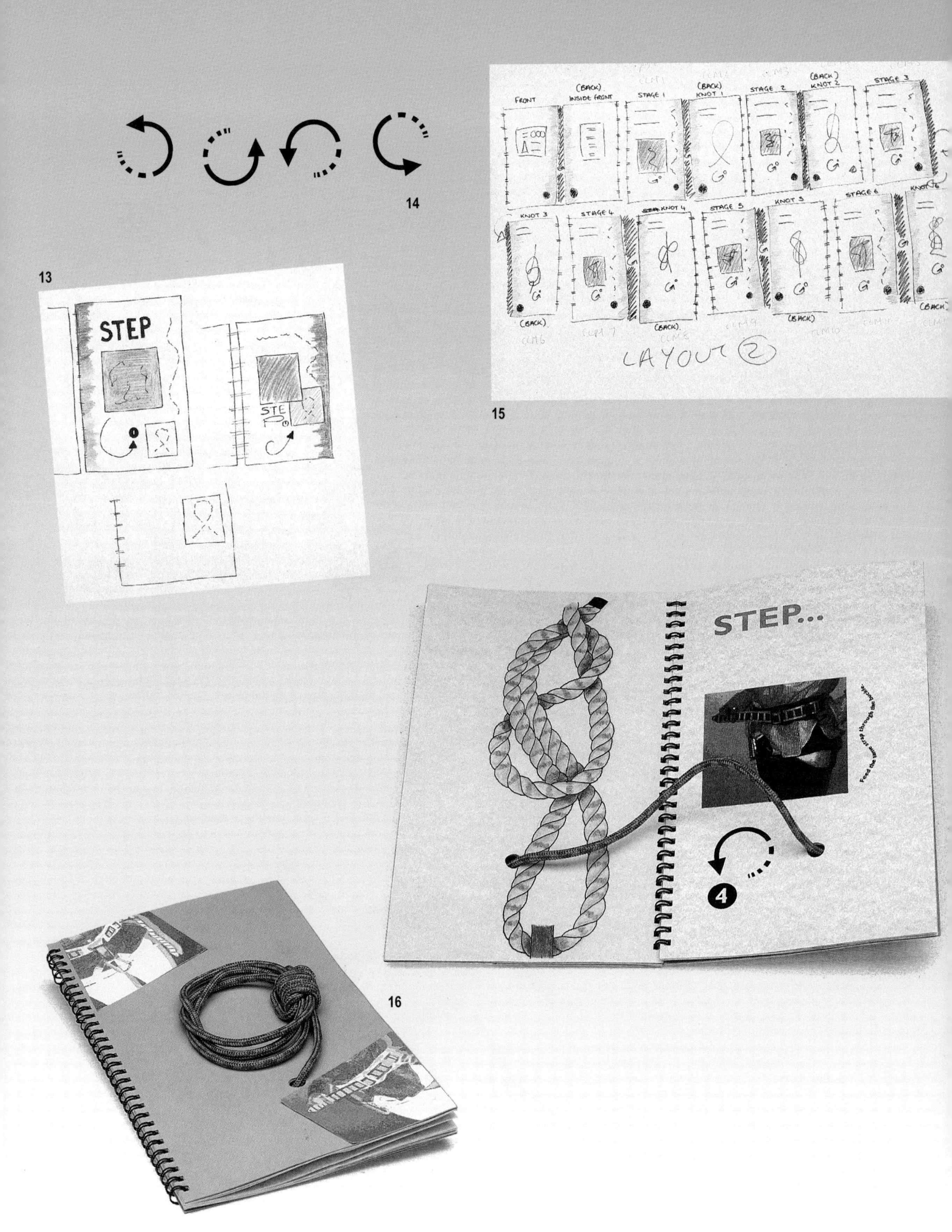
14
13
STEP
STE
FRONT
(BACK) INSIDE FRONT
STAGE 1
(BACK) KNOT 1
STAGE 2
(BACK) KNOT 2
STAGE 3
KNOT 3
STAGE 4
KNOT 4
STAGE 5
KNOT 5
STAGE 6
(BACK)
LAYOUT 2
15
STEP...
4
16

DESIGN PROJECT 1

You are required to design and make a self propelled scale model of a male Stag beetle. The model should be 13 times larger than full size.

Depending upon the leg coordination and steering methods which you employ, the beetle's movements may be controlled either by a microcomputer, or radio control, or a combination of the two.

The beetle should have an integral power source, be constructed in light-weight materials, and appear and move in as realistic a manner as possible.

ASSESSMENT
You are required to present a scale model, preliminary drawings, and a 3 view working drawing.

PROJECT DURATION
12 weeks

1

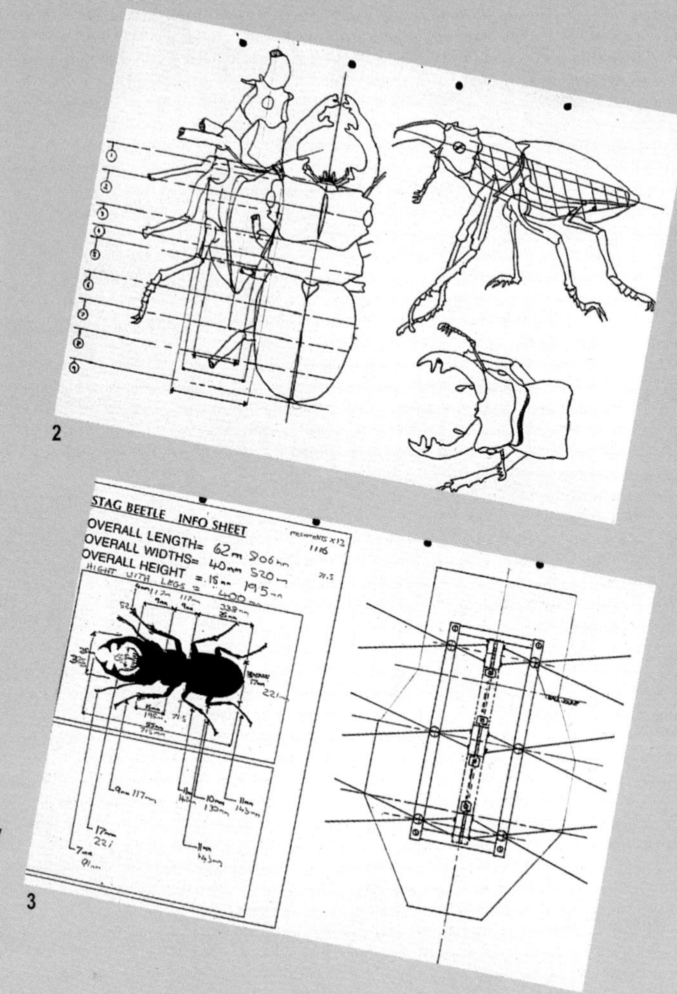

1. **Brief**
2 and 3. **Information sheets for Stag Beetle project. They show how an analysis of the structure of a stag beetle provides information for developing the 3D model.**
4. **The 3D Stag Beetle model**

4

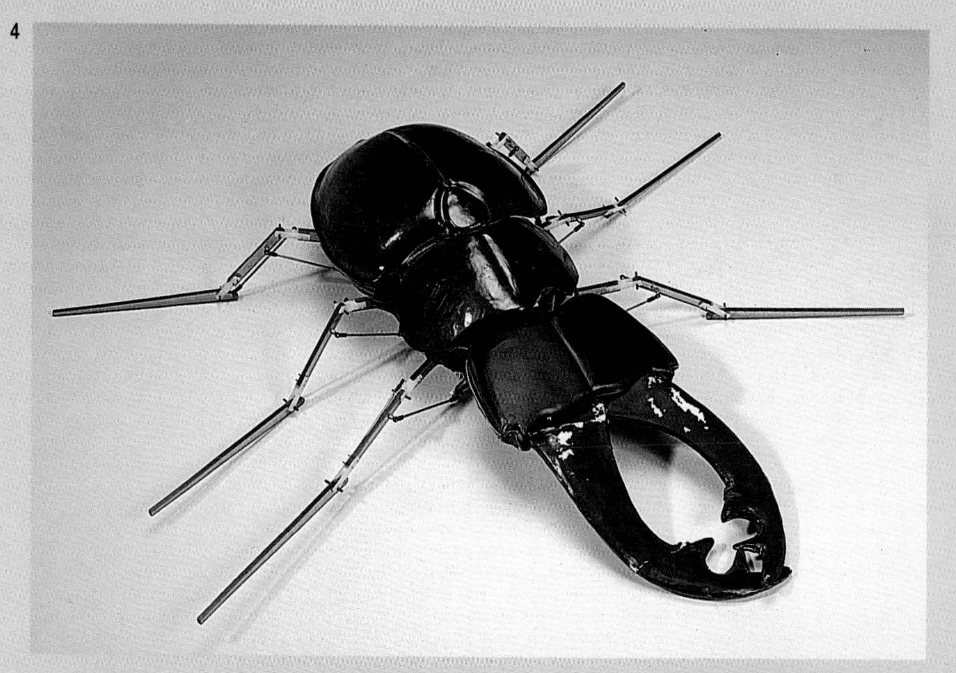

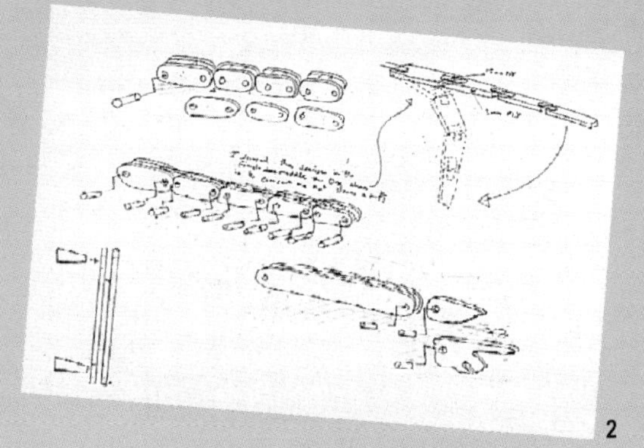

2

DESIGN PROJECT 2

You are required to research the characteristics of a particular sea creature and produce a series of drawings relating to its proportions and three-dimensional characteristics.

Based on these drawings you are to design and make a fully three-dimensional, free-standing 'interpretation' which is to be no larger than 500mm in length, width, and depth. This construction is to be produced entirely from plywood components.

You should pay particular attention to the means of joining the various components and endeavour to design joints which are visually as well as structurally acceptable, and which do not employ screws and nails.

ASSESSMENT
You are required to present a scale model, preliminary drawings, and a 3 view working drawing.

PROJECT DURATION
12 weeks

1

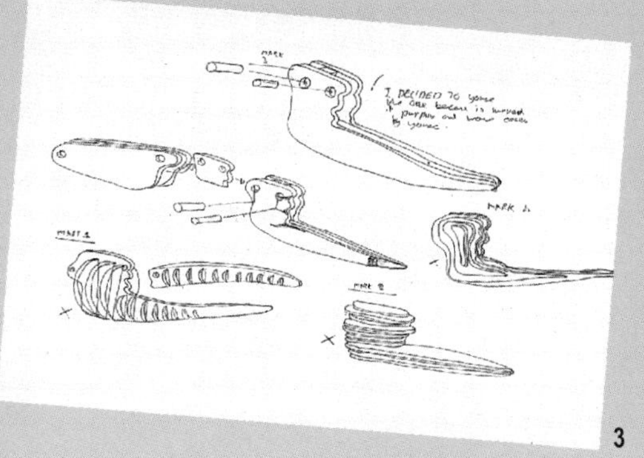

3

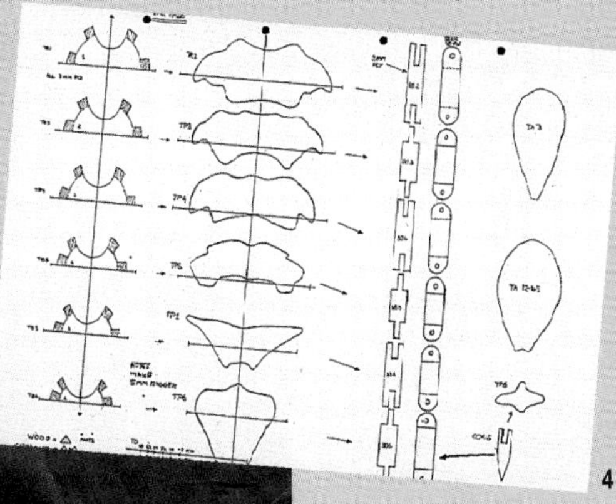

4

Lobster project

1. Brief

2–4. Drawings of the construction methods to be used in creating the articulated joints

5. The resulting 3D model of the lobster

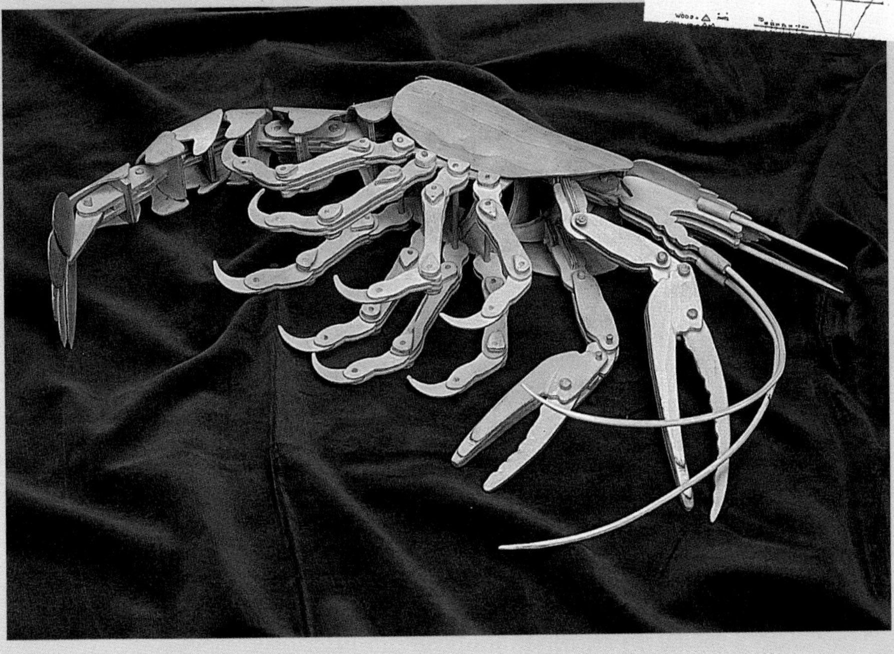

5

GNVQ Art & Design

Project/Activity Sheet

Project title
EXPERIMENTAL FRAMING

Assessment activity
WORKBOOK
PRINT PRESENTATION

Studio time allowed
8 HOURS

Self directed study time
AS REQUIRED

Date set
22 SEPTEMBER

Completion date
20 OCTOBER

Equipment requirements to carry out activity
BLACK & WHITE FILM
35MM CAMERA
WORKBOOK
DARKROOM FACILITIES

Entitled 'Experimental Framing' you are required to produce 5 photographs.

1) Shooting 'Straight Up'
2) Shooting 'Straight Down'
3) 'Tilting the Horizon'
4) 'On the Ground'
5) 'Close Up'

Through film processing, contact printing, and making final prints, you should present your 5 images at the end of the session on 20 Oct.

Your workbook should contain short statements concerning the aims of your project, and evaluation of the work produced. Keep all relevant test strips, notes, and work prints.

1

1. **Photographic brief**
2. **Workbook**
3. **Selecting images from contact prints**

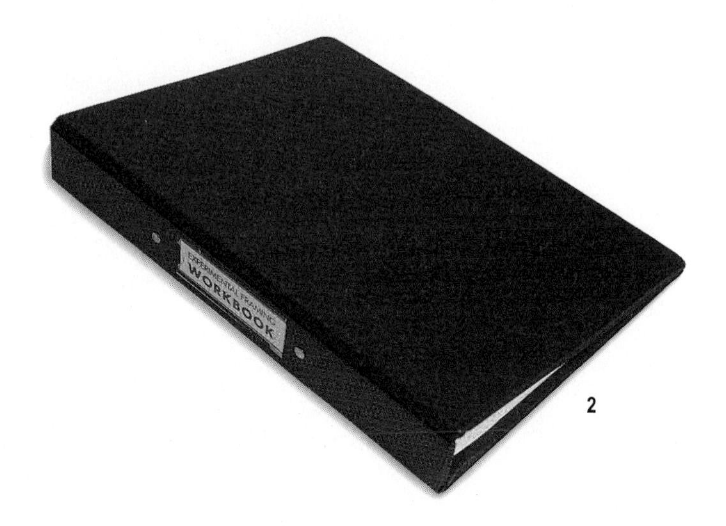

2

1A 2 2A 3 3A 4 4A 5 5A 4
ILFORD HP5 PLUS
4 8 1 7
ILFORD HP5 PLUS
ILFORD HP5 PLUS
6 6A 7 7A 8 8A 9 9A 10 10A 11
8 1 7
ILFORD HP5 PLUS
ILFORD HP5 PLUS
4 8 1 7
ILFORD HP5 PLUS
11A 12 12A 13 13A 14 14A 15 15A 16
ILFORD HP5 PLUS
4 8 1 7
ILFORD HP5 PLUS
ILFORD HP5 PLU
16A 17 17A 18 18A 19 19A 20 20A 21
4 8 1 7
ILFORD HP5 PLUS
ILFORD HP5 PLUS
4 8 1 7
ILFORD
HP5 PLUS
21A 22 22A 23 23A 24 24A 25 25A 2
ILFORD HP5 PLUS
4 8 1 7
ILFORD HP5 PLUS
6 26A 27 27A 28 28A 29 29A 30 30A 31
ILFORD HP5 PLUS
4 8 1 7
ILFORD HP5 PLUS
ILFORD HP5 PLUS
4 8 1 7
31A 32 32A 33 33A 34 34A 35 35A 36
3

4

5

6

7

The five required images

4. Shooting 'straight up'
5. Shooting 'straight down'
6. Tilting the horizon
7. On the ground
8. Close-up

8

Glossary

These are key terms commonly used in the mandatory units for all levels of GNVQ.

Assignments

These are tasks, normally set by your tutor, which you will be expected to carry out as part of your course. An assignment may last for a few days or may be spread over several weeks.

Brief

A verbal or written set of instructions which tell you what you have to do in an assignment.

Case study

This is usually a study of a particular aspect of professional practice – a case study of a designer at work for example. You can record the results of your case study in any appropriate form.

Complex activity

A complex activity is usually one in which you will be involved in a range of different processes, rather than a single activity, requiring you to manage your own time, use different materials and techniques and perhaps organize others.

Contexts

You are expected to work in aspects of *art*, *craft* and *design* – these are known as an 'art context', a 'craft context', and a 'design context'.

Art contexts: These are normally to do with making and exploring 'fine art', in which the work is often generated by you rather than from a brief. You are likely to be exploring things which are personal to you such as your own ideas, feelings, and your imagination.

Craft contexts: These usually involve you in making things for a particular purpose. Mostly the purposes would be functional, such as making pots or decorating fabrics for a specific use. A craftsperson usually controls the whole process of making things from the original idea to the finished piece of work.

Design contexts: These involve you in designing things for people's needs. Sometimes you will be improving existing designs, at others you will be expected to produce an original solution. Designers are not normally responsible for producing the things they have designed. They may supervise the making of a designed object or be involved in other ways but the process of designing is mainly concerned with originating 'plans' or art work for other people to produce.

Evaluation criteria

These are the aspects of a piece of work or study which enable you to make judgements about its effectiveness and quality. There are *aesthetic* criteria – mainly to do with its appearance, and *technical* criteria – how well it has been made and how it was made. You will normally be asked to match these criteria to your intentions – what you intended to do and how well you've done it.

Exploration

This term is used to describe those processes which enable you to find out about something, often through practical experiments – how a material can be used, what technical constraints and possibilities there are, how a thing grows or has been constructed, and what its purpose is.

Formal elements
These have been described in some detail in the book. They are the basic terms you use to discuss, think about and create the appearance of an object – its *formal qualities.*

Basic elements are: line, tone, shape/form, colour, pattern, and texture. 'Visual dynamics' involves the use of formal elements in aspects such as, movement, balance, mass, weight, rhythm, structure, proportion, and scale.

Mark-making
This is simply an all-embracing term used to describe activities such as drawing, painting, and printmaking. It is usually done on the surface of something, most commonly on paper.

Material
This is the matter out of which you make or construct something.

Media
This term is similar to 'Material' but is used to describe what you are working in – pastel, oil paint, clay, photography, video etc.

Outcome
The term used to describe the final result of your activities in art, craft, and design.

Processes
These are *sequences* of activities which often include the use of tools and equipment. They are the means by which you manipulate materials and media. They can also be used to describe the decoration of objects and the ways in which you apply media.

Project
Similar to, but usually more substantial than, an assignment, in that it will often require you to explore and develop a wider range of work over a longer period of time.

Research
Finding, collecting, collating, selecting, analysing and interpreting, information.

Sectors
Specialized activities usually related to materials – e.g. ceramics, textiles, wood, metal.

Studies
The term used to describe the outcome of learning, exploring or practising. Studies will often include written notes. They can also be drawings of something which you have tried to represent accurately or to analyse.

Techniques
The methods you use to manipulate materials and media – the way you make something.

Technology
The tools and equipment required to manipulate and use a particular material or medium.

Three-dimensional
Work which is 'in the round' or in relief in which you use the three dimensions of height, breadth, and depth.

Two-dimensional
Work which includes only height and breadth, e.g. work on paper, textiles, surfaces etc.

Visual language
The term used to describe all of the means which you have of expressing ideas, opinions, feelings and intuition *visually.* Visual language includes the use of formal elements, signs, and symbols.

Work
Usually the results of your studies, either from practical studies or from other forms of learning, such as reading and writing.

Index

Acknowledgements

Oxford University Press would like to thank the following for permission to reproduce images:

p 8 Albert Irwin (top left), Ed Barber/Crafts Council (top right and bottom left), **p 34** National Gallery/Bridgeman Art Library (bottom), Ace (top), **p 35** Angela Verren-Taunt 1996. All rights reserved DACS/Tate Gallery, **p 38** Imperial War Museum, **p 39** DACS 1996/Bridgeman Art Library, **p 40** Tate Gallery (left), Victoria & Albert Museum (right), **p 41** Images, **p 42** Norfolk Museums Services (Norwich Castle Museum) (top), ADAGP Paris and DACS, London 1996/Biblioteque Nationale, Paris/Bridgeman Art Library (right), Christies, London/BAL (left), **p 44** Cordon Art BV, **p 45** ADAGP Paris and DACS, London 1996, Philadelphia Museum of Art, Pennsylvania/BAL, **p 46** Patrick Heron 1996. All rights reserved DACS/Tate Gallery (right), Oxfam/Carol Wills (left), J. Allan Cash (bottom), **p 47** Victoria & Albert Museum/BAL (left), British Museum (right), **p 48** Ursula Edelmann, Stadelsches Kunstinstute, **p 50** Diana Rawstron, **p 51** Images (top), Sir Nicholas Bacon (centre), York City Art Gallery (bottom), **p 52** Haags Gemeentemuseum/ABC Mondrian Est/Hollyman Trust, **p 54** Tate Gallery/BAL (top), Moderna Museet, Stockholm/BAL (left), Carl Van Vechten Gallery, Fisk University (bottom), **p 55** David Nash 1996. All rights reserved DACS, **p 56** Museum of Modern Art, N.Y. (top), Fitzwilliam Museum, University of Cambridge /BAL (bottom), **p 59** Tate Gallery, **p 61** British Library/BAL (top), Guildhall Library, Corporation of London/BAL (centre), Military Picture Library (bottom), **p 62** National Gallery/BAL **p 63** Sygma (top), National Gallery/BAL (bottom), **p 65** Victoria & Albert Museum/BAL, **p 73** Science & Society Picture Library, **p 83** Museum Boymans Van Bermingen, Rotterdam (bottom), **p 84** Tate Gallery/BAL, **p 86** DACS 1996/National Gallery/BAL, **p 87** Succession Picasso/DACS 1996/Tate Gallery, **p 88** Walter Hussey Behest/BAL, **p 89** Fitzwilliam Museum/BAL, **p 90** ARS, N.Y., & DACS London 1996/Tate Gallery, **p 91** Magnum, **p 93** BBC Worldwide Publishing, **p 94** National Portrait Gallery (left), **p 104** Private Collection/BAL, **p 105** British Museum, **p 106** Crafts Council/W. Gilbert, **p 107** British Museum/BAL (bottom), Michael Macintyre (top), **p 108** Victoria & Albert Museum, **p 109** British Museum/BAL (top), Gary Alexander (bottom), **p 110** Lucy Casson/Crafts Council, **p 115** BAL, **p 116** J. Allan Cash (right), Architectural Association (left), **p 118** National Gallery of Art, Washington, **p 119** Claus Oldenburg, **p 121** Architectural Association, **p 142** Art Inst. of Chicago/BAL, **p 145** Natural History Museum (left), Royal Library (right), **p 146** Fitzwilliam Museum, **p 147** Royal Photographic Society Bath (left), National Museums & Gallerys on Merseyside/Walker Art Gallery (right), **p 148** Stapleton Collection/BAL, **p 149** Museum of Moving Image, **p 150** City Museum of Bruges (left), Memling Museum Bruges/BAL (right), **p 152** National Gallery/BAL, **p 153** Sir Allan Bowness, **p 154** Total Design (top), London Transport Museum (bottom left & right), **p 155** Portfolio Gallery, **p 156** Victoria & Albert Museum/Michael Graves, **p 160** Allen Jones (left), Victoria & Albert Museum (right), **p 161** Oxfam, **p 162** Oxfam, **p 163** Herman Miller (left), Crafts Council (right), **p 164** Phillipe Starck, **p 166** British Museum, **p 167** British Museum (top), Oxfam (bottom), **p 169** Victoria & Albert Museum, **p 178** Eileen Hogan, **p 179** Richard Long, **p 190** Ed Barber/Crafts Council, **front cover** Ed Barber/Crafts Council.

Oxford University Press would also like to thank:
Mike Blundell and past and present students at Worcester College of Art and Technology;
Polly Skinner and students at Oaklands College.

Original illustrations by Norman Binch.
Illustration on p 218 by Philip Reeve.

Interviews by Liz Robertson.
Additional photography by Norman Binch, Chris Honeywell, and Martin Sookias.